Anonymous

The School Manual

Containing the laws of Rhode Island relating to public instruction, with decisions,

remarks, and forms, for the use of school officers. 1896

Anonymous

The School Manual
Containing the laws of Rhode Island relating to public instruction, with decisions, remarks, and forms, for the use of school officers. 1896

ISBN/EAN: 9783337380502

Printed in Europe, USA, Canada, Australia, Japan

Cover: Foto ©Suzi / pixelio.de

More available books at **www.hansebooks.com**

THE SCHOOL MANUAL,

CONTAINING THE

LAWS OF RHODE ISLAND

RELATING TO PUBLIC INSTRUCTION,

WITH

DECISIONS, REMARKS, AND FORMS,

FOR THE USE OF SCHOOL OFFICERS.

1896.

Prepared, in accordance with a Resolution of the General Assembly, by
THOMAS B. STOCKWELL, Commissioner of Public Schools.

PROVIDENCE:
E. L. FREEMAN & SON, STATE PRINTERS.
1896.

RESOLUTION

AUTHORIZING AND DIRECTING THE COMMISSIONER OF PUBLIC SCHOOLS TO PREPARE A

SCHOOL MANUAL.

(Passed May Session, 1895.)

Resolved, That the commissioner of public schools be, and he is hereby, authorized and directed to prepare a manual for the use of the officers of the public schools of this state, which shall contain such portions of the General Laws of this state as relate to education, and such decisions of the supreme court and of the commissioners of public schools arising under the school laws, and such other matter including forms and rules of procedure, as he may deem advisable; and he is further authorized and directed to cause to be printed and bound three thousand copies of the same when approved by the state board of education; and the state auditor is hereby authorized and directed to draw his orders on the general treasurer for the payment of the expense of the preparation, printing, and binding of said manual upon the order of the aforesaid state board of education, and the sum of twenty-five hundred dollars, or so much thereof as may be necessary is hereby appropriated for such purpose out of any money in the treasury not otherwise appropriated.

RESOLUTION OF APPROVAL

BY THE

STATE BOARD OF EDUCATION.

AUGUST 3, 1895.

Resolved, That the state board of education, having examined the "School Manual" prepared by the commissioner of public schools, in accordance with the resolution passed at the May Session, 1895, hereby approve the same and order its publication.

CHARLES WARREN LIPPITT,
EDWIN R. ALLEN,
SAMUEL W. K. ALLEN,
JOHN E. KENDRICK,
SAMUEL H. CROSS,
FRANK E. THOMPSON,
GEORGE T. BAKER,
CHARLES J. WHITE.

} State Board of Education.

CONTENTS.

EXTRACTS FROM THE CONSTITUTION OF THE STATE.

			PAGE.
ART.	I.	Declaration of certain constitutional rights and principles..................................	1
	IX.	Of qualifications for office....................	3
	XII.	Of education.........................	3

EXTRACTS FROM THE GENERAL LAWS.

Chapter 6.

Of the rights and qualifications of voters. 5

Chapter 7.

Of the registering, listing and returning lists of voters, and of proof of their qualification to vote.................. 7

Chapter 25.

Of oaths, and by whom administered........ 10

Chapter 26.

Of the construction of statutes............................ 11

Chapter 30.

Of the permanent school fund 14

	PAGE.

Chapter 31.

Of the public records. 16

Chapter 36.

Of the powers of, and of suits by and against, towns...... 17

Chapter 43.

Of the establishment and control of free public libraries by towns....... 19

Chapter 44.

Of property liable to, and exempt from, taxation.......... 21

Chapter 47.

Of assessing and collecting poll taxes.... 23

Chapter 48.

Of the collection of taxes...... 24

Chapter 50.

General provisions concerning taxes 31

Title IX.

Chapter 51.	Of the board of education	33
	52. Of the commissioner of public schools........	36
	53. Of the appropriation for public schools......	38
	54. Of the powers and duties of towns and of the town treasurer and town clerk relative to public schools.........................	41
	55. Of the powers of school districts	46

CONTENTS. ix.

		PAGE.
56.	Of district meetings	48
57.	Of joint school districts	50
58.	Of the levy of district taxes	53
59.	Of the trustees of school districts	56
60.	Of the powers and duties of school committees	58
61.	Of teachers	65
62.	Of legal proceedings relating to public schools	67
63.	Of the normal school, teachers' institutes and lectures	71
64.	Of truant children, and of the attendance of children in the public schools	73
65.	General provisions relating to public schools.	79
66.	Of the R. I. College of Agriculture and Mechanic Arts	84
67.	Of State beneficiaries at the R. I. School of Design	88
68.	Of factory inspection	89

Chapter 85.
Of provision for the education of deaf, blind, and imbecile children.. 91

Chapter 86.
Of the Rhode Island Institute for the Deaf............ 92

Chapter 87.
Of the State Home and School for Children............ 95

Chapter 111.
Of dogs.. 100

Chapter 166.

Of bills of exchange and promissory notes, and of legal interest 104

Chapter 176.

Of incorporation 105

Chapter 278.

Of offences against public peace 108

Chapter 279.

Of offences against private property 108

Chapter 283.

Of offences against public policy 109

Decisions.

Exemption from taxation 113
Powers and duties of towns 115
Powers of districts and district officers 122
District meetings 147
District taxes 189
Trustees 208
Powers and duties of school committee, and apportionment and uses of school money 222
Teachers 249
Legal proceedings 259

REMARKS.

	PAGE.
Board of education	292
Commissioner of public schools	293
Towns	294
Town clerks	295
Town treasurers	296
School committees	297
School superintendents	324
Districts	328
Taxation	342
Teachers	348
Appeals	357
Education of the dependent and defective classes	358
Libraries	359
Forms	362
Index to General Laws	395
Index to decisions	422
Index to remarks and forms	432

EXTRACTS

FROM THE

Constitution of Rhode Island.

ARTICLE I.

DECLARATION OF RIGHTS.

SECTION
2. Object of government.—How laws should be made and burdens distributed.
3. Religious freedom secured.

ARTICLE IX.

QUALIFICATIONS FOR OFFICE.

SECTION
1. Qualified electors only eligible.

ARTICLE XII.

EDUCATION.

SECTION
1. Duty of general assembly to promote schools, etc.
2. The permanent school fund.
3. Donations for support of schools.
4. Powers of general assembly under this article.

PREAMBLE.

WE, the people of the State of Rhode Island and Providence Plantations, grateful to Almighty God for the civil and religious liberty which He hath so long permitted us to enjoy, and looking to Him for a blessing upon our endeavors to secure and to transmit the same unimpaired to succeeding generations, do ordain and establish this constitution of government.

ARTICLE I.

Declaration of Certain Constitutional Rights and Principles.

In order effectually to secure the religious and political freedom established by our venerated ancestors, and to preserve the same for our posterity, we do declare that the essential and unquestionable rights and principles hereinafter mentioned shall be established, maintained and preserved, and shall be of paramount obligation in all legislative, judicial and executive proceedings.

SECTION 2. All free governments are instituted for the protection, safety and happiness of the people. All laws, therefore, should be made for the good of the whole; and the burdens of the State ought to be fairly distributed among its citizens.

SEC. 3. Whereas Almighty God hath created the mind free; and all attempts to influence it by temporal punishments or burdens, or by civil incapacitations, tend to beget habits of hypocrisy and meanness; and whereas a principal object of our venerable ancestors, in their migration to this country and their settlement of this State, was, as they expressed it, to hold forth a lively experiment, that a flourishing civil State may stand and be best maintained with full liberty in religious concernments: we, therefore, declare that no man shall be compelled to frequent or to support any religious worship, place, or ministry whatever, except in fulfillment of his own voluntary contract; nor enforced, restrained, molested, or burdened in his body or goods; nor disqualified from holding any office;

nor otherwise suffer on account of his religious belief; and that every man shall be free to worship God according to the dictates of his own conscience, and to profess and by argument to maintain his opinion in matters of religion; and that the same shall in no wise diminish, enlarge, or affect his civil capacity.

ARTICLE IX.

Of Qualifications for Office.

SECTION 1. No person shall be eligible to any civil office, (except the office of school committee), unless he be a qualified elector for such office.

ARTICLE XII.

Of Education.

SECTION 1. The diffusion of knowledge, as well as of virtue, among the people, being essential to the preservation of their rights and liberties, it shall be the duty of the general assembly to promote public schools, and to adopt all means which they may deem necessary and proper to secure to the people the advantages and opportunities of education.

SEC. 2. The money which now is or which may hereafter be appropriated by law for the establishment of a permanent fund for the support of public schools, shall be securely invested, and remain a perpetual fund for that purpose.

SEC. 3. All donations for the support of public schools, or for other purposes of education, which may be received by the general assembly, shall be applied according to the terms prescribed by the donors.

SEC. 4. The general assembly shall make all necessary provisions by law for carrying this article into effect. They shall not divert said money or fund from the aforesaid uses, nor borrow, appropriate, or use the same, or any part thereof, for any other purpose, under any pretence whatsoever.

EXTRACTS FROM THE GENERAL LAWS

OF THE

State of Rhode Island

RELATING TO

PUBLIC INSTRUCTION.

IN THE YEAR OF OUR LORD 1896.

CHAPTER 6.

Of the Rights and Qualifications of Voters.

SECTION
1. Classification of voters as registered and unregistered, and their rights to vote.

SECTION
2. Right to vote on real estate, situated in town other than that in which voter resides.

SECTION 1. The two following classes of persons have, by the constitution, the first as registered and the second as unregistered voters, a right to vote in the election of all civil officers, and on all questions in all legally organized town, ward or district meetings :

First, Every male citizen of the United States, of the age of twenty-one years, who has had his residence and home in this state for two years, and in the town or city, in which he may offer to vote, six months next preceding the time of his voting, and whose name shall be registered, in the town or city where he resides, on or before the last day of December in the year next preceding the time of his voting : *Provided,* that no person shall at any time be allowed to vote in the election of the city council of any city, or upon any proposition to impose a tax or for the expenditure of money in any town or city, unless he shall within the year next preceding have paid a tax assessed upon his property therein, valued at least at one hundred and thirty-four dollars.

Second, Every male citizen of the United States, of the age of twenty-one years, who has had his residence and home in this state for one year, and in the town or city, in which he may claim a right to vote, six months next preceding the time of voting, and who is really and truly possessed in his own right of real estate in such town or city of the value of one hundred and thirty-four dollars over and above all incumbrances, or which shall rent for seven dollars per annum over and above any rent reserved or the interest of any incumbrances thereon, being an estate in fee-simple, fee-tail, for the life of any person, or an estate in reversion or remainder, which qualifies no other person to vote, the conveyance of which estate, if by deed, shall have been recorded at least ninety days.

SEC. 2. The following class of persons have, by the constitution, as unregistered voters, a right to vote in the election of all general officers and members of the general assembly, in the town or city in which they shall have had their residence and home for the term of six months next preceding the election:—

Every male citizen of the United States, of the age of twenty-one years, who has had his residence and home in this state for one year, and shall own any such real estate within this state, but out of the town or city in which he resides, as is described in the second clause of the first section of this chapter, and who shall produce a certificate from the clerk of the town or city in which his estate lies, bearing date within ten days of the time of his voting, setting forth that such person has a sufficient estate therein to qualify him as a voter, and that the deed, if any, has been recorded ninety days.

CHAPTER 7.

Of the Registering, Listing and Returning Lists of Voters, and of Proof of their Qualification to Vote.

SECTION
2. Registry voters to register themselves annually.
3. Names of property taxpayers to be put on voting list; and annual registry not required.
8. Proof of payment of taxes.
12. Town clerks, etc., to furnish certified copies of lists of voters on demand, etc.

SECTION
13. Town clerks to give certified copies of registration of voters and other records.
14. Electors entitled to certified lists of persons paying taxes. etc., and penalty for refusal to furnish same.

SEC. 2. Every person who is or within a year may be qualified to vote, upon being registered, shall go to the town clerk of the town in which he resides, and shall annually, on or before the last day of December, register his name, and thereby certify to the truth of the facts stated in the appropriate heads of such registry. Every person who shall knowingly make any false certificate in registering his name in any such registry book shall be fined not exceeding fifty dollars, or be imprisoned not exceeding sixty days : *Provided*, that before any person's name shall be placed upon the voting list, if such citizen shall be of foreign birth, he shall file proof, at least five days before any meeting of the board of canvassers, with the town clerk, that he is a citizen of the United States, and such proof shall be subject to the approval of the board of canvassers of the town or ward wherein such person shall claim the right to vote.

SEC. 3. The several town and ward clerks shall annually place upon the voting list the names of the several persons who have previously been upon the voting list, according to the provisions of this chapter, against whom a property tax to the amount of one dollar or upwards shall have been assessed ; and such persons need not register their names annually as is required of persons not paying a property tax.

SEC. 8. The proof of the payment of taxes upon real estate or personal property shall be the certificate of the collector of taxes or town treasurer ; and the receipt or returns of the collector of taxes shall be sufficient evidence for the purpose of procuring the certificate of the town treasurer. In case of a school-district or highway tax, when by law the same may be paid, whether in money or labor, to a surveyor of highways or to a district collector, the receipt of such surveyor or district collector shall be sufficient evidence of such payment for the purpose of procuring the certificate of the collector of taxes or of the town treasurer.

SEC. 12. Every town, ward or district clerk, upon payment or tender of his legal fees, which shall be the same for the ward and district clerks as for the town clerks, shall furnish to any one demanding the same a certified copy of any list of voters whose votes have been given in at any election.

SEC. 13. Every town clerk shall, upon like payment or tender, furnish to any person demanding the same a certified copy of any registration of voters, and shall also, upon request of any person and tender of legal fees, and without any unreasonable delay, examine the records and certify to the estate of any person, and shall furnish copies of any instrument or writing which may be on record or in the files of his office.

SEC. 14. Every officer authorized to receive taxes shall, upon like request and payment or tender, and without unreasonable delay, furnish to any elector a certified list of those who have paid to him state and town taxes, and the amounts and times of such payments; and shall grant certificates setting forth whether a certain person has or has not paid to him such taxes, and, if paid, to what amount and at what time; and every such officer who shall refuse or unreasonably delay to furnish such lists or certificates, upon payment or tender as aforesaid, shall for every such offence be fined not less than twenty-five dollars nor more than two hundred dollars.

CHAPTER 25.

Of Oaths, and by whom Administered.

SECTION
5. Form of engagement.
9. Who may administer oaths throughout the state.
10. Who may administer oaths

SECTION
within their respective counties and towns.
11. Who may administer oaths in connection with their offices.

SEC. 5. Every person, except the justices of the supreme court, elected to office by the general assembly, or by either house thereof, or by any town or town council, or under the provisions of the law in relation to public schools, or appointed to office, civil or military, by the governor, shall, before he shall act therein, take the following engagement before some person authorized to administer oaths, namely: I, [naming the person], do solemnly swear (or, affirm) that I will faithfully and impartially discharge the duties of the office of [naming the office] according to the best of my abilities, and that I will support the constitution and laws of this state, and the constitution of the United States, so help me God: [Or: This affirmation I make and give upon the peril of the penalty of perjury].

SEC. 9. The following persons may administer oaths anywhere within the state: The governor, lieutenant-governor, secretary of state, attorney-general, assistant attorney-general, general treasurer, justices of the supreme court, speaker of the house of representatives, commissioners appointed by other states to take acknowledgments of deeds and depositions within this state, notaries public, the railroad commissioner, the insurance commissioner, and the commissioners of shell fisheries.

Sec. 10. The following persons may administer oaths within the respective counties and towns for which they may be elected to office: Clerks of courts, state senators, justices and assistant justices of the district courts, justices of the peace, mayors of cities, judges of probate, presidents of town councils, or persons acting as such, town clerks and town wardens.

Sec. 11. The following persons may administer oaths in relation to all matters connected with, or in administering the duties of, their respective offices: The school commissioner, foremen of grand juries, members of committees of either house of the general assembly or of joint committees thereof, chairmen of committees of either board of a city council or of joint committees thereof, members of town councils, auditors, referees, masters in chancery, clerks of school districts, commissioners on insolvent estates, members of the board of state charities and corrections, coroners, deputy-coroners, assessors of taxes, the presiding officer of the state board of pharmacy, general and field officers, judge advocate-general and brigade judge-advocate.

CHAPTER 26.

Of the Construction of Statutes.

SECTION	SECTION
1. Rules of construction, when to be applied.	7. "United States."
2. Genders.	8. "Town," "town council," "town clerk," "ward clerk," "town treasurer," "town sergeant."
3. Numbers.	
4. Joint authority of three or more authorizes a majority.	9. "Land" or "lands," "real estate."
5. "Person."	
6. "Insane person."	10. "Oath," "sworn," "engaged."

Section	Section
11. "Month." "year."	lic acts for purposes of pleading.
12. Computation of time.	
13. "Justice of the peace," "district court."	16. Repeal. effect of, in civil cases.
	18. Repeal not to revive statutes repealed.
14. "Seal."	
15. Acts of incorporation are pub-	19. Statutes, when to take effect.

SECTION 1. In the construction of statutes the provisions of this chapter shall be observed, unless the observance of them would lead to a construction inconsistent with the manifest intent of the general assembly, or be repugnant to some other part of the same statute.

SEC. 2. Every word importing the masculine gender only, may be construed to extend to and to include females as well as males.

SEC. 3. Every word importing the singular number only, may be construed to extend to and to include the plural number also ; and every word importing the plural number only, may be construed to extend to and to embrace the singular number also.

SEC. 4. All words purporting to give a joint authority to three or more officers or persons shall be so construed as to give such authority to a majority of them.

SEC. 5. The word "person" may be construed to extend to and include copartnerships and bodies corporate and politic.

SEC. 6. The words "insane person" shall be construed to include every idiot, person of unsound mind, lunatic and distracted person.

SEC. 7. The words "United States" shall be construed to include the several states and the territories of the United States.

SEC. 8. The word "town" may be construed to include city, or the District of Narragansett; the words "town council," board of aldermen or the district council of the District of Narragansett; the words "town clerk," city clerk or the clerk of the District of Narragansett; the words "ward clerk," clerk of election district; the words "town treasurer," city treasurer or the treasurer of the District of Narragansett; and the words "town sergeant," city sergeant or the district sergeant of the District of Narragansett.

SEC. 9. The word "land" or "lands," and the words "real estate," may be construed to include lands, tenements and hereditaments, and rights thereto and interests therein.

SEC. 10. The word "oath" shall be construed to include affirmation; the word "sworn," affirmed; and the word "engaged," either sworn or affirmed.

SEC. 11. The words "month" and "year" shall be construed to mean a calendar month and year.

SEC. 12. Whenever time is to be reckoned from any day, date, or act done, or the time of any act done, such day, date, or the day when such act is done, shall not be included in such computation.

SEC. 13. The words "justice of the peace" may be construed to include warden of the peace, and the words "district court" to include warden's court.

SEC. 14. Whenever a seal is required to be affixed to any paper, the word "seal" shall be construed to include an impression of such seal made with or without the use of wax or wafer on the paper.

SEC. 15. Every act of incorporation shall be so far deemed a public act, that the same may be declared on and given in evidence, without specially pleading the same.

SEC. 16. The repeal of any statute shall in no case affect any act done, or any right accrued, acquired or established, or any suit or proceeding had or commenced in any civil case before the time when such repeal shall take effect.

SEC. 18. The repeal of any statute shall not be construed to revive any other statute which has been repealed.

SEC. 19. Every statute which does not expressly prescribe the time when it shall go into operation, shall take effect on the tenth day next after the rising of the general assembly at the session thereof at which the same shall be passed.

CHAPTER 30.

Of the Permanent School Fund.

SECTION
1. Custody and investment.
2. Money from auctioneers to be added to the fund.
3. School money forfeited by towns, to be added to the fund.

SECTION
4. Additions, how they are to be invested.
5. Income to be appropriated for support of public schools.

SECTION 1. The general treasurer, with the advice of the governor, shall have full power to regulate the custody and safe keeping of the fund now constituting the permanent fund for the support of public schools, and shall keep the same securely invested in the capital stock of some safe and responsible bank or banks or in bonds of towns or cities within this state.

SEC. 2. The money that shall be paid into the state treasury by auctioneers, for duties accruing to the use of the state, is appropriated, and the same shall annually be added to said school fund, for the permanent increase thereof.

SEC. 3. Whenever any money appropriated to any town from the state treasury, for the support of public schools therein, shall have been forfeited by such town, the same shall be added to said school fund, and shall forever remain a part thereof.

SEC. 4. The general treasurer, with the advice of the governor, shall from time to time securely invest all sums of money hereby directed to be added to said fund, in the capital stock of some safe and responsible bank or banks or in bonds of any town or city within this state.

SEC. 5. The income arising from said fund so invested shall annually be appropriated for the support of public schools in the several towns.

CHAPTER 31.

Of the Public Records.

SECTION
1. Officers to deliver official records, etc., to their successors in office, or to secretary of state, when. Penalty for neglect.

SECTION
2. Penalty for neglect by other than the lawful custodian, to deliver official records, etc.

SECTION 1. Every person who shall hold a public office shall, upon leaving the same, deliver to his successor in office, or, if there be no successor, to the secretary of state, all records, books, writings, letters and documents, kept or received by him in the transaction of his official business, and all moneys in his hands which he shall have received as trust funds from any person or otherwise in the course of his official business; and every such person who shall, without just cause, refuse or neglect for the space of ten days after request made in writing by any citizen of the state, to deliver as herein required such records, books, writings, letters or documents, or to pay over such moneys, to the person authorized to receive the same, shall be fined not exceeding five hundred dollars and be imprisoned not exceeding five years.

SEC. 2. Every person, other than the lawful custodian thereof, who shall have in his possession, or under his control, any such record, book, writing, letter or document as is designated in section one of this chapter, and who shall, without just cause, refuse or neglect for the space of ten days after request made in writing by any citizen of the state, to deliver such record, book, writing, letter or document to the lawful custodian of the same, shall be fined not exceeding five hundred dollars and be imprisoned not exceeding five years.

CHAPTER 36.

Of the Powers of, and of Suits by and against, Towns.

SECTION
4. Towns may grant money for schools, schoolhouses and school libraries.
5. Towns may establish free public libraries.
6. May appropriate money for the maintenance, etc., of such libraries.

SECTION
7. May appropriate money for free public library not its own.
21. Town indebtedness limited to three per centum of taxable property.
22. Town taxes limited to one per centum of ratable property.

SEC. 4. Towns may, at any legal meeting, grant and vote such sums of money as they shall judge necessary :—

* * * * * *

For the support of schools, purchase of sites for and the building and repair of schoolhouses; and for the establishing and maintaining of school libraries;

* * * * * *

SEC. 5. The electors in any town or city qualified to vote upon any proposition to impose a tax, or for the expenditure of money in such town or city, may, by a majority vote of such electors voting at the annual meeting for the election of town officers, or members of the city council therein, appropriate a sum not exceeding twenty-five cents on each one hundred dollars of the ratable property of such city or town in the year next preceding such appropriation, for the foundation therein of a free public library, with or without branches, for all the inhabitants thereof, and to provide suitable rooms for such library, which shall be used under such regulations as may from time to time be prescribed by the town council of such town, or city council of such city.

SEC. 6. Any town or city having established a free public library therein, in manner as aforesaid, may annually, by the majority vote of the electors of said town, qualified as aforesaid and voting on the proposition, or by vote of the city council of said city, appropriate a sum not exceeding thirty cents on each one thousand dollars of its ratable property, in the year next preceding such appropriation, for the maintenance and increase of such library therein, and may take, receive, hold and manage any devise, bequest or donation for the establishment, increase or maintenance of a public library therein, to be under such regulations for its government, when they are not prescribed by its donor, as may from time to time be prescribed by the town council of such town, or the city council of such city.

SEC. 7. Every town not owning a free public library may, at the annual town meeting, appropriate a sum not exceeding thirty cents on each one thousand dollars of its ratable property in the year next preceding such appropriation, for the maintenance and increase of any free public library therein.

SEC. 21. No town shall, without special statutory authority therefor, incur any debt in excess of three per centum of the taxable property of such town, including the indebtedness of such town on the tenth day of April, one thousand eight hundred seventy-eight, but the giving of a new note or bond for a pre-

LAWS RELATING TO PUBLIC INSTRUCTION. 19

existing debt, or for money borrowed and applied to the payment of such pre-existing debt, is excepted from the provisions of this section, and the amount of any sinking fund shall be deducted in computing such indebtedness.

SEC. 22. No town shall assess its ratable property in any one year in excess of one per centum of its ratable value, except for the purpose of paying the indebtedness of such town or the interest thereon, or for appropriations to any of the sinking funds, or for extraordinary repairs for damages caused by the elements; but assessments for specific benefits conferred by the opening or improving of any public highway, or for any public sewer, shall not be taken to be within the provisions of this section.

CHAPTER 43.

Of the Establishment and Control of Free Public Libraries by Towns.

SECTION
1. Town or city council may accept gift of public library, or funds for.
2. Town or city council to elect trustees, and may fill vacancies.

SECTION
3. Duties and powers of trustees.
4. Appropriation for support of library to be made annually.
5. Trustees to accept and receipt for legacies.

SECTION 1. In case any library, or funds for the establishment thereof, may be offered to any city or town on the condition that said library shall be maintained as a free public library, the city council of any city, or town council of any town, is hereby authorized to accept such gift in behalf of the city or town.

SEC. 2. Whenever any city or town shall establish a free public library, or shall become possessed, as above provided, of any such library, the aforesaid city council or town council, as the case may be, shall proceed to elect a board of trustees, to consist of not less than three members nor more than seven. As soon as possible after the election of the first board, the members thereof shall meet and be divided by lot into three groups or classes, the terms of office of one group expiring in one year from the date of their election, those of another group in two years, and those of the remaining group in three years. With the expiration of the term of office of any member the vacancy shall be filled by the city council or town council, as the case may be, for the term of three years. Vacancies occurring by resignation, removal, death, or otherwise, shall be filled as above for the unexpired term thereof.

SEC. 3. The aforesaid trustees shall take possession of said library, and shall thereafter be the legal guardians and custodians of the same. They shall provide suitable rooms for the library, arrange for the proper care of the same, choose one or more competent persons as librarians and fix their compensation, and make all needful rules and regulations for the government of the library and the use of the books: *Provided*, that no fee for the use of the books shall ever be exacted.

SEC. 4. Each city or town acting under this chapter shall annually appropriate for the support of the public library an amount at least as much as that which the library shall receive from the state. All appropriations from the city or town and state, and the income of all funds belonging to the library, shall be subject to the exclusive control of the trustees, and the several city and town treasurers shall pay, within the limits of the appropriations and other library funds in their hands, all bills properly certified by the said trustees.

Sec. 5. In case of any bequest, legacy, or gift to, or in favor of, a public library, the trustees thereof are hereby authorized and empowered to accept the same in behalf of, and for the use of, the library, and their receipt shall be a full and sufficient discharge and release to any executor, administrator, or other person authorized to make the payment thereof.

CHAPTER 44.

Of Property Liable to and Exempt from Taxation.

SECTION
1. Property liable to taxation.

SECTION
2. Property exempt from taxation.

Section 1. All real property in the state and all personal property belonging to the inhabitants thereof shall be liable to taxation unless otherwise specially provided.

Sec. 2. The following property and no other, shall be exempt from taxation: Property belonging to the state; lands ceded or belonging to the United States; buildings for free public schools, buildings for religious worship and the land upon which they stand and immediately surrounding the same, to an extent not exceeding one acre, so far as said buildings and land are occupied and used exclusively for religious or educational purposes ; the buildings and personal estate owned by any corporation used for a school, academy or seminary of learning, and of any incorporated public charitable institution, and the land upon which said buildings stand and immediately surrounding the same, to an extent not exceeding one acre, so far as the same is used exclusively for educational purposes, but no property or estate whatever shall hereafter be exempt from taxation, in any case, where any part of the income or profits thereof or of the business carried on thereon, is divided among its owners or stockholders ; the estates, persons and families of the president and professors, for the time being, of Brown University, for not more than ten thousand dollars for each such officer, his estate, person and family included; property specially exempt by charter, unless such exemption shall have been waived in whole or in part ; lots of land used exclusively for burial grounds ; the property, real and personal, held for or by any incorporated library society, or any free public library, or any free public library society, so far as said property shall be held exclusively for library purposes, or for the aid or support of poor friendless children, or for the aid or support of the aged poor, or for the aid or support of the poor generally, or for a hospital for the sick or disabled, and any fund given or held for the purpose of public education ; almshouses and the land and buildings used in connection therewith, except that almshouse-estates, when belonging to the town, shall be subject to taxation for school purposes, in the school district in which they are situated ; the estate of any person who in the judgment of the assessors is unable, from infirmity or poverty, to pay the tax ;

the bonds and other securities issued and exempted from taxation by the government of the United States.

CHAPTER 47.

Of Assessing and Collecting Poll Taxes.

SECTION
1. Poll tax to be assessed, when and upon whom.
2. Assessors entitled to certain information from inhabitants of towns and cities.

SECTION
  Penalty for refusing to give such information.
3. Collection of poll tax. Tax to be applied to support of public schools.

SECTION 1. The assessors of taxes of each town and city shall, at the time of the annual assessment of town and city taxes therein respectively, assess against every person in said town or city, who, if registered, would be qualified to vote, a tax of one dollar, or so much thereof as with his other taxes shall amount to one dollar.

SEC. 2. The assessors of taxes of each town or city, or either of them, or any person by them authorized, may, at any time within three months preceding the time of assessing the poll tax in their respective towns or cities, require from any and every inhabitant of such town or city such information as may be deemed necessary by them, or either of them, to enable said assessors to decide whether or not any inhabitant is liable to assessment for said tax ; and any person who shall refuse to give such information, or shall wilfully make any false statements for the purpose of deceiving in the giving of such information, shall be punished by fine not exceeding twenty dollars, or imprisonment in the county jail for a term not exceeding ninety days.

Sec. 3. The assessors of taxes on completing the assessment of taxes as prescribed in this chapter, shall date and sign, and within three days thereafter deposit the same in the office of the town clerk, except in the city of Providence, and in the city of Providence deposit the same with the city treasurer thereof. The town clerk shall forthwith make a copy of the same, and deliver it to the town treasurer, and the town treasurer shall forthwith issue and affix to said copy a warrant under his hand, and which need not be under seal, directed to the collector of taxes of the town commanding him to proceed and collect the several sums of money therein expressed, of the persons liable therefor, by the time directed by the town, and to pay over the same to him or to his successor in office. Whenever any town shall elect its town treasurer collector of taxes for such town, such warrant shall be issued to the town treasurer as collector of taxes by the town clerk. The tax assessed according to the provisions of this chapter, shall be applied to the support of the public schools in such town or city.

CHAPTER 48.

Of the Collection of Taxes.

Section	Section
2. Taxes a lien on real estate.	9. Collector may advertise and sell.
3. Lien, how long to continue.	10. Real estate may be sold after notice; notice how given.
7. Tax may be collected from either real or personal estate.	11. Notice, how given in case of residents.

LAWS RELATING TO PUBLIC INSTRUCTION.

Section		Section	
12.	Notice to persons not taxed who have an interest in the property taxed.	19. 20.	Sales of personal property; notice of, how given.
13.	If non-residents, a copy of notice to be sent by mail.	21.	Property to be sold by auction if tax is not paid.
14.	Entry upon the land not necessary; return to be made to town clerk under oath; effect of return.	22.	Surplus to be returned to owner.
		23.	Collector may remove personal property for sale.
		24.	May follow persons or property to any town.
15.	Deed of real estate sold by collector or sheriff for taxes, what title vests in purchaser.	25.	Sale may be adjourned.
		26.	Collector may recover tax, how.
		27.	Judgment, execution and levy.
		28.	Proceedings, where person taxed is out of state.
16.	Owner may redeem within one year.	29.	Warrant of distress to issue, when.
17.	Collector may distrain and sell personal property.	34.	Warrant is in force until tax is collected.
18.	Property exempt from distraint.	35.	Collector may require aid.

SECTION 2. All taxes assessed against any person in any town for either personal or real estate shall constitute a lien on his real estate therein.

SEC. 3. All taxes assessed against the owner of any real estate shall constitute a lien on such real estate in any town, for the space of two years after the assessment, and, if such real estate be not aliened, then until the same is collected.

SEC. 7. If any person is taxed for several parcels of real estate, or for personal and real estate in the same tax, the whole of such person's tax may be collected, either out of the real or personal estate, or any part thereof: *Provided*, that no land aliened shall be sold, if the person taxed have other sufficient property.

SEC. 9. The collector may advertise and sell any real estate liable for taxes in the manner hereinafter directed.

SEC. 10. In all cases where any parcel of real estate is liable for payment of taxes, so much thereof as is necessary to pay the tax, interest, costs and expenses, shall be sold by the collector, at public auction, to the highest bidder, after notice has been given of the levy, and of the time and place of sale, in some newspaper published in the town, if there be one, and if there be no newspaper published in the town, then in some newspaper published in the county, at least once a week for the space of three weeks, and the collector shall also post up notices in two or more public places in the town for the same period.

SEC. 11. If the person to whom the estate is taxed be a resident of this state, the collector shall, in addition to the foregoing, cause notice of his levy, and of the time and place of sale, to be left at his last and usual place of abode, or personally served on him, at least twenty days previous to the day of sale.

SEC. 12. In case the collector shall advertise for sale any property, real, personal or mixed, in which any person other than the person to whom the tax is assessed has an interest, he shall, provided the interest of such other person appears upon the records of the town, leave a copy of the notice of such sale at the last and usual place of abode, or personally with such other person, if within this state, twenty days prior to the time of such sale.

SEC. 13. If such other person have no last and usual place of abode within this state, then a copy of said notice shall be sent by mail to such person, at his place of residence, if known, twenty days prior to the time of such sale.

Sec. 14. No entry upon the land by the collector shall be deemed necessary; but the collector, in all cases of sales of real estate, shall make a return of all his proceedings under oath into the town clerk's office, within ten days after the sale; which return shall be evidence of the facts therein stated.

Sec. 15. The deed of any real estate, or of any interest therein, sold for the payment of taxes, made and executed by the sheriff or collector who shall sell the same, shall vest in the purchaser, subject to the right of redemption hereinafter provided, all the estate, right and title the owner thereof had in and to such real estate at the time said tax was assessed, free from any interest or incumbrance thereon of any person to whom the notice required by the provisions of this chapter shall have been given; and the recitals in such deed shall be evidence of the facts stated.

Sec. 16. The person who owned any real estate sold for taxes, at the time of the assessment, or any interest therein, his heirs, assigns or devisees, may redeem the same upon repaying to the purchaser the amount paid therefor, with twenty per centum in addition, within one year after the sale, or within six months after final judgment has been rendered in any suit in which the validity of the sale is in question: *Provided*, said suit be commenced within one year after such sale.

Sec. 17. The collector may distrain personal property, except as provided in the section following, and may sell the same in the manner hereinafter directed.

SEC. 18. Property exempt from attachment or distress by the laws of this state or of the United States shall not be liable to be distrained for any taxes whatsoever.

SEC. 19. In all cases where personal property shall be levied on by any collector, he shall cause notice thereof, and of the time and place of sale, to be left at the last and usual place of abode of the owner, or personally to be given to him, at least five days previous to the appointed time of sale, if such owner have a last and usual place of abode in the state or if personal notice can be given to him.

SEC. 20. The collector shall also in all cases advertise the same for three successive weeks in a newspaper, if there be one published in the town, if not, in the county, and shall also post up notices in three public places in said town, at least twenty days previous to the appointed time of sale.

SEC. 21. If such owner do not pay the amount of the tax, with the interest or percentage and all costs and charges, by the time appointed for the sale, the collector shall sell the same, or enough to pay said sums, at public auction.

SEC. 22. Any property or surplus of money remaining shall be returned to the owner or person entitled to receive it. If no owner or person entitled to receive the same can be found by the collector, he shall deliver such property or surplus of money to the town treasurer, who shall hold the same subject to the call of the owner thereof.

SEC. 23. Any collector may, with consent of the

owner, remove personal property for sale to any town or place, where it may be sold to the best advantage, giving notice to the owner as before provided, and giving notice as provided by section twenty of this chapter, in the town or place where the sale is to be made.

Sec. 24. If any person or property taxed in one town removes or is removed into another town before the tax is collected, the collector may follow such person or property into any town, and levy or collect the tax with the same power as if not removed.

Sec. 25. Any sale of real or personal estate or of any interest therein, liable for the payment of taxes by the provisions of this chapter, may be adjourned from time to time.

Sec. 26. The collector of any tax may recover the amount thereof in an action of the case against the person taxed, and in the declaration it shall be sufficient to set forth that the action is to recover a specified sum of money, being a tax assessed against the defendant, specifying the town in which said tax was assessed and the time of ordering and assessing the same.

Sec. 27. If judgment be rendered in favor of the collector, he shall have an allowance for his reasonable trouble in attending to the suit, to be taxed by the court in the bill of costs, and execution shall issue against the real and personal estate of the defendant, and the levy of the execution upon any real estate, upon which a lien for such tax is created by this chapter, shall be deemed to relate back, and take effect from the time of commencement of such lien.

Sec. 28. If any person legally taxed shall be out of the state, or depart therefrom, leaving no property liable for the tax, the collector may summon the attorney, agent, factor, trustee or debtor of such person before the district court of the district in which the town where the tax is assessed is situated, to declare on oath how much property, if any, of such absent person, he has in his possession ; and if he has sufficient property he shall forthwith pay such tax and charges, or deliver to the collector sufficient property therefor.

Sec. 29. If any person so summoned shall neglect to appear, or refuse to make oath, or having made oath shall refuse to pay such tax and charges, or to deliver to the collector sufficient property therefor, if such he has, such district court shall forthwith grant to the collector a warrant of distress against the proper goods and chattels of such person so summoned, and the collector may distrain and sell the same wherever found, or so much thereof as will pay the tax and all interest and expenses, in manner provided by this chapter; and said district court shall have jurisdiction in the premises, although the amount involved shall exceed three hundred dollars.

Sec. 34. All warrants for the collecting of taxes shall continue in force until the whole tax is collected, notwithstanding the time appointed for collecting the tax, or the year of office, may have expired, and notwithstanding the collector may have paid the tax into the town treasury.

Sec. 35. Every collector shall have the same right to require the aid or assistance of the persons present, in the performance of his duty, which a sheriff now has by law.

CHAPTER 50.

General Provisions Concerning Taxes.

SECTION
1. Towns may provide for deduction, if tax is paid; and impose percentage, if tax is not paid.
2. Officers neglecting to perform duties required of them, liable to be indicted.

SECTION
3. Town taxes to have preference, in cases of insolvency.
4. Compensation of assessors, town clerks and collectors.
5. School district taxes.

SECTION 1. Any town may provide for such deduction from the tax assessed against any person, if paid by an appointed time, or for such penalties by way of percentage on a tax, if not paid at the time appointed, not exceeding twelve per centum per annum, as they shall deem necessary to insure punctual payment.

SEC. 2. Every officer who shall neglect or refuse to perform any duty imposed on him in this title, or who shall not comply with the provisions thereof, or who shall in any wise knowingly violate any provisions thereof, shall be imprisoned not exceeding one year or be fined not exceeding five hundred dollars, which fine, in case it be a state tax, shall be paid into the state treasury, or if a town tax, into the town treasury, or if a school district tax, into the school district treasury, or if a fire corporation tax, into the fire corporation treasury.

SEC. 3. Whenever any person shall become insolvent, or die insolvent, town taxes due from him or his estate shall have preference, after debts or taxes due the United States and this state, over all other debts or demands, save those due for necessary funeral charges, and for attendance and medicine during his last sickness.

SEC. 4. Assessors shall receive such compensation as the town shall allow; town clerks shall be paid for copying tax bills as for other copies; and collectors shall be paid for collecting at the rate of five per centum, unless they shall have agreed with the town for a less sum; which fees shall be paid out of the town treasury. In case of distraint of personal property, or levy on land, the collector shall have the same fees as sheriffs have in similar cases.

SEC. 5. The provisions of this title shall apply to all school district taxes, so far as they may be applicable.

TITLE IX.

OF PUBLIC INSTRUCTION.

CHAPTER 51. Of the board of education.
CHAPTER 52. Of the commissioner of public schools.
CHAPTER 53. Of the appropriation for public schools.
CHAPTER 54. Of the powers and duties of towns and of the town treasurer and town clerk relative to public schools.
CHAPTER 55. Of the powers of school districts.
CHAPTER 56. Of district meetings.
CHAPTER 57. Of joint school districts.
CHAPTER 58. Of the levy of district taxes.
CHAPTER 59. Of the trustees of school districts.
CHAPTER 60. Of the powers and duties of school committees.
CHAPTER 61. Of teachers.
CHAPTER 62. Of legal proceedings relating to public schools.
CHAPTER 63. Of the normal school, teachers' institutes and lectures.
CHAPTER 64. Of truant children and of the attendance of children in the public schools.
CHAPTER 65. General provisions relating to public schools.
CHAPTER 66. Of the Rhode Island college of agriculture and mechanic arts.
CHAPTER 67. Of state beneficiaries at the Rhode Island school of design.
CHAPTER 68. Of factory inspection.

CHAPTER 51.

Of the Board of Education.

SECTION
1. Board of education, how constituted, and duties of.
2. How divided, and term of office of members.
3. Vacancies, how filled.
4. Officers of the board.
5. To hold quarterly meetings, and prescribe rules.
6. Appropriation for free public libraries.
7. Board to prescribe conditions on which libraries may receive aid.

SECTION
8. Payments, how to be made.
9. Annual reports to be made to the board, by officers of schools receiving state aid.
10. Private schools to be registered.
11. Board to furnish forms for returns under preceding two sections.
12. Chapter 86 unaffected.
13. Board to report annually.
14. Travelling expenses of the board to be paid, and how.

SECTION 1. The general supervision and control of the public schools of the state, with such high schools, normal schools and normal institutes, as are or may be established and maintained wholly or in part by the state, shall be vested in a state board of education, which shall consist of the governor and the lieutenant-governor, as members by virtue of their office, and of one other member from each of the counties of the state, with the exception of Providence county, which shall have two other members. The board of education shall elect the commissioner of public schools.

SEC. 2. The members of the board of education shall continue to be divided into three classes, and to hold their offices until the terms for which they were respectively elected shall have expired.

SEC. 3. Two members of the board of education shall be elected annually at the May session of the general assembly, in grand committee, from the counties in which vacancies shall occur in said board, who shall hold office for three years, and until their successors shall have been elected and qualified ; vacancies in said board shall be filled for any unexpired term by an election from the county for which the member whose office is vacant was elected, in the same manner, at any session of the general assembly.

SEC. 4. The governor shall be president, and the commissioner of public schools shall be secretary of the board of education.

SEC. 5. The board of education shall hold quarterly meetings in the first week of March, June, September and December of each year, at the office of the commissioner of public schools, and may hold special meetings at the call of the president or secretary. They shall prescribe, and cause to be enforced, all rules and regulations necessary for carrying into effect the laws in relation to public schools.

SEC. 6. The board of education may cause to be paid annually to and for the use of each free public library established and maintained in the state, and to be expended in the purchase of books therefor, a sum not exceeding fifty dollars for the first five hundred volumes included in such library, and twenty-five dollars for every additional five hundred volumes therein : *Provided*, that the annual payment for the benefit of any one such library shall not exceed the sum of five hundred dollars.

SEC. 7. The board of education shall from time to time establish rules prescribing the character of the books which shall constitute such a library as will be entitled to the benefits conferred by the preceding section, regulating the management of such library so as to secure the free use of the same to the people of the town and neighborhood in which it shall be established, and directing the mode in which the sums paid in pursuance of this chapter shall be expended. No library shall receive any benefit under the foregoing provisions, unless such rules shall have been complied with by those in charge thereof, nor until they shall have furnished to said board satisfactory evidence of the number and character of the books contained in said library.

SEC. 8. Every payment herein authorized shall be made by the general treasurer upon the order of the commissioner of public schools, approved by the board of education, and payable to the librarian or other person having charge of such library or of the funds applied to its support designated by said board.

SEC. 9. The trustees, officers, or persons in charge of all schools and educational institutions supported wholly or in part by this state, whether entirely devoted to education or only partially so, shall make a report annually in the month of July to the state board of education, of such facts as shall show the number of pupils and instructors, the courses of study, the cost of maintenance, and general needs and conditions of the school or institution.

SEC. 10. All private schools or institutions of learning in this state shall be registered at the office of the state board of education, said registry showing location, name, officers or persons in charge, grade of instruction, and common language used in teaching. They shall also make a report annually in the month of July, to the state board of education, showing the number of different pupils enrolled, the average attendance, and the number of teachers employed.

Sec. 11. The board shall provide registers for all such schools and institutions, and shall prepare blank forms of inquiry for the facts called for in the two sections next preceding, and in doing so shall have special reference to the requirements of the bureau of education at Washington.

Sec. 12. Nothing in the three sections next preceding shall be so construed as to repeal, affect, or modify the provisions of chapter eighty-six.

Sec. 13. The board of education shall make an annual report to the general assembly at the adjourned session at Providence.

Sec. 14. The members of said board shall receive no compensation for their services, but the general treasurer shall pay, upon the order of the state auditor, the necessary expenses of the members, when attending the meetings of the board, or when traveling on official business within the state, after the bills have been approved by the general assembly.

CHAPTER 52.

Of the Commissioner of Public Schools.

Section
1. Commissioner, how elected.
2. May employ a clerk.
3. Duties of the commissioner.
4. To secure uniformity of textbooks.

Section
5. To prepare and distribute programme for Arbor Day.
6. To report to the general assembly.

SECTION 1. There shall be annually elected a commissioner of public schools in the manner prescribed in the preceding chapter, who shall devote his time exclusively to the duties of his office. In case of sickness, temporary absence, or other disability, the governor may appoint a person to act as commissioner during such absence, sickness or disability.

SEC. 2. He may employ a clerk to assist in the duties of his office.

SEC. 3. The commissioner of public schools shall visit, as often as practicable, every school district in the state, for the purpose of inspecting the schools, and diffusing as widely as possible, by public addresses and personal communications with school officers, teachers and parents, a knowledge of the defects, and of any desirable improvements, in the administration of the system and the government and instruction of the schools.

SEC. 4. He shall, under the direction of the board of education, recommend and bring about, as far as practicable, a uniformity of text-books in the schools of all the towns; and shall assist in the establishment of, and selection of books for, school libraries.

SEC. 5. The commissioner of public schools shall prepare each year a programme of exercises suitable for the observance of Arbor Day, and shall distribute the same among all of the public schools of the state at least four weeks previous to said day.

SEC. 6. He shall annually, in December, make a

report to the board of education, upon the state and condition of the schools and of education, with plans and suggestions for the improvement of said schools.

CHAPTER 53.

Of the Appropriation for Public Schools.

SECTION
1. Appropriation from treasury to be paid annually.
2. How apportioned.
3. How expended.
4. Conditions upon which towns shall receive their proportion.
5. Forfeiture of town's proportion, when.
6. Orders on the general treasurer.

SECTION
7, 8. Appropriation for reference books and illustrative apparatus. How apportioned.
9. Of future apportionments in case applications exceed the amount of appropriation.
10. Evening schools.

SECTION 1. The sum of one hundred and twenty thousand dollars shall be annually paid out of the income of the permanent school fund, and from other money in the treasury, for the support of public schools in the several towns, on the order of the commissioner of public schools.

SEC. 2. This sum of one hundred and twenty thousand dollars shall be apportioned by the commissioner of public schools among the several towns, as follows: The sum of one hundred dollars shall be apportioned for each school, not to exceed fifteen in number in any one town; the remainder shall be apportioned in proportion to the number of children from five to fifteen years of age, inclusive, in the several towns, according to the school census then last preceding.

SEC. 3. The money appropriated from the state as aforesaid shall be denominated "teachers' money," and shall be applied to the wages of teachers, and to no other purpose.

SEC. 4. No town shall receive any part of such state appropriation, unless it shall raise by tax, for the support of public schools, a sum equal to the amount it may receive from the treasury for the support of public schools.

SEC. 5. If any town shall neglect or refuse to raise or appropriate the sum required in the preceding section, on or before the first day of July, in any year, its proportion of the public money shall be forfeited, and the general treasurer, on being informed thereof in writing by the commissioner of public schools, shall add it to the permanent school fund.

SEC. 6. The commissioner of public schools shall draw orders on the general treasurer for their proportion of the appropriation for public schools, in favor of all such towns as shall on or before the first day of July annually comply with the conditions of section four of this chapter.

SEC. 7. The sum of three thousand dollars shall be annually appropriated for the purchase of dictionaries, encyclopedias and other works of reference, maps, globes and other apparatus, for the use of the public schools of the state.

SEC. 8. Said sum of three thousand dollars shall be apportioned among the several towns and districts as follows: Every town or district desiring to avail itself of this appropriation shall make application therefor to the commissioner of public schools, stating the amount that has been raised or appropriated for the same purpose by the town or district. Upon the receipt of said application and vouchers for the amount actually expended, the commissioner of public schools may draw his order on the general treasurer in favor of said applicant for half of the amount of said vouchers, to an amount not to exceed twenty dollars in any one year, in favor of any district, or, in case of any town not divided into districts, at the rate of not more than ten dollars for each school, to an amount not to exceed two hundred dollars in any one year: *Provided*, that the gross amount in any one fiscal year shall not exceed three thousand dollars.

SEC. 9. In case the number and amount of applications in any one fiscal year shall exceed the limit of the appropriation, the commissioner of public schools shall record the date of each application, and in the apportionment for the following year such recorded applications shall have the preference in the order of their dates.

SEC. 10. There shall be an annual appropriation for the support and maintenance of evening schools in the several towns of this state, under the general supervision of the state board of education, who shall apportion said appropriation annually among the several towns and draw orders therefor on the general treasurer.

CHAPTER 54.

Of the Powers and Duties of Towns and of the Town Treasurer and Town Clerk Relative to Public Schools.

SECTION
1. Towns to maintain schools with or without districts.
2. Towns may be divided into districts.
3. Schoolhouses, how to be provided.
4. Towns may abolish school districts.
5. Powers and liabilities of discontinued district.
6. Control of public schools to then vest in school committee.
7. School committee, how and when chosen.
8. Superintendent, how appointed, his duties and compensation.

SECTION
9. Town treasurer to receive and keep account of school money.
10. To submit statement of school money to committee.
11. To transmit statement of money raised and paid out, to commissioner.
12. Town clerk to record boundaries of districts, and distribute school documents.
13. Annual census of children of school age to be taken.
14. Blanks, by whom provided, and to call for what information.
15. Census returns, how arranged and disposed of.

SECTION 1. Every town shall establish and maintain, with or without forming districts, a sufficient number of public schools, at convenient places, under the management of the school committee, subject to the supervision of the commissioner of public schools as provided by this title.

SEC. 2. Any town may be divided by a vote thereof into school districts.

SEC. 3. Any town may vote, in a meeting notified for that purpose, to provide schoolhouses, together with the necessary fixtures and appendages thereof, in all the districts, if there be districts, at the common expense of the town: *Provided*, that if any district shall provide, at its own expense, a schoolhouse approved by the school committee, such district shall not be liable to be taxed by the town to provide or repair schoolhouses for the other districts.

SEC. 4. Any town may at any town meeting, or at district meetings for the election of town officers, the subject having been duly inserted in the warrant for said meeting or meetings, abolish all of the school districts therein; and forthwith all title and interest in all of the schoolhouses, land, furniture, apparatus and other property which was vested in the several districts shall be vested in the town. The property so taken by the town shall be appraised by a commission of three disinterested persons to be appointed by the common pleas division of the supreme court in the county in which such town is situated, and, at the next annual assessment of taxes thereafter, a tax shall be levied upon the whole town equal to the amount of said appraisal; and there shall be remitted to the taxpayers of each district their proportional share of the appraised value of the school property in such district: *Provided*, that if any district be in debt, and said debt be assumed by the town, the amount of said debt shall be deducted from the whole amount to be remitted to the taxpayers of said district. If, however, the parties in interest prefer, the differences in the value of the property of the several districts may be adjusted in such manner as they may agree upon.

SEC. 5. Upon the abolition or discontinuance of

any district, its corporate powers and liabilities shall continue and remain so far as may be necessary for the enforcement of its rights and duties.

SEC. 6. When a town shall abolish the school districts therein, the entire control, management and care of all the public school interests of the town shall be vested in the school committee of that town, and the number of the school committee in any town abolishing the district system may be, by vote of the town, increased to a number not exceeding seven.

SEC. 7. The school committee of each town shall consist of three residents of the town, or of such number as at the present time constitute the committee, and they shall be divided as equally as may be into three classes, whose several terms of office shall expire at the end of three years from the dates of their respective elections; and in the case of the first election of a school committee under this chapter, the terms of office of the three classes shall be respectively one year, two years and three years; the classes and their terms of office to be determined by lot by the committee at their first meeting after their election. As the office of each class shall become vacant, such vacancy or vacancies shall be filled by the town at its annual town meeting for the election of state or town officers, or by the town council at its next meeting thereafter. In case of a vacancy by death, resignation, or otherwise than as is above provided, such vacancy shall be filled by the town council until the next annual town meeting for state or town officers, when it shall be filled for the unexpired term thereof as is above provided.

SEC. 8. The school committee of each town shall elect a superintendent of the public schools of the town, to perform, under the advice and direction of the committee, such duties, and to exercise such powers, as the committee shall assign him, and to receive such compensation out of the town treasury as the town shall vote. Said superintendent shall be elected at the first regular meeting of the school committee succeeding the annual election of school committee; but the committee shall have power to fill a vacancy at any meeting duly called.

SEC. 9. The town treasurer shall receive the money due the town from the state for public schools, and shall keep a separate account of all money appropriated by the state or town or otherwise for public schools in the town, and shall pay the same to the order of the school committee, and he shall credit the public school account, on the first Monday of May in each year, with the total amount of money received by him for poll taxes during the year ending the thirtieth day of April last preceding.

SEC. 10. The town treasurer shall, before the first day of July in each year, submit to the school committee a statement of all moneys applicable to the support of public schools for the current school year, specifying the sources of the same.

SEC. 11. The town treasurer shall, on or before the first day of July, annually, transmit to the commissioner of public schools a certificate of the amount which the town has voted to raise by tax for the support of public schools for the current year; and also a statement of the amount paid out to the order of the school committee, and from what sources it was derived, for the year ending the thirtieth day of April next preceding; and until such return is made to the commissioner, he may, in his discretion, withhold the order for the money in the state treasury belonging to such town.

SEC. 12. The town clerk shall record the boundaries of school districts and all alterations thereof in a book to be kept for that purpose, and shall distribute such school documents and blanks as shall be sent to him, to the persons for whom they are intended.

SEC. 13. The town clerks, or some person whom the board of aldermen of any city, or the town council of any town, shall appoint for the purpose, shall annually, in the month of January, take or cause to be taken a census of all persons between the ages of five and fifteen years, inclusive, residing within the limits of their respective towns on the first day of said January.

SEC. 14. The blank forms required to carry out the requirements of the preceding section shall be furnished by the commissioner of public schools to each town on or before the first day of December in each year, and they shall call in substance for the following information, namely, the name, age, number of weeks' attendance upon any school, parents' name and residence, of each person enumerated; and if any parent or guardian shall refuse to give the above information in regard to his children or wards, or shall knowingly and wilfully falsify such information, he shall be fined not exceeding twenty dollars.

SEC. 15. The returns of said census shall be alphabetically arranged and deposited in the hands of the school committees of the several towns on or before the first day of March in each year; and the receipt of the chairman or clerk of the school committee to the effect that the above returns have been so received by him shall be forwarded to the commissioner of public schools before he shall draw his order for the payment of any portion of the public money to that town.

CHAPTER 55.

Of the Powers of School Districts.

SECTION
1. School districts are bodies corporate.
2. Powers of school districts.
3. District may build and repair schoolhouses.
4. May raise money by tax.
5. Officers of the district.
6. Powers and duties of district officers.

SECTION
7. District taxes, how collected.
8. Town collector may collect.
9. Districts neglecting to organize, committee may establish the school.
10. District may devolve its duties and powers on the committee.

SECTION 1. Every school district shall be a body corporate, and shall be known by its number or other suitable designation.

SEC. 2. Every school district may prosecute and defend in all actions in which said district or its officers are parties, may purchase, receive, hold and convey, real or personal property for school purposes, and may establish and maintain a school library.

SEC. 3. Every such district may build, purchase, hire and repair schoolhouses, and supply the same with blackboards, maps, furniture and other necessary and useful appendages, and may insure the house and appendages against damage by fire : *Provided*, that the erection and repairs of the schoolhouse shall be made according to the plans approved by the school committee or, on appeal, by the commissioner of public schools.

SEC. 4. Every such district may raise money by tax on the ratable property of the district, to support public schools, and to carry out the powers given them by any of the provisions of this title : *Provided*, that the amount of the tax shall be approved by the school committee of the town.

SEC. 5. Every such district shall annually elect a moderator, a clerk, a treasurer, a collector and either one or three trustees, as the district shall decide, and may fill vacancies in either of said offices at any legal meeting. The moderator may administer the oath of office to all the other officers of the school district.

SEC. 6. The clerk, collector and treasurer, within their respective school districts, shall have the like power, and shall perform like duties, as the clerk, collector and treasurer of a town ; but the clerk, collector and treasurer need not give bond, unless required by the district.

SEC. 7. All district taxes shall be collected by the district or town collector, in the same manner as town taxes are collected.

SEC. 8. Any district may vote to place the collection of any district tax in the hands of the collector of town taxes, who shall thereupon be fully authorized to proceed and collect the same, upon giving bond therefor to the district satisfactory to the school committee.

SEC. 9. If any school district shall neglect to organize, or, if organized, shall for any space of six months neglect to establish a school and employ a teacher, the school committee of the town may themselves or by an agent establish a school in the district schoolhouse, or elsewhere in the district, in their discretion, and employ a teacher.

SEC. 10. Any district may, with the consent of the school committee, devolve all the powers and duties relating to public schools in the district on the school committee.

CHAPTER 56.

Of District Meetings.

SECTION
1. Meetings, notice of, how and by whom to be given.
2. Annual meeting, when held.
3. Special meetings, how called.
4. District meeting, where held.

SECTION
5. Notice of time and place, how to be given.
6. Qualification of voters.
7. Clerk to record names of voters on request.

SECTION 1. Notice of the time, place and object of holding the first meeting of a district for organization or for a meeting, either annual or special, to choose officers or to transact any other business, shall be given by the trustees or, in case of the death, removal, resignation or disability of the trustees, by the clerk of the district; in case there be no trustee or clerk authorized to call a meeting such notice shall be given by the school committee of the town.

SEC. 2. Every school district when organized, shall hold an annual meeting in the month of April of each year for choice of officers and for the transaction of any other business relating to schools.

SEC. 3. The trustees or, in case of the death, removal, resignation or disability of the trustees, the clerk may call a special meeting for election or other business at any time, and shall call one to be held within seven days on the written request of any five qualified electors stating the object for which they wish it called; and if the trustees or clerk, as above provided, neglect or refuse to call a special meeting when so requested, the school committee may call it and fix the time therefor: *Provided*, that no special district meeting shall be called without the consent of the school committee, to consider any subject which shall have been acted on by the district at any time within six months previous to the time of such proposed meeting.

SEC. 4. District meetings shall be held in the schoolhouse, unless otherwise ordered by the district. If there be no schoolhouse or place appointed by the district for its meetings, the trustee or, in case of the death, removal, resignation or disability of the trustees, the clerk, and, if there be no trustees or clerk, the school committee, shall determine the place, which shall always be within the district.

SEC. 5. Notice of the time and place of every annual meeting, and of the time, place and object of every special meeting, shall be given, either by publishing the same in a newspaper published in the district, or by posting the same in two or more public places in the district for five days before holding the same.

SEC. 6. Every person residing in the district may vote in district meetings to the same extent and with the same restrictions as he might at the time vote in town meeting; but no person shall vote upon any question of taxation of property, or expending money raised thereby, unless he shall have paid or be liable to pay, a portion of the tax.

SEC. 7. The clerk of the district shall record the number and names of the persons voting, and on which side of the question, at the request of any qualified voter.

CHAPTER 57.

Of Joint School Districts.

SECTION
1. Adjoining districts may establish advanced school.
2. Such districts to constitute a district as to such school.
3. Organization.
4. Public money, how drawn.
5. Adjoining districts in the same town may consolidate.
6. To receive public money as if not united.
7. Organization.
8. Adjoining districts, or parts,

SECTION
in adjoining towns may be formed into joint districts, and discontinued.
9. Organization.
10. Powers of such joint district.
11. Public money to be apportioned.
12. Corporate property, how owned.
13. Apportionment, when district is divided.
14. Payment, when, by part of a district added to district.

SECTION 1. Any two or more adjoining school districts in the same or adjoining towns may, by a concurrent vote, establish a school for the older and more advanced children of such districts.

Sec. 2. Such associating districts shall constitute a school district for the purposes of providing a schoolhouse, fuel, furniture and apparatus, and for the election of a board of trustees, to consist of one member from each district so associating, and for levying a tax for school purposes, with all the rights and privileges of a school district, so far as such school is concerned.

Sec. 3. The time and place for the meeting for organization of such associate district may be fixed by the school committees, and any one or more of the associating districts may delegate to the trustees of such school the care and management of its primary school.

Sec. 4. The school committee of the town or towns in which such school shall be established, shall draw an order in favor of the trustees of such school, to be paid out of the public money appropriated to each district interested in such school, in proportion to the number of scholars from each.

Sec. 5. Any two or more adjoining school districts in the same town may, by concurrent vote, with the approbation of the school committee, unite and be consolidated into one district for the purpose of supporting public schools, and such consolidated district shall have all the powers of a single district.

Sec. 6. Such consolidated district shall be entitled to receive the same proportion of public money as such districts would receive if not united.

SEC. 7. The mode of organizing such consolidated district and calling the first meeting thereof shall be regulated or prescribed by the school committee, and notice thereof given as prescribed in section five of chapter fifty-six.

SEC. 8. Two or more adjoining districts, or parts of districts, in adjoining towns may be formed into a joint school district by the school committees of such towns concurring therein; and all joint districts which have been or shall be formed may by them be altered or discontinued.

SEC. 9. The meeting for organization of such joint district shall be called by the school committees of such towns, and notice thereof shall be given as prescribed in section five of chapter fifty-six.

SEC. 10. Such joint district shall have all the powers of a single school district, and shall be regulated in the same manner, and shall be subject to the supervision and management of the school committee of the town in which the school is located.

SEC. 11. A whole district making a portion of such joint district shall be entitled to its proportion of public money, in the same manner as if it had remained a single district; and whenever part of a district is taken to form a portion of such joint district, the school committee of the town of which such district is a part shall assign to it its reasonable proportion.

SEC. 12. Whenever any two or more districts shall be consolidated, the new district shall own all the corporate property of the several districts.

SEC. 13. Whenever a district is divided and a portion taken from it, the funds and property, or the income and proceeds thereof, shall be divided among the several parts in such manner as the school committee of the town or towns to which the districts belong may determine.

SEC. 14. Whenever a part of one district is added to another district or part of a district owning a schoolhouse or other property, such part shall pay to the district or part of a district to which it is added, if demanded, such sum as the school committee may determine, towards paying for such schoolhouse and other property.

CHAPTER 58.

Of the Levy of District Taxes.

SECTION	SECTION
1. District taxes, how levied.	6. Abatement of taxes, when and how made.
2. Town assessors to assess value of property in what cases.	7. Schoolhouse taxes and expenses by joint districts, by whom to be approved.
3. Notice of assessment.	
4. Commissioner in certain cases may order assessment.	8. Assessment of taxes in joint or associated districts.
5. Errors in assessment, how corrected.	

SECTION 1. District taxes shall be levied on the ratable property of the district, according to its value in the town assessment then last made, unless the district shall direct such taxes to be levied according to the next town assessment; and no notice thereof shall be required to be given by the trustees.

SEC. 2. The trustees of any school district, if unable to agree with the parties interested with regard to the valuation of any property in such district, shall call upon one or more of the town assessors not interested, and not residing in the district, to assess the value of such property so situated, in the following cases, namely: Whenever any real estate in the district is assessed in the town tax bill with real estate out of the district, so that there is no distinct or separate value upon it; whenever any person possessing personal property shall remove into the district after the last town assessment; whenever a division and apportionment of a tax shall become necessary by reason of the death of any person, or the sale of such property; whenever a person has invested personal property in real estate and shall call upon the trustees to place a value thereon; and whenever property shall have been omitted in the town valuation.

SEC. 3. The assessors shall give notice of such assessment by posting up notices thereof for ten days next prior to such assessment in three public places in the district; and after notice is given as aforesaid, no person neglecting to appear before the assessors shall have any remedy for being overtaxed.

SEC. 4. If a district tax shall be voted, assessed and approved of, and a contract legally entered into under it, or such contract be legally entered into without such vote, assessment, or approval, and said district shall thereafter neglect or refuse to proceed to assess and collect a tax sufficient to fulfill such contract, the commissioner of public schools, after notice to and hearing of the parties, may appoint assessors to assess a tax for that purpose, and may issue a warrant to the collector of the district, or to a collector by him appointed, authorizing and requiring him to proceed and collect such tax.

SEC. 5. Errors in assessing a tax may be corrected, or the tax re-assessed, in such manner as may be directed or approved by the commissioner of public schools.

SEC. 6. Whenever any person who has paid a tax for building or repairing a schoolhouse in one district shall, by alteration of the boundaries thereof, become liable to pay a tax in any other district, if such person cannot agree with the district, such abatement of the tax may be made as the school committee, or in case of a district composed from different towns, as the commissioner of public schools, may deem just and proper.

SEC. 7. Whenever a joint district shall vote to build or repair a schoolhouse by tax, the amount of the tax and the plan and specifications of the building and repairs shall be approved by the school committees of the several towns, or, in case of their disagreement, by the commissioner of public schools.

SEC. 8. In case of assessing a tax by a joint or associate district, if the town assessments be made on different principles, or the relative value be not the same, the relative value and proportion shall be ascertained by one or more persons, to be appointed by the commissioner of public schools, and the assessment shall be made accordingly.

CHAPTER 59.

Of the Trustees of School Districts.

SECTION
1. Trustees to have charge of the school property, and to employ teachers.
2. To provide school facilities, visit the schools, and report.
3. To furnish bookcases.
4. To make out tax bills and issue tax warrants.
5. To make returns to school committee.
6. The trustees to receive no compensation out of the school moneys for their services.

SECTION
7. May admit scholars from without the town or state, when.
8. School committee, similarly empowered, if town is not divided into districts.
9. Disposition of money received for tuition.
10. Attendance of scholars from without the district, where reckoned.

SECTION 1. The trustees of school districts shall have the custody of the schoolhouse and other district property, and shall employ one or more qualified teachers for every fifty scholars in average daily attendance.

SEC. 2. The trustees shall provide schoolrooms and fuel, and shall visit the schools twice at least during each term, and notify the committee or superintendent of the time of opening and closing the schools.

SEC. 3. The trustees shall provide a suitable cabinet or bookcase in each schoolroom, for the reception and care of such text-books and school supplies as may be furnished by the school committee.

SEC. 4. The trustees shall make out the tax bill against the persons liable to pay the same, and deliver the same to the collector with a warrant by them signed annexed thereto, requiring him to collect and pay over the same to the treasurer of the district.

Sec. 5. The trustees shall make returns to the school committee in manner and form prescribed by them or by the commissioner, or as may be required by law, and perform all other lawful acts required of them by the district, or necessary to carry into full effect the powers and duties of districts.

Sec. 6. The trustees shall receive no compensation for services out of the money received from either the state or town appropriations, nor in any way, unless raised by tax by the district.

Sec. 7. The trustees of any school district may allow scholars from without the town or the state to attend the public schools of such district, on such terms as the trustees may determine : *Provided*, that such terms shall be approved by the school committee.

Sec. 8. Whenever a town shall not be divided into school districts, or whenever public schools shall be provided without reference to such division, the school committee may exercise the powers provided in the preceding section to be exercised by trustees.

Sec. 9. All moneys received for tuition as hereinbefore provided shall be paid into the district or town treasury, as the case may be, and shall be used for school purposes only.

Sec. 10. No attendance upon the public schools authorized by the preceding three sections shall be reckoned in determining the average attendance for the purpose of regulating the distribution of school money; but such average attendance shall be returned to the district where such scholars reside, and be there reckoned with the average attendance of the schools of that district, upon demand by the trustee thereof.

CHAPTER 60.

Of the Powers and Duties of School Committees.

SECTION
1. Chairman and clerk, how chosen and removed.
2. Stated meetings, when held.
3. Committee may alter and discontinue districts.
4. To locate all schoolhouses.
5. Land for schoolhouse sites, if taken without owners' consent, how appraised.
6. Owner of land may petition for relief.
7. Instruction to be given in physiology and hygiene.
8. Committee to examine teachers; and to annul certificates, when.
9. To visit schools, when and how often.
10. To make rules and regulations for schools.
11. May authorize children to attend school in adjoining town or district.

SECTION
12. May suspend pupils.
13. Committee to manage schools, if town is not divided into districts.
14. Apportionment of the town's share of the state school money to the districts.
15. Notice of apportionments to be given to trustees.
16—18. Orders on town treasurer, in what cases and on what conditions to be given.
19. Money forfeited or unexpended, to be divided.
20. Annual report of school committee.
21. Expense of printing report, how to be paid.
22. School committee to furnish books and supplies.
23. Change in school books, how made.

SECTION 1. The school committee of each town shall choose a chairman and clerk, either of whom may sign any orders or official papers, and may be removed at the pleasure of said committee.

Sec. 2. The school committee of each town shall hold at least four regular meetings in every year, at such time and place within the town as the committee shall by general order fix and determine.

Sec. 3. The school committee may alter and discontinue school districts, and shall settle their boundaries when undefined or disputed ; but no change shall be made in the boundaries of any district except at a meeting, notice of which, with the proposed changes, has been posted upon the schoolhouses and sent to the trustees of the districts whose boundaries are liable to be affected, for at least five days before holding the same ; and no new district shall be formed with less than forty children between the ages of four and sixteen, unless with the approbation of the commissioner of public schools ; and the clerk of the committee shall transmit to the town clerk a certified copy of all votes affecting the boundary lines of the districts immediately on the passage thereof.

Sec. 4. The school committee shall locate all schoolhouses, and shall not abandon or change the location of any without good cause.

Sec. 5. In case the school committee shall fix upon a location for a schoolhouse in any town or district, or shall determine that the schoolhouse lot ought to be enlarged, and the town or district shall have passed a vote to erect a schoolhouse, or to enlarge the schoolhouse lot, and the committee shall fix upon a location for a schoolhouse, and the proprietor of the land shall refuse to convey the same, or cannot agree with the town or district for the price thereof, the school committee of their own motion, or on application of the town or district, may appoint three disinterested persons, who shall notify the parties and decide upon the valuation of the land ; and upon the tender or payment of the sum so fixed on, to the proprietor, the title to the land so fixed on by the school committee, not exceeding one acre, shall vest in the town or district for the purpose of maintaining thereon a schoolhouse and the necessary appendages thereof.

SEC. 6. Any person aggrieved thereby may, within six months after any tender as aforesaid (but not after any payment as aforesaid), petition the common pleas division of the supreme court in the county for such relief in the premises, by way of damages or otherwise, as to law and justice shall appertain, in the manner and with the same procedure prescribed in sections fifteen and sixteen of chapter forty-six in the case of petition for relief for over-assessment for taxes.

SEC. 7. The school committee of the several towns shall make provision for the instruction of the pupils in all schools supported wholly, or in part, by public money, in physiology and hygiene, with special reference to the effect of alcoholic liquors, stimulants and narcotics upon the human system.

SEC. 8. The school committee may examine, by themselves or by some one or more persons by them appointed, every applicant for the situation of teacher in the public schools of the town, and may, after five days' notice in writing, annul the certificate of such as upon examination by them prove unqualified, or will not conform to the regulations of the committee, and in such case shall give immediate notice thereof to the trustee of the district in which such teacher is employed.

SEC. 9. The school committee shall visit, by one or more of their number, every public school in the town at least twice during each term, once within two weeks of its opening and once within two weeks of its close; at which visits they shall examine the register and matters touching the schoolhouse, library, studies, books, discipline, modes of teaching and improvement of the school.

SEC. 10. The school committee shall make and cause to be put up in each schoolhouse, rules and regulations for the attendance and classification of the pupils, for the introduction and use of text-books and works of reference, and for the instruction, government and discipline of the public schools, and shall prescribe the studies to be pursued therein, under the direction of the commissioner of public schools.

SEC. 11. Whenever the school committee of any town shall find that it is more convenient or expedient for any child residing in said town to attend school in an adjoining town or district, said committee may arrange with the school authorities of such town or district for the attendance of such child at their schools, and may pay for such tuition out of the town appropriation for public schools. The amount so paid shall be used for school purposes only.

SEC. 12. The school committee may suspend during pleasure all pupils found guilty of incorrigibly bad conduct or of violation of the school regulations.

SEC. 13. Where a town is not divided into districts, or shall vote in a meeting duly notified for that purpose to provide schools without reference to such division, the school committee shall manage and regulate said schools, and draw all orders for the payment of their expenses.

SEC. 14. Whenever the public schools are maintained by district organization, the committee shall apportion among the districts, equally, according to the number of schools maintained in each, the whole of the town's proportion of the one hundred and twenty thousand dollars received from the state, and in addition thereto at least one-fourth as much more from the town appropriation for the support of public schools; the remainder of the town appropriation, and the moneys received from poll and dog taxes, from school funds, and from other sources, shall be divided into two equal parts, one part to be apportioned to the several districts, according to the average attendance of the schools therein, for the year preceding; the other part to be apportioned at the discretion of the committee: *Provided always*, that the total apportionment for each school shall not be less than one hundred and eighty dollars.

SEC. 15. The school committee shall make the apportionment among the several districts as provided in the preceding section on or before the first Monday of July in each year, and immediately thereafter give notice to the trustees of the amount so apportioned to each district.

Sec. 16. The school committee shall draw an order on the town treasurer in favor of such districts only as shall have made a return to them in manner and form prescribed by them or by the commissioner of public schools, or as may be required by law, from which it shall appear that for the year ending on the first day of May previous one or more public schools have been kept for at least six months by a qualified teacher in a schoolhouse approved by the committee or commissioner, that the money designated "teachers' money," received the year previous, has been applied to the wages of teachers and to no other purpose, and that the register properly kept has been deposited with the committee or with some person by them appointed to receive the same.

Sec. 17. Such orders may be made payable to the trustees or their order, or to the district treasurer, or teacher; and if the treasurer receive the money, he shall pay it out to the order of the trustees.

Sec. 18. The school committee shall give no such order, until they are satisfied that the services have actually been performed for which the money is to be paid; and they shall have power, in case the average attendance of any school falls below five, to suspend said school in their discretion and to make such other provisions as they may deem best for the attendance of the children, properly belonging to said school, upon some other public school; but such suspension shall not work the forfeiture of the public money to any district provided for by section sixteen of this chapter. The school committee may allow scholars residing in one district to attend school in any other district.

SEC. 19. At the end of the school year, any money appropriated to any district which shall be forfeited and the forfeiture not remitted, or which shall remain unexpended, shall be divided by the committee among the districts the following year.

SEC. 20. The school committee shall prepare and submit annually to the commissioner of public schools, on or before the first day of July, a report in manner and form by him prescribed ; and until such report is made to the commissioner, he may refuse to draw his order for the money in the state treasury belonging to such town : *Provided*, that the necessary blank for said report has been furnished by the commissioner on or before the first day of May next preceding ; they shall also prepare and submit annually, at the annual town meeting, a report to the town, setting forth their doings, the state and condition of the schools and plans for their improvement, which report, unless printed, shall be read in open town meeting ; and if printed, at least three copies shall be transmitted to the commissioner on or before the first day of July in each year.

SEC. 21. The school committee may reserve annually out of the public appropriation, a sum not exceeding forty dollars to defray the expense of printing their annual report.

SEC. 22. The school committee of every city and town shall purchase, at the expense of such city or town, text-books and other school supplies used in the public schools; and said text-books and supplies shall be loaned to the pupils of said public schools free of charge, subject to such rules and regulations as to care and custody as the school committee may prescribe.

SEC. 23. A change may be made in the schoolbooks in the public schools of any town by a vote of two-thirds of the whole school committee ; and in the city of Providence by a vote of a majority of all the members elected to the school committee, notice of the proposed change having been given in writing at a previous regular meeting of said committee : *Provided*, that no change be made in any text-book in the public schools of any town oftener than once in three years, unless by the consent of the board of education.

CHAPTER 61.

Of Teachers.

SECTION
1. Certificate of qualification required.
2. Certificate valid for how long.
3. Qualifications of teachers.
4. When teachers may be dismissed.

SECTION
5. Teachers to keep register of scholars and certain records, and make report.
6. School officers ineligible to teach in public schools.
7. Moral instruction.

SECTION 1. No person shall be employed by any trustee to teach as principal or assistant in any school supported entirely or in part by the public money, unless he shall have a certificate of qualification signed either by the school committee of the town, or by some person appointed by said committee, or by the trustees of the normal school.

SEC. 2. Such certificate, unless annulled, if signed by the school committee, shall be valid within the town for one year or for such portion thereof as shall be specified in said certificate.

SEC. 3. The school committee shall not sign any certificate of qualification unless the person named in the same shall produce evidence of good moral character and be found on examination qualified to teach the various branches required to be taught in the school.

SEC. 4. The school committee of any town may, on reasonable notice and a hearing of such teacher, dismiss any teacher for refusal to conform to the regulations by them made, or for other just cause; and in such case shall give immediate notice to the trustees of the district.

SEC. 5. Every teacher in any public school shall keep a register of the names of all the scholars attending said school, their sex, age, names of parents or guardians, the time when each scholar enters and leaves the school, the daily attendance, together with the days of the month on which the school is visited by any officer connected with public schools, and shall prepare the return of the district to the school committee of the town.

SEC. 6. No superintendent of schools or member of the school committee of any town, or trustee of any school district, shall, so long as he continues in said office of superintendent, member of the school committee or trustee of school district, be eligible or employed to teach as principal or assistant in any school supported entirely or in part by the public money, within the town where said superintendent, member of the school committee or trustee resides.

SEC. 7. Every teacher shall aim to implant and cultivate in the minds of all children committed to his care the principles of morality and virtue.

CHAPTER 62.

Of Legal Proceedings Relating to Public Schools.

SECTION
1. Appeals from decisions relating to public schools, to whom made: duty of commissioner to hear and decide.
2. Statement of facts may be presented to justice of supreme court.
3. Appeals, rules of to be prescribed by commissioner.
4. Matters in dispute may be submitted to commissioner by agreement.
5. Votes ordering district taxes, final unless appealed from.

SECTION
6. Costs, in what cases not to be taxed against school officers.
7. Suit against district may be answered by inhabitant or taxpayer.
8. 9. Judgment against school district, how satisfied.
10. Process against school district, how to be served.
11. Record of clerk of district is prima facie evidence.
12. Commissioner may remit certain fines, penalties and forfeitures.

SECTION 1. Any person aggrieved by any decision or doings of any school committee, district meeting, trustees, or in any other matter arising under this title, may appeal to the commissioner of public schools who, after notice to the party interested of the time and place of hearing, shall examine and decide the same without cost to the parties : *Provided,* that nothing contained in this section shall be so construed as to deprive such aggrieved party of any legal remedy.

SEC. 2. The commissioner of public schools may, and if requested on hearing such appeal by either party shall, lay a statement of the facts of the case before one of the justices of the supreme court, whose decision shall be final.

SEC. 3. The commissioner of public schools may from time to time prescribe rules regulating the time and manner of taking such appeals, and rules to prevent appeals for trifling and frivolous causes.

SEC. 4. Parties having any matter of dispute between them arising under this title, may agree in writing to submit the same to the adjudication of said commissioner, and his decision therein shall be final.

SEC. 5. If no appeal be taken from a vote of a district relating to the ordering of a tax, or from the proceedings of the officers of the district in assessing the same, or if, on appeal, such proceedings are confirmed, the same shall not again be questioned before any court of law or magistrate whatsoever : *Provided*, that this section shall not be so construed as to dispense with legal notice of the meeting, or with the approval of the votes or proceedings by the school committee or commissioner of public schools, whenever the same is required by law.

SEC. 6. In any civil suit before any court against any school officer for any matter which might by this chapter have been heard and decided by the commissioner of public schools, no costs shall be taxed for the plaintiff if the court are of opinion that such officer acted in good faith.

SEC. 7. Any inhabitant of a district, or person liable to pay taxes therein, may be allowed by any court to answer a suit brought therein against the district, on giving security for costs, in such manner as the court may direct.

SEC. 8. Whenever judgment shall be recovered in any court of record against any school district the court rendering judgment shall order a warrant to be issued, if no proceedings operating as a stay be taken, to the assessors of taxes of the town in which such district is situated, or, in case of a joint district composed of parts of towns, then to one or more of the assessors of each town, with or without designating them, requiring them to assess upon the ratable property in said district a tax sufficient to pay the debts or damages, costs, interest and a sum in the discretion of the court sufficient to defray the expenses of assessment and collection. Said assessors shall, without a new engagement, proceed to assess the same, giving notice as in case of other district taxes.

SEC. 9. Said warrant shall also contain a direction to the collector of the town, or in case of joint district, then to the collector of either town, as the court may direct, requiring him to collect said tax; and said warrant with the assessment annexed thereto, shall be a sufficient authority for the collector, without a special engagement, to proceed and collect the same with the same power as in the case of a town tax; and when collected, he shall pay over the same to the parties to whom it may belong, and the surplus, if any, to the district. And the court may require a bond of the collector.

SEC. 10. Whenever any writ, summons or other process shall issue against any school district in any civil suit, the same may be served on the treasurer or clerk; and if there are no such officers to be found, the officer charged with the same may post up a certified copy thereof on the door of the schoolhouse, and, if there be no schoolhouse, then in some public place in the district, and the same, when proved to the satisfaction of the court, shall constitute a sufficient service thereof.

SEC. 11. The record of the district clerk that a meeting has been duly or legally notified shall be prima facie evidence that it has been notified as the law requires. The clerk shall obtain at the expense of the district a suitably bound book for keeping the record therein.

SEC. 12. The commissioner of public schools may, by and with the advice and consent of the board of education, remit all fines, penalties and forfeitures incurred by any town, district or person, under any of the provisions of this title, except the forfeiture incurred by any town for not raising its proportion of money.

CHAPTER 63.

Of the Normal School, Teachers' Institutes and Lectures.

SECTION
1. Normal school, management of.
2. Qualification of applicants for tuition.
3. Diploma, who to receive.
4. Trustees to examine applicants to teach.
5. When may pay travelling expenses of pupils.

SECTION
6. Teachers' institutes, and educational publications, etc., appropriation for.
7. Commissioner of public schools to account to state auditor for expenditures.

SECTION 1. The normal school shall be under the management of the board of education and the commissioner of public schools as a board of trustees.

SEC. 2. All applicants from the several towns in the state shall be admitted to free tuition in said school, after having passed such an examination as may be prescribed by the board of trustees, and after having given to such board satisfactory evidence of their intention to teach in the public schools of this state for at least one year after leaving the said school.

SEC. 3. Persons who shall have passed the regular course of studies at the normal school shall, on the written recommendation of the principal, receive a diploma signed by the trustees of the school.

SEC. 4. The said trustees may, by themselves or by a committee of their board, examine all applicants to teach in the public schools, and shall give certificates to such as are found qualified to teach school.

SEC. 5. The trustees of the normal school may

pay to each pupil who shall reside within the state and not within five miles of said school, who shall have been duly admitted thereto, and who shall have attended the regular sessions of said school and complied with the regulations thereof during the term next preceding such payments, not exceeding ten dollars for each quarter year for traveling expenses; but such payments in the aggregate for such traveling expenses shall not exceed the sum of fifteen hundred dollars in any one year, and shall be made to the respective pupils entitled to the same in proportion to the distance they may reside from said school.

SEC. 6. A sum not exceeding five hundred dollars shall be annually paid for defraying the necessary expenses and charges for teachers and lecturers for teachers' institutes, to be holden under the direction of the commissioner of public schools; and a sum not exceeding three hundred dollars shall be annually paid under the direction of the board of education for publishing and distributing among the several towns educational publications, providing lectures on educational topics and otherwise promoting the interests of education in the state.

SEC. 7. The commissioner of public schools shall render an annual account to the state auditor of his expenditures under the provisions of this chapter with his vouchers therefor.

CHAPTER 64.

Of Truant Children, and of the Attendance of Children in the Public Schools.

SECTION
1. Attendance at day schools required.
2. Private school may be approved.
3. Truant officers, and their appointment, duties and fees.
4. Inquiry to be made into causes of neglect to attend school.
5-7. Employment of children between twelve and fifteen years of age forbidden, when, unless, etc. Penalty.
8, 9. Duties of truant officers, as to children employed.
10. Penalty for employment of

SECTION
children unable to read or write, when.
11. Ordinances to be made concerning truancy and idle children.
12, 13. Commitment and discharge of minors convicted under such ordinances.
14. School committee to report of action of town under this chapter.
15. Fines, how to inure.
16. Jurisdiction of district court.
17. Officers need not give surety for costs.

SECTION 1. Every person having under his control a child between the ages of seven and fifteen years shall annually cause such child to regularly attend for at least eighty full school days some public day school in the town or city in which such child resides ; and while such child is not lawfully employed to labor at home or elsewhere said person shall cause such child to attend a public day school regularly during the days and hours that the public schools are in session in the city, town, or district where such child resides ; and for every neglect of such duty the person so offending shall be fined not exceeding twenty dollars : *Provided,* that if the person so charged shall prove, or shall present a certificate, made by or under the direction of the school committee of the city or town wherein he resides, setting forth that the child has attended for the required period of time a private day school approved by the school committee of the city or town where said school is located, or that the child has been otherwise furnished for a like period of time with the means of education, or has already acquired the elementary branches of learning taught in the public schools, or that his physical or mental condition was such as to render his attendance inexpedient or impracticable, or that the child was destitute of clothing suitable for attending school and that the person in charge of said child was unable to provide such clothing, or that the child has been excused from attending school by the school committee of the city or town where he resides, then such penalty shall not be incurred.

SEC. 2. For the purposes of this chapter the school committees of the several towns and cities shall approve a private school only when the teaching therein is in the English language and when they are satisfied that such teaching is thorough and efficient, and when the persons in charge of said school shall keep the record of the attendance of the pupils thereof upon the blanks provided by the state for such purpose and shall render to the school committee of the town or city where said school is located a detailed report of the attendance of any pupil for any specified time : *Provided*, that the request for such report is made in writing and sets forth that such pupil is suspected of irregular attendance or truancy.

SEC. 3. The town council of each town, and the board of aldermen of each city, shall annually appoint one or more special constables, and fix their compensation, who shall be truant officers and who shall, under the direction of the school committee, inquire into all cases arising under the provisions of this chapter, or under any ordinances made in pursuance thereof by the town or city by which such officers were appointed, and shall alone be authorized, in case of violation of any of the provisions of this chapter, or of any such ordinances, to make complaint therefor; they shall also serve all legal processes issued in pursuance of this chapter or of any such ordinances, but shall not be entitled to receive any fees for such service: *Provided, however*, that in case of the commitment of any person under the provisions of any section of this chapter, or of any ordinance made in pursuance thereof, or for default of payment of any fine and costs imposed thereunder, such officer shall be entitled to the regular fees allowed by law for similar service.

SEC. 4. The truant officers and the school committees of the several towns and cities shall inquire into all cases of neglect of the duty prescribed in section one of this chapter within their respective towns and cities, and ascertain the reasons, if any, therefor; and such truant officers, or any of them, shall, when so directed by the school committee, prosecute any person liable to the penalty provided for in said section one.

SEC. 5. No child between the ages of twelve and fifteen years shall be employed in any manufacturing, mechanical or mercantile establishment, or by any telegraph or telephone company in this state, except during the vacations of the public schools of the city, town or district in which such child resides, unless, during the twelve months next preceding such employment, he shall have attended school as provided for in section one of this chapter, or shall have already acquired the elementary branches of learning taught in the public schools, or shall have been excused by the school committee of the town or city in which such child resides; nor shall such employment continue unless such child shall attend school as above provided each year, or until he shall have acquired the elementary branches of learning taught in the public schools.

SEC. 6. No child between the ages of twelve and fifteen years shall be so employed who does not present a certificate made by or under the direction of the school committee of the city or town in which such child resides, of his compliance with the requirements of section five of this chapter; and said certificate shall also give the place and date of birth of such child as nearly accurate as may be; and every owner, superintendent or overseer, of any establishment or company employing any such child shall keep such certificate on file so long as such child is employed therein. The form of said certificate shall be furnished by the secretary of the state board of education.

SEC. 7. Every owner, superintendent or overseer of any such establishment or company who employs or permits to be employed any child in violation of either of the two next preceding sections, and every parent or guardian who permits such employment, shall be fined not exceeding twenty dollars.

SEC. 8. The truant officers shall, at least once in every school term, and as often as the school committee require, visit the establishments or companies employing such children in their respective towns and cities, and ascertain whether the provisions of the three next preceding sections hereof are duly observed, and report all violations thereof to the school committee.

SEC. 9. The truant officers shall demand the names of the children under fifteen years of age employed in such establishments or companies in their respective towns and cities, and shall require the certificates of age and school attendance, prescribed in section six of this chapter, to be produced for their inspection; and a refusal to produce such certificates shall be punished by a fine not exceeding ten dollars.

SEC. 10. Every owner, superintendent or overseer of any such establishment or company who employs or permits to be employed therein a child under fifteen years of age who cannot write his name, age and place of residence legibly, while the public schools in the town or city where such child lives are in session, shall for every such offence be fined not exceeding twenty dollars.

SEC. 11. The town council of each town, and the city council of each city, shall make all needful provisions and arrangements concerning habitual truants and children who may be found wandering about in the streets or public places therein, having no lawful occupation or business, not attending school and growing up in ignorance, and shall make such ordinances as will be most conducive to the welfare of such children and to the good order of such town or city; and shall designate or provide suitable places for the confinement, discipline and instruction of such children.

SEC. 12. Every minor convicted, under an ordinance made under the provisions of section eleven of this chapter, of being an habitual truant, or of wandering about in the streets and public places of a town or city, or of having no lawful employment or business, or of not attending school and of growing up in ignorance, shall be committed to any institution of instruction or suitable place designated or provided for the purpose under the authority of said section eleven, for a period not exceeding two years.

SEC. 13. Children so committed may, on satisfactory proof of amendment or for other sufficient cause, be discharged from such institution or place by the court which committed them.

SEC. 14. The school committees of the several towns and cities shall annually report to the state board of education whether their towns or cities have made the provisions required by this chapter; and in case the town council of any town, or the board of aldermen and city council of any city, shall in any year refuse or neglect to comply with the provisions of section three and section eleven of this chapter, or of either of them, after having been duly notified by the commissioner of public schools, fifty per centum of the money apportioned to such city or town from the state for school purposes shall be withheld until the provisions of said section three and section eleven of this chapter have been complied with.

SEC. 15. All fines under the provisions of this chapter shall inure and be applied to the support of the public schools in the town or city where the offence was committed.

SEC. 16. The district courts of the state shall have jurisdiction in their respective districts of all cases arising under this chapter and all ordinances passed in conformity with this chapter.

SEC. 17. No officer complaining under any of the provisions of this chapter, or under the provisions of any ordinance that may be passed in pursuance hereof, shall be required to give surety for costs ; and such officer shall not in anywise become liable for any costs that may accrue on such complaint.

CHAPTER 65.

General Provisions Relating to Public Schools.

SECTION
1. Exclusion from school to be by general rule.
2, 3. District officers to be engaged in office; record of district clerk is prima facie evidence.
4. Tenure of office of such officers.
5. Penalty for neglect of duties.
6. School committee, board of education and commissioner may visit schools incorporated or aided by the state.
7. Penalty for refusing to permit such visitation.
8. Nuisances near schoolhouse, prohibited.
9. Construction of the word "town," as to the city of Providence.

SECTION
10. Public schools in city of Providence, how governed.
11. Taking of fees, etc., for promoting sale or exchange of school books, etc., prohibited.
12. Offering of fees, etc., to public school officers for such purpose, prohibited.
13. Children of deceased soldiers and sailors, when admitted free to public schools.
14. Pupils not allowed to attend public schools without certificate of vaccination.
15. Penalty for violation of provisions of this chapter.
16. Special statutes prevail.

SECTION 1. No person shall be excluded from any public school in the district to which such person belongs, if the town is divided into districts, or, if not so divided, from the nearest public school, on account of race or color, or for being over fifteen years of age, nor except by force of some general regulation applicable to all persons under the same circumstances.

SEC. 2. Every school district officer elected or appointed under the provisions of this title, except the moderator of a district meeting, shall take an engagement, before some person authorized to administer oaths, to support the constitution of the United States, the constitution and laws of this state, and faithfully to discharge the duties of his office so long as he shall continue therein.

SEC. 3. The record of the district clerk that any school district officer has been duly engaged shall be prima facie evidence thereof; and no school district officer shall enter upon the duties of his office without taking an engagement.

SEC. 4. Every school district officer elected or appointed under the provisions of this title shall, without a new engagement, hold his office until the time of the next annual election or appointment for such office and until his successor is elected or appointed and qualified.

SEC. 5. Every officer who shall make any false certificate, or appropriate any public school money to any purpose not authorized by law, or who shall refuse for a reasonable charge to give certified copies of any official paper, or to account for or deliver to his successor any accounts, papers or money in his hands, or shall wilfully or knowingly refuse to perform any duty of his office, or violate any provisions of any law regulating public schools, except where a particular penalty may be prescribed, shall be fined not exceeding five hundred dollars or be imprisoned not exceeding six months, and shall be liable to an action of the case for damages to be brought by any person injured thereby.

SEC. 6. Any school receiving aid from the state, either by direct grant or by exemption from taxation, may be visited and examined by the school committee of the town in which such school is situated, and by the members of the board of education and the commissioner of public schools, whenever they shall deem it advisable.

SEC. 7. Whenever such school shall refuse to permit such visitation, when requested, its exemption from taxation shall thereafter cease and be determined.

SEC. 8. No person shall keep any swine in any pen or other enclosure, or shall keep or suffer to be kept any other nuisance, within one hundred feet of any schoolhouse or within one hundred feet of any fence enclosing the yard of any such schoolhouse.

SEC. 9. In the construction of this title, except in the construction of chapter sixty-four, and sections six and seven of this chapter, and section twenty-three of chapter sixty, the word "town" shall include the city of Providence only so far as to entitle said city to a distributive share in the public money, upon making a report to the commissioner in the same manner as the school committees of other towns are required to do.

SEC. 10. The public schools in said city shall continue, as heretofore, to be governed according to such ordinances and regulations as the proper city authorities may from time to time adopt.

SEC. 11. No superintendent or school committee of any town, or any person officially connected with the government or direction of the public schools, shall receive any private fee, gratuity, donation or compensation in any manner whatsoever for promoting the sale or the exchange of any schoolbook, map or chart in any public school, or be an agent for the sale or the publisher of any school text-book, or be directly or indirectly pecuniarily interested in the introduction of any school text-book; and any such agency or interest shall disqualify any person so acting or interested from holding any school office whatsoever.

SEC. 12. No person shall offer to any public school officer any fee, commission or compensation whatsoever, as an inducement to effect through such officer any sale or promotion of sale, or exchange, of any schoolbook, map, chart or school apparatus.

SEC. 13. All the public schools in the state, including the State Normal School, shall be open to the children of officers and soldiers belonging to the state, mustered into the service of the United States, and of those persons belonging to the state, and serving in the navy of the United States, who died in said service during the late rebellion against the authority of the United States, or who were discharged from said service in consequence of wounds or disease contracted in said service, or who were killed in battle, without any cost or expense for taxes or other charges imposed for purposes of public education.

SEC. 14. No person shall be permitted to attend any public school in this state as a pupil, unless such person shall furnish to the teacher of such school a certificate of some practicing physician that such person has been properly vaccinated as a protection from smallpox; and every teacher in the public schools shall keep a record of the names of such pupils in their respective schools as have presented such certificate.

SEC. 15. Every person violating any provision of this chapter shall be fined not exceeding fifty dollars or be imprisoned not exceeding thirty days, unless herein otherwise provided.

SEC. 16. The foregoing provisions of this title are subject to the provisions of any special statutes respecting schools, or the management of schools, in any particular town or city, none of which are repealed hereby.

CHAPTER 66.

Of the Rhode Island College of Agriculture and Mechanic Arts.

SECTION
1. Continued a body corporate for what purposes.
2. Location. To have moneys received from the United States.

SECTION
3. Board of managers; term of office, vacancies, and residence.
4. Officers of the board.
5. Duties of officers and teachers.

SECTION 1. The present board of managers of the Rhode Island College of Agriculture and Mechanic Arts, and their successors, for the terms for which they have been or for which they hereafter may be appointed or elected as such managers, shall continue to be a body politic and corporate for the purpose of continuing and maintaining said college corporation as a college where the leading object shall be, without excluding other scientific and classical studies, and including military tactics, to teach such branches of learning as are related to agriculture and the mechanic arts, in order to promote the liberal and practical education of the industrial classes in the several pursuits and professions of life, as provided in the act of the Congress of the United States approved July 2, 1862, entitled "An act donating public lands to the several states and territories which may provide colleges for the benefit of agriculture and the mechanic arts," and for the purpose of continuing and maintaining an agricultural experiment station as a department of said college under and in accordance with, and to carry out the purposes of, the act of Congress approved March 2, 1887, entitled "An act to establish agricultural experiment stations in connection with the colleges established in the several states under the provisions of an act approved July 2, 1862, and of the acts supplementary thereto," by the said name of "Rhode Island College of Agriculture and Mechanic Arts," with all the powers and privileges, and subject to all the duties and liabilities set forth in chapter one hundred seventy-seven.

SEC. 2. Said college and experiment station shall until otherwise ordered continue to be located in the town of South Kingstown upon the estate now occupied by them, and all moneys hereafter received under said act of Congress approved March 2, 1887, and under the act of Congress approved August 30, 1890, entitled "An act to apply a portion of the proceeds of the public lands to the more complete endowment and support of the colleges for the benefit of agriculture and the mechanic arts, established under the provisions of an act of Congress approved July 2, 1862," and all other moneys which shall be received by the state for the promotion of agriculture or the mechanic arts under or by virtue of any act of Congress, shall, as and when received, be paid over to the treasurer for the time being of said college corporation, to be used and applied and accounted for by the managers and officers of said corporation for the time being, as required by the respective acts of Congress under which the same are received. And the managers and officers of said corporation shall perform all the duties, and make and publish, distribute and render all bulletins and reports required by said acts of Congress, or by any acts in amendment thereof or supplementary thereto; and shall also report to the general assembly annually at its January session.

SEC. 3. The several members of said present board of managers of said college corporation shall continue to hold their respective offices during the terms for which they were last appointed and until their respective successors are qualified to act; and upon the expiration of the term of office of that member of said board whose term shall expire next after the General Laws shall go into operation, and in every year thereafter, there shall be one member of said board appointed by the governor, with the advice and consent of the senate, for the term of five years and until his successor shall be qualified to act. In case of a vacancy in said board such vacancy shall be filled, if the general assembly be in session, by the governor with the advice and consent of the senate, if not in session by the governor until the next session of the general assembly, when, as soon as may be, an appointment shall be made by the governor with the advice and consent of the senate, to fill such vacancy, and the person so appointed shall hold his office for the remainder of the unexpired term. And every future member of said board shall be a domiciled inhabitant of the same county as was the retiring member of the board whose place he is appointed to fill.

SEC. 4. Said board of managers shall annually elect one of their own number to be president of the board, who shall also be the president of the corporation and shall continue in office until his successor is elected. They shall also from time to time appoint a treasurer and a clerk, who shall also be officers of the corporation, and who may be, but need not necessarily be, the same person or members of the board, and who shall hold their respective offices at the pleasure of the board. The treasurer before entering upon his office shall give bond to the state for the faithful discharge of his duties, in form to be approved by the attorney-general, in a penal sum to be fixed by the said board of managers and with surety or sureties to be approved by the governor; such bond to be filed and to be kept on file in the office of the secretary of state, and which bond shall be renewed whenever required by the board of managers or by the governor. And the treasurer shall make a full detailed report annually to the general assembly, at its January session, of all his receipts and expenditures, properly audited by the board of managers or a committee thereof.

SEC. 5. Said board of managers shall have the general care and management of said estate in South Kingstown and of said college and experiment station, and may employ professors, teachers and other persons in and about the same and prescribe their duties and fix their compensation, and from time to time make rules and regulations for their government; and may also make by-laws, rules, and regulations to govern their own meetings and proceedings. Said board of managers shall from time to time appoint the faculty of said college; and such faculty shall from time to time arrange the courses of study, conforming to said acts of Congress in this behalf, and prescribe such qualifications for admission of students, and such rules of study, exercise, discipline, and government, as they shall deem proper;

they may also grant academical degrees and diplomas appropriate to the courses of study to those students of good moral character who shall have pursued the prescribed courses and passed satisfactory examinations.

CHAPTER 67.

Of State Beneficiaries at the Rhode Island School of Design.

SECTION
1. Appropriations for.
2. Annual report.
3. Ex-officio directors.

SECTION
4, 5. State beneficiaries, and how appointed.
6. Tuition fees, how paid.

SECTION 1. Such sums as shall be from time to time appropriated by the general assembly to the Rhode Island School of Design, shall be paid by the general treasurer upon the orders of the state board of education, who are hereby empowered and authorized to visit and examine said school at their pleasure.

SEC. 2. The directors of the above-named school of design shall make an annual report to the state board of education in manner and form prescribed by said board of education.

SEC. 3. The state board of education are hereby authorized and empowered to elect two of their number who, by virtue of said election, shall be members of the board of directors of said school of design.

SEC. 4. The state board of education are hereby authorized to appoint as state beneficiaries at the Rhode Island School of Design, persons of proper age, character and acquirements, who have not the means of defraying the expense of instruction in said school themselves.

SEC. 5. The secretary of the board of education shall receive and file in their order the applications of all persons who desire to receive such appointment; and in making their appointments the board shall, as far as practicable, make them so that the people of the several counties may participate in the advantages as nearly as possible in proportion to the respective populations of the counties according to the last United States census.

SEC. 6. The board of education are hereby authorized to draw their orders on the general treasurer for the payment of the tuition fees of the beneficiaries appointed by them as above.

CHAPTER 68.

Of Factory Inspection.

SECTION
1, 2. Children under 12 years of age not to be employed in factories.

SECTION
3. Factory inspectors; appointment, tenure of office and duties.

SECTION 1. No child under twelve years of age shall be employed in any factory, manufacturing or mercantile establishment, within this state. It shall be the duty of every person, firm or corporation employing children, to keep a register in which shall be recorded the name, birthplace, age and place of residence of every person employed under the age of sixteen years; and said register shall be produced for inspection on demand by either of the inspectors appointed under this chapter.

SEC. 2. No person, firm or corporation employing less than five persons who are women or children shall be deemed a factory, manufacturing or mercantile establishment within the meaning of this chapter.

SEC. 3. The governor shall, between the fifteenth and thirtieth days of June, in the year eighteen hundred ninety-seven, and between the fifteenth and thirtieth days of June in every third year thereafter, appoint two factory inspectors, one of whom shall be a woman, whose term of office shall be three years from date of their appointment and until their successors shall qualify. They shall at all times be subject to removal by the governor for neglect of duty or malfeasance in the discharge of duty; and in case of removal as aforesaid, or of vacancies in said offices from any cause, the governor shall appoint successors to fill such vacancies for the unexpired term of said office. The said inspectors shall be empowered to visit and inspect, at all reasonable hours, and as often as practicable, the factories, workshops and other establishments in the state employing women or children, and shall report to the general assembly of this state at its January session in each year, including in said report the names of the factories, the number of such hands employed, and the number of hours' work performed each week. It shall also be the duty of said inspectors to enforce the provisions of this chapter, and to prosecute all violations of the same before any court of competent jurisdiction in the state. The said inspectors shall devote their whole time and attention to the duties of their respective offices. In case of any conflict of authority between the said inspectors, either of them may apply for instructions to the governor, whose decision of the controversy, after hearing the statement of each inspector and making such further investigation of the circumstances as he may deem necessary, shall be final.

CHAPTER 85.

Of Provision for the Education of Deaf, Blind, and Imbecile Children.

SECTION
1. State beneficiaries.
2. Supervision, and annual report.

SECTION
3. Clothing, how furnished.
4. Bills, how approved and paid.

SECTION 1. The governor, on recommendation of the state board of education, upon application of the parent or guardian, may appoint any deaf, blind or imbecile child, being a legal resident of this state, who shall appear to said board to be a fit subject for education, as a state beneficiary at any suitable institution or school now established, or that may be established, either within or without the state, for such period as he may determine : *Provided,* that no beneficiary shall receive educational aid for a longer time than ten years ; and the governor shall have the power to revoke any such appointment at any time for cause.

SEC. 2. The board of education are hereby clothed with the duty and responsibility of supervising the education of all such beneficiaries, and no child appointed as above shall be withdrawn from any institution or school except with their consent, or the consent of the governor ; and said board shall annually report to the general assembly their doings under this chapter, with such further information in relation to the several institutions at which these beneficiaries have been placed as may be deemed desirable.

SEC. 3. The board of education may expend in the purchase of necessary clothing for such beneficiaries a sum not exceeding twenty dollars, in any calendar year, for a single child.

SEC. 4. All bills arising under this chapter shall be examined and approved by the board of education, and the state auditor is hereby authorized to draw his orders on the general treasurer for the payment thereof when properly certified by the secretary of the board and approved by the governor, and a sum not to exceed twelve thousand dollars, or so much thereof as may be needed, is hereby annually appropriated therefor out of any money in the treasury not otherwise appropriated.

CHAPTER 86.

Of the Rhode Island Institute for the Deaf.

SECTION
1. Management and control vested in trustees.
2. Trustees, how appointed and term of office.
3. Power of board of trustees to admit.
4. Who may be admitted. Objects

SECTION
of the institute, and how managed.
5. Trustees to report annually to general assembly.
6. This chapter not affected by chapter 51, sections 9, 10 and 11.

SECTION 1. The governor and lieutenant-governor together with nine citizens of this state, of whom six shall be men and three women, to be appointed as hereinafter provided, shall constitute a board of trustees in whom shall be vested the management and control of a state institution for the instruction and maintenance of deaf children in accordance with the provisions of this chapter. Such institution shall be known as the Rhode Island Institute for the Deaf.

SEC. 2. Said trustees, other than the governor and lieutenant-governor, shall be appointed by the governor; and said trustees now in office shall continue to serve, in classes of three each, for and during the terms for which they were appointed, respectively; and in the year eighteen hundred ninety-seven, and once in every two years thereafter, three trustees in the said board shall in the same manner be appointed for a term of six years, to fill the places of those whose terms shall have expired; and vacancies which may occur from death and resignation shall be filled by the governor for the remainder of the unexpired term. The members of said board of trustees shall receive no compensation for their services.

SEC. 3. The board of trustees may admit such persons therein as hereinafter is provided.

SEC. 4. Deaf persons between the ages of three and twenty years, and of sufficient capacity for instruction, who are legal residents of the state, shall be entitled to the privilege of the school without charge, and for such period of time in each individual case as may be deemed expedient by the board of trustees; residents of other states may be admitted upon the payment of such rates of board and tuition as may be fixed by the board of trustees. The primary object of the school shall be to furnish to the deaf children of this state, oral instruction, and the best known facilities for the enjoyment of such a share of the benefits of the system of free public education as their afflicted condition will admit of. The board of trustees shall have charge of the affairs of the institution, with power to make such by-laws and regulations for the government thereof (not inconsistent with the provisions of this chapter) as they may deem expedient. They shall elect from their own number a president and secretary, together with such standing committees as they may deem necessary. They shall appoint a principal who shall be chief executive officer of the institution, and shall have charge of the educational and internal affairs of the institution, and shall also, upon the nomination of the principal, appoint teachers and subordinate officers, prescribe the duties and terms of service of the same, and fix their salaries, and for just cause remove any or all of them. They shall likewise employ the requisite number of servants and other assistants, and fix the wages of the same, and shall purchase all furniture, schoolbooks, school apparatus and other supplies necessary to the equipment and carrying-on such institution.

SEC. 5. The board of trustees shall annually in the month of January make a report to the general assembly, of the state and condition of the school, and a statement of all expenses incurred for salaries, maintenance, tuition and other items of current expense, together with an estimate of the amount of money necessary to meet the current expenses of the next year.

SEC. 6. The provisions of this chapter are not repealed, affected or modified by the provisions of sections nine, ten and eleven of chapter fifty-one.

CHAPTER 87.

Of the State Home and School for Children.

SECTION
1-3. Board of control; number, term of office, and how appointed.
4. Secretary, duties and term of office.
5. Compensation to secretary only, but traveling expenses to all.
6. Government of the school.
7. What children to be received;

SECTION
what may be returned, when, to authorities.
8. Object of school, and duty of the board.
9. Jurisdiction of probate courts.
10. Board to keep a register of the children in the school.
11. To make annual report to board of education.

SECTION 1. The control and maintenance of the state home and school for dependent and neglected children shall continue to be vested in a board of control, to be called the "board of control of the state home and school." Said school shall be known as the State Home and School for Children.

SEC. 2. The said board shall consist of seven persons, four of whom shall be men and three women, and, in addition, of such person as may be secretary of said board. The terms of office of the members of said board shall begin on the first day of July.

SEC. 3. The governor, by and with the advice

and consent of the senate, shall appoint the members of said board, other than the secretary; and he shall annually, upon the expiration of the term of office of any of said board, appoint persons to such office in place of those whose terms shall expire, and every person so appointed shall hold his office for three years, unless sooner removed. Every appointment to fill a vacancy shall be for the remainder of the term.

Sec. 4. Said board may appoint a secretary, who shall by virtue of his office be a member of the board; he shall give bond to the state in such sum as the board may require, for the faithful performance of his duties; he shall keep a record of all the doings of said board, and shall perform such other duties as may be by them required. Such secretary shall hold his office during the pleasure of the board.

Sec. 5. No member of the board, except the secretary, shall receive any compensation for his services, but every member shall be paid out of the state treasury his necessary traveling expenses.

Sec. 6. The said board shall establish a system of government for the institution, and shall make all necessary rules and regulations for imparting instruction, and for the proper training of the children. They shall appoint such officers, teachers and employees as shall be necessary, and prescribe their duties, and fix their salaries.

Sec. 7. They shall receive, in accordance with rules by them established, such children as may be declared vagrant, neglected and dependent on the public for support. as provided in this chapter, who are over four and under fourteen years of age, and who are in suitable condition of mind and body to be instructed; for exceptional reasons, children under four years may be received, should the board deem it advisable. Any child who shall be found by the board to be of unsound mind, or who may be considered by the board an improper inmate of said institution, shall be forthwith returned by them to the authorities from whom said child was received, who are hereby required to receive the same; and all children admitted shall remain until they are eighteen years of age, unless otherwise ordered by the board.

SEC. 8. It is declared to be the object of this chapter to provide for neglected and dependent children, not recognized as vicious or criminal, such influences as will lead toward an honest, intelligent and self-supporting manhood and womanhood, the state, so far as possible, holding to them the parental relation. But if at any time, in the discretion of the board, this object can be better attained by placing a child in a good family, they shall have the power to do so on condition that its education shall be provided for by such family in the public schools of the town or city where they may reside. The board are hereby made the legal guardians of all the children who may become inmates of the home and school, and charged with the duty of following such children as may be placed in families, with watchful care, and of taking them back to their own immediate supervision if at any time they fail to receive kind and proper treatment and a fair elementary education; and in case any child shall leave without permission, or be taken by any person unauthorized from said institution or from any family where it shall have been placed by said board, then said board is hereby authorized to take and restore said child to said institution or to the family.

SEC. 9. It shall be the duty of the superintendents or overseers of the poor in the several towns to, and any agent of the Rhode Island Society for the Prevention of Cruelty to Children may, bring before the courts of probate of such towns for examination, children supported in poorhouses or otherwise dependent on the public for support, or other children found to be in a state of vagrancy, want or suffering, or abandoned by their parents or guardians, or not having any home or settled abode or proper guardianship; and thereupon it shall be the duty of the court of probate before whom any such child is brought, to investigate the facts and ascertain if the child is so supported, or is in a state of vagrancy, want, and suffering, or is abandoned by its parents or guardians, or is without home or settled abode or proper guardianship, and also to ascertain its name, age and place of birth, and the names and residence of its parents or guardians, if it have any, and where and for what length of time, if at all, it has been supported at the expense of the town or state; and said courts of probate shall have power to compel attendance of witnesses. The parents or any friend may appear in behalf of any child, and the court of probate in its discretion may request some suitable person to appear in behalf of any child; and if on such examination the court shall find that such child is so supported or dependent, or is in a state of vagrancy, want, and suffering, or is so abandoned, or without home or settled abode or proper guardianship, it shall make a proper order containing a statement of the facts ascertained as to said child, and entrusting said child to the care and custody of the said board, together with a direction to the superintendent or overseer of the poor to take said child to the state home and school, and shall deliver to the superintendent or overseer of the poor, or other person procuring such examination, a certified copy thereof. Such certified copy of such order shall then be delivered with the child at the home and school, to the presiding officer thereof. All expenses attending the foregoing proceedings shall be paid by the town or city in which the child belongs: *Provided*, that children between the ages of four and fourteen supported in the state almshouse may be brought before the probate court of the town of Cranston by the agent of the board of state charities and corrections, and said court is hereby clothed with the same power over such children, and such proceedings may be had, as if they were regularly domiciled in said town; and all expenses incident to the hearings in said cases before said probate court shall be paid by the state, and the state auditor is hereby authorized to draw his orders for the payment of all such bills, when certified by the secretary of the board of control of the state home and school, out of any money in the treasury not otherwise appropriated.

SEC. 10. The board shall provide a book in which shall be registered the names, ages and places of birth of the children under their care; the residence of the parents or guardians as nearly as can be ascertained; the date when each child is received and from what town, and when he leaves the school; and whenever a child is placed in a family, the name, residence and occupation of such family; and such book shall be open at all times for the inspection of the probate clerks and the overseers of the poor of the several cities and towns of the state.

SEC. 11. The said board of control shall annually report to the state board of education, in the month of November, upon the condition of the school, the number of inmates thereof, the expenditures for the year, and their estimates for the year ensuing, together with such other matters as may seem desirable; which report shall be included by said state board of education in its annual report to the general assembly.

CHAPTER 111.

Of Dogs.

SECTION
10. Dogs to be licensed, fees; penalty.
15, 16. Mode of appraising damage

SECTION
by dogs. Balance to be applied for support of public schools.

SEC. 10. Every owner or keeper of a dog, of what age soever, shall annually in the month of April cause such dog to be registered, numbered, described and licensed from the first day of the ensuing June, in the office of the town clerk of the town wherein such owner or keeper resides; and shall cause it to wear a collar around its neck distinctly marked with its owner's name and with its registered number; and shall pay to such clerk, for such license, one dollar and fifteen cents for a male dog and five dollars and fifteen cents for a female dog; and all licenses granted under the provisions of this chapter shall be valid in every town during the then current year; *Provided, however*, that any owner or keeper of a dog of what age soever may, in the month of May in any year, have such dog licensed as aforesaid, upon paying to such clerk two dollars and fifteen cents for a male dog and six dollars and fifteen cents for a female dog; *and provided further*, that any person who shall become the owner or keeper of a dog, of what age soever, after the last day in May in each year, and prior to the first day of April following, shall cause the same to be registered, numbered, collared and licensed, within thirty days after he becomes such owner or keeper, upon the payment of one dollar and fifteen cents for a male dog and five dollars and fifteen cents for a female dog. Every person owning or keeping a dog not registered, licensed and collared according to the provisions of this section shall be fined ten dollars, one-half thereof to the use of the complainant and one-half thereof to the use of the town wherein such dog shall have been kept, to be applied by the said town to the support of public schools therein.

SEC. 15. Each town or city council, excepting town and city councils in the county of Newport, shall annually in the month of April appoint one or more suitable persons appraisers, who shall be sworn to the faithful discharge of their duties, to appraise the damage that may be done to any owner of any sheep or lambs, cattle or horses, hogs or fowls, suffering loss by reason of the biting, maiming or killing thereof by any dog or dogs, and to give a statement thereof in writing to the owner suffering such loss; and such owner, suffering loss as aforesaid, shall, within two days after such loss shall come to his knowledge, notify the appraiser, so appointed and sworn, living nearest to him in the town wherein such owner resides, of such loss; and said appraiser shall, on receipt of twenty-five cents for each mile's travel and the sum of one dollar from such owner, appraise the damage and give a statement thereof in writing, with his lawful fees taxed thereon, to such owner; and said owner shall, within sixty days thereafter, present the same to the town council of such town, who shall draw an order on the town treasurer for the amount of such appraisal and fees, or for such other amount as they, in their discretion, after careful examination, shall deem just; and said order, when presented to the town treasurer, shall be paid in the same manner as any other order made by the town council upon the town treasurer; and should any money, received under the provisions of this chapter, remain in the town treasury after April first, the town treasurer shall, on the first Monday in May following, pay over the whole of such money so remaining to the school fund of such town for the support of the public schools therein: *Provided, however*, that any town, at its annual meeting or at a town meeting specially called for that purpose, may vote to retain such money as a separate fund for the payment of damages done as aforesaid.

SEC. 16. Each town or city council in the county of

Newport shall annually in the month of April appoint one or more suitable persons appraisers, who shall be sworn to the faithful discharge of their duties, to appraise the damage that may be done to any owner of any sheep or lambs, cattle, horses, hogs or fowls, suffering loss by reason of the biting, maiming or killing thereof by any dog, and to give a statement thereof in writing to the owner suffering loss; and such owner, suffering loss as aforesaid, shall, within two days after such loss shall come to his knowledge, notify the appraiser, so appointed and sworn, living nearest to him in the town wherein such owner resides, of such loss; and said appraiser shall, on receipt of twenty cents for each mile's travel and the sum of one dollar from such owner, appraise the damage and give a statement thereof in writing, with his lawful fees taxed thereon, to such owner; and said owner shall, within sixty days thereafter, present to the town or city council of the town or city where such damage is done the appraisal thereof, and thereupon the town or city council of such town or city shall draw an order on the town or city treasurer for the amount of such appraisal and fees, or for such other amount as they, in their discretion, after careful examination, shall deem just. And such town or city treasurer shall annually, on the last Monday in March, pay all such orders in full, if the gross amount thus received by such town or city under the provisions of this chapter, after deducting all sums previously laid out under such provisions, is sufficient therefor; otherwise the town or city treasurer shall divide such amount, after deducting as aforesaid, pro rata among said orders, and the payment thereof shall be in full discharge of such orders; and should any money, received under the provisions of this chapter, remain in the town treasury after payment provided for herein, the town or city treasurer shall, on the first Monday in May following, pay over the whole of such money so remaining to the school fund of such town or city for the town or city for the support of the public schools therein : *Provided, however*, that any town in said county at its annual meeting, or at a town meeting specially called for that purpose, or any city in said county by its city council, may vote to retain such money as a separate fund for the payment of damages done as aforesaid.

CHAPTER 166.

Of Bills of Exchange and Promissory Notes, and of Legal Interest.

SECTION 8. What days shall be holidays.

SEC. 8. The twenty-second day of February (as Washington's birthday), the first Wednesday of April (as State election day), the thirtieth day of May (as Memorial day), the fourth day of July (as Independence day), the first Monday of September (as Labor day), the twenty-fifth day of December (as Christmas day), and each of said days in every year, such day as the governor of this state shall appoint as Arbor day in every year, the Tuesday next after the first Monday of November in the year eighteen hundred ninety-six and in every second year thereafter (as National election day), or when either of the said days falls on the first day of the week, then the day following it, the first day of every week (commonly called Sunday), and such other days as the governor or general assembly of this state, or the president or the congress of the United States, shall appoint as holidays for any purpose, days of thanksgiving, or days of solemn fast, shall be holidays.

CHAPTER 176.

Of Incorporation.

SECTION
11. Miscellaneous corporations are formed by what articles of agreement, how executed, and, with certificate of fee paid, where filed. Form of certificate of incorporation.
12. Certificate of incorporation confers what powers.

SECTION
13. Such corporation may hold property to what amount.
14. Articles of agreement may be amended, how.
15. Certified copies of incorporations are admissible in evidence.

SEC. 11. All libraries, lyceums, fire engine companies, and corporations formed for religious, charitable, literary, scientific, artistic, social, musical, agricultural or sporting purposes, not organized for business purposes, and all other corporations of like nature not hereinbefore otherwise provided for, shall be created in the following manner, viz.: Five or more persons of lawful age shall associate by written articles which shall express :

First. Their agreement to form said corporation ;

Second. The name by which it shall be known, which name shall not then be in use by any existing corporation of the state ;

Third. The purpose for which it is constituted;

Fourth. The town or city in which it is to be located.

Said agreement shall be signed and acknowledged by all the members named therein, and shall prescribe the manner in which the first meeting shall be held and organized. Said agreement shall be filed in the office of the secretary of state, and said persons shall pay a fee of five dollars into the general treasury of the state. When said agreement has been so filed, together with the certificate of the general treasurer that the fee of five dollars has been paid, and the sum of one dollar has been paid to said secretary of state for the certificate hereinafter required, the secretary of state shall thereupon issue to said corporation his certificate, under the seal of the state, substantially in the following form:—

STATE OF RHODE ISLAND AND PROVIDENCE PLANTATIONS.

I,   secretary of state, hereby certify that [*here insert names of all the corporators*] have filed in the office of secretary of state their agreement to form a corporation under the name of [*here insert name of corporation*] for the purpose [*here insert purpose*] in accordance with law, and have also filed the certificate of the general treasurer that they have paid into the general treasury of the state the fee required by law.

Witness my hand and the seal of the State of Rhode Island this   day of   in the year   .

SEC. 12. When said certificate has been issued as aforesaid said corporators shall be authorized to carry out the purpose of such agreement with all the powers and subject to all the duties and liabilities as provided herein and in chapter one hundred seventy-seven and all amendments thereof and additions thereto, so far as not inconsistent with the provisions of this chapter, and so far as the provisions of said chapter one hundred seventy-seven shall be applicable to such corporation.

SEC. 13. Said corporation shall be entitled to take, hold, transmit and convey real and personal estate to an amount not exceeding in all one hundred thousand dollars. But if such corporation desires to take and hold property to an amount exceeding one hundred thousand dollars either originally or by amendment, such privilege shall be granted only by the general assembly on petition thereto.

SEC. 14. Such agreement may be amended in any particular not inconsistent with the provisions of this chapter, excepting as provided in the preceding section, by vote of the corporation and the filing in the office of the secretary of state of a copy of such vote duly attested by the president and secretary of said corporation.

SEC. 15. Copies of agreements to form corporations, when formed by agreement, or of any amendment thereof, and the fact of their being filed in the office of the secretary of state and the date of such filing, and the filing of the certificate of the general treasurer, shall, when certified to by the secretary of state, be received in evidence before any court, tribunal or authority.

CHAPTER 278.

Of Offences Against Public Peace.

SECTION 7. Disturbing town, ward, religious, scientific, etc., meetings, how punished.

SEC. 7. Every person who shall wilfully interrupt or disturb any town or ward meeting, any assembly or people met for religious worship, any public or private school, any meeting lawfully and peaceably held for purposes of moral, literary or scientific improvement, or any other lawful meeting, exhibition or entertainment, either within or without the place where such meeting or school is held, shall be imprisoned not exceeding one year or be fined not exceeding five hundred dollars.

CHAPTER 279.

Of Offences Against Private Property.

SECTION
52. Of malicious mischief to books, etc., of free public libraries.

SECTION
53. Of neglect to return to such libraries, books, pamphlets, etc., after due notice.

SEC. 52. Every person who, wilfully and maliciously or wantonly and without cause, writes upon, injures, defaces, tears or destroys any book, pamphlet, plate, picture, engraving or statue or other property belonging to any law, town, city or other free public library, or suffers any such injury to be inflicted while said property is in his custody, shall be fined not less than one dollar nor more then ten dollars, the same to be for the use of the library.

SEC. 53. Every person who shall take or borrow from any law, town, city or other free or public library any book, pamphlet, paper or other property of said library and who, upon neglect to return the same within the time required and specified in the by-laws, rules or regulations of the library owning the property, has been notified by the librarian or other proper custodian of the property that the same is overdue, shall, upon further neglect to return the same within two weeks from the date of such notice, be considered to have unlawfully converted the property of the library to his own use. A written or printed notice, given personally or sent by mail to the last known or registered place of residence, shall be considered a sufficient notice.

CHAPTER 283.

Of Offences against Public Policy.

SEC. 29. Flags or emblems of foreign countries not to be displayed upon public buildings and schoolhouses.

SEC. 29. It shall be unlawful to display the flag or emblem of any foreign country upon the flagstaff of any State, county, city or town building or public schoolhouse within this State : *Provided, however,* that when any foreigner shall become the guest of the United States, or of this State, the flag of the country of which such public guest shall be a citizen or subject may be displayed upon public buildings, except public schoolhouses. Every person who shall violate the provisions of this section shall be fined not less than twenty-five nor more than one hundred dollars.

DECISIONS.

In the following pages will be found, so far as it has been possible to collect them, a digest of such decisions, rendered since the establishment of the present school system, both by the commissioners of public schools and by the Supreme Court, as interpret the school law and unfold the principles of its application.

A great many of them were made by the late Hon. Elisha R. Potter, formerly Commissioner and subsequently Associate Justice of the Supreme Court, to whose deep interest in the subject of public education it is in great part owing that the present law was enacted, and whose very intimate knowledge of the design and bearing of the law eminently qualified him to give authoritative opinions concerning it.

In those cases which were published in full in the preceding manuals, it has been deemed best in this edition usually to print only the conclusions and the reasons therefor, so far as they were given; but in cases decided since 1882, the plan of giving a fuller statement of the case has been followed.

These decisions will be found arranged topically according to the principal subjects of the several chapters of the General Laws, with cross references in cases where the decisions cover two or more distinct subjects.

It is sincerely hoped that this exposition of the law will be found adapted to the needs of the various school officers of the State and that it will tend to a vigorous enforcement of its varied provisions, and thus to a more healthy and efficient system of public schools.

EXEMPTION FROM TAXATION.

DECISION No. 1.

Saint Mary's Church vs. Benjamin Tripp, City Treasurer of the City of Providence.

A building for religious purposes is exempt from taxation although used for educational purposes, so long as the use is merely incidental or occasional, or so long as the use, if habitual, is purely permissive and voluntary and does not interfere with the use for religious purposes, there being no alienation of the building in whole or part for educational uses, as e. g. by lease.

The question here arises on Pub. Stat. R. I. cap. 41, § 2, which exempts certain classes of property from taxation, and among them "buildings for free public schools, buildings for religious worship, and the land upon which they stand and immediately surrounding the same to an extent not exceeding one acre, so far as said buildings and land are occupied and used exclusively for religious or educational purposes." The defendant contends that the words "religious or educational," at the close of this citation, are used distributively, the word "educational" being applicable exclusively to buildings for free public schools, and the word "religious" being applicable exclusively to buildings for religious worship; so that if any free public schoolhouse be used for religious purposes, or any building for religious worship be used for educational purposes, however incidental or occasional the use may be, the exemption is forfeited. We do not think the statute is to be so strictly construed. The statute seems to recognize the close connection which exists between religion and education as auxiliary to one another. It is well known that much of our Sunday school teaching, though it may be auxiliary to religion, is not purely religious. Buildings for religious worship or parts of them are frequently permitted to be used on week days for literary or scientific lectures, or for industrial instruction. It cannot be supposed that the General Assembly, which must have been familiar with these uses, some of them prompted by religion, though not religious, intended to proscribe or discourage them. We think a building for religious purposes may be used for educational purposes, without any forfeiture of its exemption, so long as the use is merely incidental or occasional, or, if habitual, so long as it is purely permissive and voluntary, and is so managed as not to interfere with the uses of the building for religious worship, there being no alienation of the building or any part of it to the educational uses, as there would be if it were leased for such uses and thus secularized, if the word may be permitted. In the case at bar, if we rightly understand the agreed statement, the use was such that it did not interfere with the needs of religious worship, and such, too, that it might have been terminated at any time, being purely permissive and voluntary. We think that under these circumstances there was no forfeiture of the exemption.

THOMAS DURFEE, C. J. S. C.

1883.

POWERS AND DUTIES OF TOWNS.

DECISION No. 2.

District of Narragansett.

"District of Narragansett is entitled to same consideration in distribution of school money as if it were styled a town."

I am of the opinion that the District of Narragansett is entitled to the same share in the apportionment of the one hundred and twenty thousand dollars appropriated for the support of public schools as provided by Public Laws R. I. cap. 426, as though it had been styled a town instead of a district in the act by which it was incorporated.

CHARLES MATTESON, A. J. C. S.
1889.

DECISION No. 3.

On Petition of Town Council of Cranston for Opinion of the Court.

1. The act authorizing any town to abolish the school districts therein does not violate the provision in Art. 1, § 2, of the Constitution of Rhode Island, which declares that "the burdens of the state ought to be fairly distributed among its citizens."
2. The assessment of the tax, deduction for debts, and remissions are required by the act to be made by the assessors of taxes, whose duty arises when the town has taken action under the act, and does not depend upon any vote of the town levying the tax.
3. The words "next annual assessment" in the act mean, and are equivalent to saying, "when the assessors begin to make their next annual assessment."
4. The remission required by the act to be made is to the individual taxpayers.

Case stated for an opinion of the court under the Judiciary Act. cap. 20, § 24, asking for a construction of Pub. Laws R. I. cap. 447.

In April, 1892, the town of Cranston voted to abolish the school district system and to adopt the town system. Thereupon, pursuant to Public Laws, cap. 447, the title to all the school property vested in the town, subject to an appraisal to be made by a commission to be appointed by this court. The act provides for the payment of such property as follows: "At the next annual assessment of taxes thereafter, a tax shall be levied upon the whole town equal to the amount of said appraisal; and there shall be remitted to the taxpayers of each district their proportional share of the appraised value of the school property in such district; provided that if any district be in debt, and said debt be assumed by the town, the amount of such debt shall be deducted from the whole amount to be remitted to the taxpayers of said district." A commission was appointed and a report made, which was confirmed September 12, 1893. Upon these facts the following questions are presented to the court for an opinion :

1. "Is so much of section 1 of said chapter 447 of the Public Laws as requires that 'at the next annual assessment of taxes thereafter, a tax shall be levied upon the whole town equal to the amount of the said appraisal; and there shall be remitted to the taxpayers of each district their proportional share of the appraised value of the school property in such district,' constitutional?"

It is suggested that the statute violates the provision in Art. 1, § 2, of the Constitution that "the burdens of the state ought to be fairly distributed among its citizens." The argument is that taxation is a public burden; that the statute provides for a tax for other than a public purpose; and that it is oppressive and unequal in that it does not apply to the district taxed; or, in other words, that the citizens of one district, having a small school property, are taxed for the benefit of other districts having more school property. We do not think the statute is open to the objection of unconstitutionality.

School districts have been recognized by this court as quasi corporations. Bull v. School Committee, 11 R. I. 244. As such corporations they are respectively the owners of their schoolhouses. Under the act these were to become the property of the town, and to be paid for by the town by way of a proportionate remission of tax. It is true that the taxpayers in a particular district may not, at the present time, be the same persons who paid the tax from which a schoolhouse was built; and yet it is fair to presume that purchasers of property have indirectly paid for the same in an enhanced value of land and property by reason of the erection of a schoolhouse within the district; and they are the present corporators of the district.

The apportionment may not be absolutely just, but it is evidently as nearly so as practicable. The remission provided for is not a tax raised for the benefit of individuals, but in payment of property which is virtually purchased by the town. Neither is it a tax for the benefit of one part of the town at the expense of another part, for schoolhouses are for the benefit of all and not for a part. Some sections may have required and built larger and more expensive buildings than others, but this may be so under direct taxes to build schoolhouses, and surely no one can question the right of a town to do the same thing. The increased expense in such cases is usually offset by the increased number and amount of contributing taxes. The compensation for the more costly buildings under this act is therefore as nearly equitable as it can be made. The tax and remission is virtually a tax paid into the town for the schoolhouses purchased and paid back again to the members of the respective school districts in proportion to their interest in the same.

But here comes the objection that, because none of the money goes into the town treasury, it is a tax for the benefit of individuals and not a tax for a public purpose. This objection was disposed of In the matter of Dorrance Street, 4 R. I. 230, 243, where the court says: "Certainly it approaches very near an absurdity, if he (an owner of land) is constitutionally liable, on the one hand, to pay a sum of money to the public for the benefits he has received from the improvement, and the public is constitutionally liable, on the other hand, to pay him in money for the damages which he has sustained by the improvement, to say that he is constitutionally wronged because in such a case the public,—instead of clumsily collecting the money due from him, and putting it into the treasury with one of its numerous hands, and then taking it out again and paying him for his damages with another of its numerous hands,—pays him the balance due him, if his damages exceed his benefits, or exacts from him the balance due to them, if his benefits exceed his damages. It is a mere mistaking of words for things to say, in such case, that he is compensated contrary to one clause of the Constitution, by benefits instead of money,—if under the general power of the government, and in accordance with the spirit of another clause of the same Constitution, he is liable to pay money for those benefits."

There is no difference in principle between that case and the case at bar. Here all the taxpayers would be liable to pay for schoolhouses built or purchased by the town, and as members of the school districts the act recognizes that some payment should be made by the town for the property taken from the districts. This much certainly is equitable and within the general principles of taxation. It is not compensation in the strict sense of the term, as when private property is taken, although it resembles that. It is rather an attempted equalization as between the taxpayers of the town, as members of one corporation, and the taxpayers of the districts as members of other corporations; and we fail to see that the adjustment of debit and credit is not fair and reasonable. A similar statute has been sustained in Massachusetts, Whitney v. Stow, 111 Mass. 368; Rawson v. Spencer, 113 Mass. 40. The case of Freeland v. Hastings, 10 Allen 570, is similar in principle.

2. "Does chapter 447 give the collector of taxes power under the appraisal made, to compute, collect and remit without any act on the part of the assessors?"

We think the act clearly implies that the assessment, deduction for debts and remissions are to be made by the assessors at the same time as the annual assessment.

3. "Is it the duty of the assessors to assess the amount of the appraised value of the district school

property until the voters of the town in town meeting have levied, ordered or voted such amount as a tax?"

We think it is. The act of the general assembly is superior to the vote of a town, and commands the assessment when the town has taken action under it. Of course the more orderly way would be for the town to vote the tax; but an omission to do so would not defeat the operation of the law which imposes it.

4. "If a vote of the electors of the town in town meeting is necessary before the amount of such appraised value can be assessed by the assessors, can such tax be levied, ordered or voted at a special town meeting called for the purpose at any time, or must it be levied, ordered or voted at the annual town meeting to be holden next after the commissioners' report has been confirmed by the court?"

5. "Can the amount of such appraised value be assessed by the assessors prior to the levy and assessment of the next annual tax, whether levied, ordered or voted by the electors of the town or not, without such proceedings being had as are prescribed by sections 6, 7 and 8 of chapter 43 of the Public Statutes?"

These two questions may be answered together. Strictly, the assessment is not fully made until the list is completed and delivered by the assessors. But Pub. Stat. cap. 43, § 6, provides that the assessment is not to begin until after the time given to the taxpayers for bringing in their accounts. We think the statute contemplates that the assessment of this special tax is to be made along with the general tax, and hence that the intention was to fix the time of making it at the beginning of the assessment. It would be unreasonable to suppose, if, as in this case, a report should be made after the assessment list had been practically completed but before it had been delivered, that the assessors must do the work all over again, and thus delay the collection of the tax. We think the "next annual assessment" means, and is equivalent to saying, "when the assessors begin to make their next annual assessment." There might, therefore, be an interval after the annual town meeting, within which a special meeting could be held, but it should be at a time to allow for the bringing in of lists by taxpayers as provided in said section 6.

6. "Are these amounts remitted to be deducted from the taxes of the individual taxpayers, or are they payable to the treasurer of each school district as a fund from which to pay and cancel debts and obligations of the respective districts?"

The act clearly provides for a remission to taxpayers, which means, we think, the individual taxpayers. There is no provision for the proportionate amount of any district to go to its treasurer for any purpose. The liability of a district for debts continues, notwithstanding such remission, although the act presupposes an assumption of district debts by the town and the retention of an amount sufficient to cancel them, thus saving the trouble of proceedings against the district or of an assessment and collection of a special district tax to pay its debts.

JOHN H. STINESS, A. J. S. C.

1893.

POWERS OF DISTRICTS AND DISTRICT OFFICERS.

DECISION No. 4.

The district has power, with approval of committee, to open a second school, provided that there be money enough in the treasury to the credit of the district to pay for both schools.

ELISHA R. POTTER, C. P. S.

1851.

DECISION No. 5.

School District No. 10, North Kingstown.

Schoolhouse may not be used for any purposes other than those directly connected with public education.

This case involves the right of the district or trustees to use the schoolhouse for other purposes than an ordinary school, and depends partly upon the provisions of the general school laws, and partly upon the conditions of the deed of the lot upon which this particular schoolhouse stands.

The following remark upon this subject is made in the notes to the school act: "A schoolhouse, built or bought by taxation on the property of the district, should not be used for any other purpose than keeping a school, or for purposes directly connected with education, except by the general consent of the tax-paying voters."

The rule laid down here is believed to be substantially correct and sound. The district holds the property in trust for educational purposes. The money has been taken from the taxpayers by force of law for certain purposes, and for those only, and cannot be applied by either district or trustee to any other use.

I am of opinion that under the school law the house may be used for educational purposes collateral to the main purpose, such as meetings of the district for school business, lectures upon literary or scientific subjects, debating societies for the people or children of the district, etc. It may not be easy in all cases to draw the line between legal and illegal cases, but it would be perfectly clear that the district could not use the house for trade or religious meetings if any person objected to it.

The question then arises, whether the deed in the present case varies the rights of parties from what they would be if the deed contained no conditions.

By the deed from Joseph Case and others, dated October 11, 1848, the schoolhouse lot is conveyed to the district "for the purpose of maintaining thereon a district schoolhouse and appurtenances, for the benefit of the district school of said district, and for no other use or purpose whatever, except religious meetings," and it is provided "that when said lot of land shall cease to be occupied for the purposes of a district school aforesaid, the same shall revert to the grantors, their heirs and assigns forever."

The exception in regard to religious meetings may

be left out of consideration in the present case. It cannot affect it in any way. If the district have no right to religious meetings there, independent of the deed, the deed cannot give it to them. And if the district would have such a right otherwise, it may admit of question whether a provision in a deed would deprive them of it.

Leaving out of consideration the words, "except religious meetings," the remainder of the first passage quoted from the deed appears to me, on the maturest reflection, to express no more and no less than the school law, according to the construction herein given to it, would have expressed without the deed; the provision in the deed is exactly in the spirit of the law, and neither adds to nor lessens the rights and powers of the district or trustees.

If the first passage quoted from the deed does not vary the rights of the district from what they would be, if there was no such provision in the deed, the latter proviso appears for the same reason to contain no limitation, as to the use of the house, which would prevent its being used for the purposes for which I have said the law, apart from the deed, would authorize.

ELISHA R. POTTER, C. P. S.

I have carefully considered the above opinion and approve of the same. I have also consulted with Judges Haile and Brayton, who concur with me in opinion.

RICHARD W. GREENE, C. J. S. C.

1853.

See No. 12.

DECISION No. 6.

School District No. 12, Burrillville.

A vote of a school district to tax cannot be rescinded after a lawful contract has been made under it.

The fact of the tax being assessed, or of its having been approved by the committee, would not take from the district the right to rescind it. The whole turns upon the question whether a contract was legally entered into under the vote of the district, and I am of opinion that it was. The district, therefore, could not rescind it after the contract was made, without being liable to a suit for damages or to a process like that now applied for.

As a general rule, it is not advisable for district officers to proceed in expending money or making a contract unless they are satisfied that a majority of the taxpayers, absent as well as present, are fairly in favor of it. A mere accidental majority occasioned by absence of opponents is unsafe. And if a case should arise where district officers should undertake to avail themselves of such an accidental majority, and there should be any appearance of a design to anticipate or prevent a repeal of the tax by entering into a contract before there could be time for having another meeting, the commissioner of public schools would not lend the aid of his office to the enforcement of it, but would leave the parties to their action at law.

ELISHA R. POTTER, C. P. S.
1853.

I approve of the above decision.

RICHARD W. GREENE, C. J. S. C.

See No. 7.

DECISION No. 7.

School District No. 7, Burrillville.

1. A district may rescind a vote ordering a tax, and postpone the payment of it.
2. A district may borrow money and give a note.
3. Costs of suits in court against a district must be paid by the district.

The question is presented whether a district having voted a tax according to a particular town valuation, can rescind the vote, postpone the payment, and hire the money upon a note of the district.

I cannot see any objection to the right of a district to rescind a vote ordering a tax and postpone the payment of it. The object and effect may sometimes be to include property and persons afterwards coming into the district. Whoever comes into a school district becomes a sharer in all the advantages of the school and district property. If, by their coming, an addition to the schoolhouse is made necessary, such new comers or new property do not pay the whole expense of such addition: the former inhabitants and property have also to pay a portion, and, sharing in all the advantages of former taxation, it does not seem unreasonable that the new property should also share in the burdens. In the present case the schoolhouse was probably built larger than would have been necessary if it had not been expected that there would be an addition to the population of the district.

Any creditor of the district who may be injured by such postponement has a remedy provided by law.

As to giving notes, a district has the undoubted right to make contracts for certain purposes, upon which contracts they may be sued and the debt and interest recovered of them. A note given to such a contractor would be only additional evidence of his claim. And there seems to be no legal objection to the district hiring money of a third person to pay a just debt contracted for purposes authorized by law. This has been the construction always put upon the law in practice, and it appears to me sound.

An objection is also made to costs and attorney's fees. The costs of court in a suit decided against the district must of course be paid by the district. And the reasonable charges of an attorney for defending the suit are proper to be allowed. But services rendered by an attorney to any person in contests with other persons in the district about district business must be paid for by the person for whom they are performed.

Objection is also made to allowance of compound interest. This could not be recovered of the district at law, but I see no objection to the district's agreeing to pay it, and paying it if they see fit, as it would be in the power of the school committee to prevent any excess or abuse of the right.

I therefore confirm the vote of the committee approving of said tax.

ELISHA R. POTTER, C. P. S.

1853.

See No. 6.
See No. 10.
See No. 41.

DECISION No. 8.

School District No. 3, North Providence.

1. A person who has the legal qualifications may vote in district meetings even though his name is not on the town voting list.
2. A district has no right to build on a lot till it has a legal title to that lot.
3. Registry voters may vote to ask division of a district.
4. The power to divide a district lies with the school committee.
5. A district should not make a contract to build till a lot has been secured and the plan approved.

It appears from the statement and admissions of the parties, that a meeting duly notified was held August 17th, to reconsider all action relating to building the house, etc. At this meeting a motion was made to rescind the former proceedings, and as declared by the moderator, the vote stood 22 to 22, and the motion was declared rejected. It is admitted that five who voted for rescinding, and four who voted against it, had no right to vote. It is contended that Asa M. Allen, who voted for rescinding, had no right to vote. He was a resident and owned real estate, and according to previous decisions he had a right to vote without his name being on the town registry. A certificate is produced from the assessors to show that Charles Leonard and Crawford Martin, two who voted against rescinding are not taxed for real or personal property. Of course, not being liable to pay a portion of the tax, their votes should have been rejected. The vote, therefore, stands seventeen for rescinding and sixteen against rescinding, and the votes for building, etc., were legally rescinded.

This of course disposes of all questions relating to building, but the following points were made and argued, and therefore, to prevent further agitation, I give my opinion upon them.

I am of opinion that a district has no right to build upon a lot until they have acquired a legal title to it, either by lease, deed, or by taking it by process of law. And in the latter case, either the time for appeal to the Court of Common Pleas should have elapsed or the appeal have been decided. The latter caution is necessary because the jury on appeal have a right to alter the location or wholly reverse all the proceedings.

It has been previously decided that a district has no right to take a deed of a house for religious purposes.

If the question of the propriety of dividing the district be proposed in district meeting, registry voters have a right to vote, because it merely amounts to an expression of opinion, and the whole power to divide rests with the school committee to whom the vote of the district is a mere recommendation to be weighed according to its deserts. And registry voters can by law vote upon all questions except taxing or expending money.

It was also contended that the location must be made, a lot legally procured, and the plans approved before a contract can be legally made to build. In the present case the contract was made first. The question is a most important one, because, if a district proceeds before these things are done, it would often lead to a wasteful expenditure of the district's money, if the lot was not procured or the proceedings approved of, and also because innocent parties who contract to build may suffer in consequence. In regard to claims of contractors against building committees or districts, those cases must of course be decided by the courts of law; but I think it is the duty of the school committees and school commissioner to guard against a wasteful expenditure of money by a district majority in all cases where they can do it, and it may frequently be in the power of the commissioner to do it on appeal. And it seems to me plain (without undertaking to decide how innocent third parties may be affected by their acts,) that neither the district nor its officers have any right to make a contract until the lot is fixed and procured and the plans approved of.

The appeal was also made from all doings of the committee in relation to dividing the district; but I do not see anything upon which the commissioner can act. The committee merely decided that the district had not asked to be divided. They did not reject the application. Any individual has a right to petition the committee for a division, and it would be a matter of discretion in the committee to adopt or reject it.

ELISHA R. POTTER, C. P. S.

1854.
See No. 18.
See No. 20.
See No. 23.
See No. 25.
See No. 26.
See No. 27.
See No. 39.

DECISION No. 9.

A qualified voter, if he be not a property holder, is eligible to office.

ELISHA R. POTTER, C. P. S.

1854.
See No. 57.

DECISION No. 10.

Joseph O. Clarke vs. School District No. 7.

A school district may borrow money upon the note of the district.

The facts material of this case are these:

That this school district contracted debts to a considerable amount, in building a schoolhouse, and for other school purposes, and for expenses incurred in certain actions and suits in which the district was concerned, which debts, it was conceded, the district was in law bound to pay; that instead of levying a tax on the ratable property of the district to raise the money for the payment thereof, the district hired of the several individuals named as payees of the promissory notes, declared upon in this action, for the purpose of paying said debts with the money borrowed; that the said promissory notes were given by the district for the money so borrowed, and that the money borrowed was applied to the payment of said debts.

The question was raised, whether these promissory notes are valid and binding upon the district, or are void; whether a school district has power to raise money by borrowing, for the payment of its debts lawfully contracted, and to give its promissory notes therefor.

A corporation may bind itself by a negotiable promissory note or bill of exchange for any debt contracted in the course of its legitimate business; that is, in any matter which is not foreign to the purposes of its creation.

A school district (a corporation under the school act) by giving its promissory notes for moneys hired to discharge debts, incurred in the building of a schoolhouse and otherwise, in so doing was not contracting debts in a manner foreign to the purposes of its creation; and the provision of the school act giving this class of corporations power to raise money by taxation, cannot be construed to forbid a borrowing of money for a legitimate purpose.

GEORGE A. BRAYTON, A. J. S. C.

1855.
See No. 7.

DECISION No. 11.

Building committee ordinarily has power to give orders on treasurer for payment of bills contracted by them.

If a district vote to build or repair a schoolhouse, and appoint a building committee for that purpose, and the building committee be empowered by general terms as "to build" or "repair" as distinguished from merely *contracting* for the same, that is, be armed with general powers to carry through the project of the district, such powers would include as incidental the power to give orders on the district treasurer for the payment of those employed by them.

If, however, the power of the committee be so restricted by the form of the vote as to exclude, or not naturally to include, this power, then it belongs to the trustees of the district, in whom is the general custody, in the sense of care, of the property of the district, and who are expressly armed with all powers necessary to carry out the powers and duties of the district.

SAMUEL AMES, C. J. S. C.

1858.

DECISION No. 12.

School District No. 1, Barrington.

A schoolhouse may be occupied for a singing school, when such occupation does not interfere with the ordinary school, without the consent, or even against the vote, of the district.

The question at issue is manifestly without the jurisdiction of the district, and has already been decided upon by the proper tribunal, viz.: by the commissioner of public schools, approved by the Chief Justice of the Supreme Court.

With regard to the instance cited in said appeal, the use of the house for a singing school, as a violation of such decision, I am of opinion that the use of said house for such instruction is perfectly legitimate "to purposes connected with public instruction."

Instruction in vocal music is a part of our system of public education, and is so recognized and paid for by the city of Providence out of the "teachers' money," and is recognized and employed as an important element of education in nearly all the rural districts of our commonwealth. Many of our school committees insist upon its introduction into the public schools, and nearly all the school reports which reach the office are emphatic in its recommendation. And certainly if the younger children may be instructed in vocal music in the public schoolhouse, and this too during school hours, there can be no legal objection why their older brothers and sisters and friends may not receive such instruction at the same place out of school hours.

Nor is the fact that the teacher receives pecuniary

compensation from his pupils pertinent to the question; for to allow it to be so would be to question the legal use of schoolhouses for public schools, many of the sessions of which are prolonged by *private* subscriptions, and are of course kept, in the same sense in which the one is kept to which reference is made, by "private" individuals.

The manner in which any teacher is paid, or whether his services are gratuitous, does not affect the question in point. Moreover, such a legitimate use of the schoolhouse would not require "the general consent of the tax-paying voters," said "private individual" having permission for occupancy from the trustees of said district, in whom the law places the custody of the schoolhouse.

JOSHUA B. CHAPIN, C. P. S.
1860.

Approved.   SAMUEL AMES, C. J. S. C.

See No. 5.

DECISION No. 13.

The same person may hold the office of clerk and that of either treasurer or collector, but the same person cannot be *both* treasurer and collector.

SAMUEL AMES, C. J. S. C.
1863.

DECISION No. 14.

School District No. 8, North Providence.

A call for a meeting signed by a de facto trustee is valid.

In appeal of Waterman B. Angell and others from acts of trustees in calling the meetings of said district held on the 18th and 27th of June.

The facts upon the points at issue were these. At the annual meetings of said district for the years 1862, 1863 and 1864, as appears by the clerk's record, Ralph P. Devereux, Charles A. Boyd and Henry Armington were successively elected trustees. It was contended by appellants and admitted by respondents that Charles A. Boyd was not at the time of his election eligible (Art. IX, § 1, Constitution of R. I.), to the office of trustee, he being a certificate voter, and by the Constitution (Art. II, § 1,) entitled to vote for general officers only.

It was also contended that a school district must elect either one or three trustees (Title X, cap. 61, § 5, Revised Statutes,) and in this case, inasmuch as the district had decided to elect, and did elect, *three* trustees, only *two* of whom were eligible, the *third* not being qualified to hold the office, therefore all the acts of these trustees were void.

It did not appear that there was the slightest suspicion, during the entire period for which said Boyd had held the office of trustee, either upon the part of the voters of the district or of the trustees, that he was not a legal and legally elected officer, or that he acted otherwise than in good faith. It has been decided that "a person by *color of election*, may be an officer *de facto*, though indisputably ineligible."

I am therefore of opinion that the said Charles A. Boyd, though ineligible to the office of trustee, was by *color of election, de facto* one of the trustees, that his office was *voidable* only and not *void*, and that the acts of said trustees in calling the meetings held respectively on the 18th and 27th of June, 1864, and from which appeal was taken, were legal and binding acts.

JOSHUA B. CHAPIN, C. P. S.

1864.

Approved.   SAMUEL AMES, C. J. S. C.

See No. 31.
See No. 45.
See No. 58.

DECISION No. 15.

A district has no right to expend the money of the coming year.

ELISHA R. POTTER, A. J. S. C.

1868.

DECISION No. 16.

In cases of temporary absence, declining or refusing to serve, or misconduct, unless the declination or refusal is in writing, or capable of positive proof, reasonable notice should be given to the officer to appear and show cause why the office should not be declared vacant.

ELISHA R. POTTER, A. J. S. C.

1873.

See No. 60.

DECISION No. 17.

Edward W. Howland vs. School District No. 3, of Little Compton.

1. A vote by the district to locate is not a vote to erect.
2. The district has no power to locate; this must be done by the committee.
3. A delegated power of condemning property must be exercised strictly in accordance with terms of its delegation.

This is trespass and ejectment for a lot of land in Little Compton, which it is admitted belongs to the plaintiff unless the defendant has acquired title by taking it for a schoolhouse lot under Gen. Stat. R. I. cap. 53, § 5, being the same as Pub. Stat. R. I. cap. 56, § 5. We think that § 5, though not quite clear in all respects, is clear in this respect, namely, that, where a town has a district organization, the school committee is authorized to appoint appraisers to decide upon the value of land fixed upon by the committee as the site of a schoolhouse in any district, after the district has voted to erect a schoolhouse, no authority to make the appointment being given until after such vote. It follows that in such a case an appointment before the vote is unauthorized and void, and consequently that any valuation of the land by the appraisers so appointed, and any tender to the owner in pursuance thereof, are ineffectual to divest the title of such owner and vest it in the district.

We think the proceeding under which the defendant claims is defective in this particular. The records of the defendant district and of the school committee, copies of which were put in evidence at the trial, show that the proceeding was as follows, to wit : A meeting of the district was held April 14, 1875, for the purpose, among other things, of "considering the expediency of building or repairing the schoolhouse in said district." At the meeting it was voted "to repair the schoolhouse," and that "Charles Staples hire money for the present use, if needed, for the repairs of the said schoolhouse." Subsequently a special meeting was notified for May 22, 1875, "for the purpose of taking such measures as may be deemed necessary for the location of a district schoolhouse."

At the meeting held pursuant to this notice it was voted, "that we locate the district schoolhouse on the ground of the old schoolhouse," and "that the trustee petition the school committee to lay out a lot of a suitable size for a district schoolhouse." Under the latter vote the trustee petitioned the school committee, which was in session the same day, "to locate a site for a district schoolhouse for district No. 3." The school committee, acting on this petition, fixed upon the old schoolhouse lot, being the lot in suit, and defined its bounds. An attempt was then made to agree with the plaintiff as owner, which failed. Thereupon, on application of the trustee, the school committee appointed appraisers who valued the land at $45. Upon their report the district voted to tender the $45 to the plaintiff as owner, which was done June 10, 1875.

The recital shows no vote of the district to erect a schoolhouse. There is no proof of any such vote prior to the appointment of the appraisers. Possibly it may be thought that the vote to locate implies a vote to erect, and is therefore equivalent to it. We do not think so. The vote to locate was, in point of law, a mere nullity, the power to locate being in the school committee. The vote was merely an expression of preference. The statute contemplates that the selection of the site shall precede the vote to build. Moreover, it does not appear that the district ever supposed or claimed that the vote to locate was equivalent to a vote to erect. On the contrary, the record shows that at a special meeting of the district, August 27, 1875, held pursuant to notice, "for the purpose of considering the question of building or repairing the district schoolhouse," it was voted " to recede from repairing the old schoolhouse," and "to build a new schoolhouse." The inference is that the district then considered the vote to repair as still in force, and that the vote to build still remained to be adopted. It is hardly necessary to say that if the appraisal was unauthorized, and consequently void, when made, for want of a precedent vote to build, this subsequent vote was without effect, as against the plaintiff at least, to ratify or confirm it. The power to take property *in invitum* is a sovereign power, and, when delegated, must be exercised in strict conformity with the terms of its delegation, or otherwise the exercise will be invalid.

THOMAS DURFEE, C. J. S. C.

1885.

See No. 19.

DECISION No. 18.

Edward W. Howland vs. School District No. 3, Little Compton.

1. Pub. Stat. R. I. cap. 56, § 5, does not imperatively require that the location of a district schoolhouse shall be fixed by the school committee before the district votes to build the schoolhouse.
2. On a motion to quash proceedings, only defects apparent on the record can be considered.

After the rendering of decision No. 17, the district instituted new proceedings to condemn for school purposes the lot in question. From this condemnation Howland appealed to the Court of Common Pleas for the County of Newport, at its May Term, A. D. 1886. The Court of Common Pleas, on motion of the appellant, quashed the proceedings of condemnation, and the school district, the appellee, brought its exceptions to the Supreme Court.

OPINION.

This is an appeal from proceedings instituted by school district No. 3, in Little Compton, to acquire by condemnation a lot of land in said district belonging to the appellant Howland, for the erection of a public schoolhouse thereon. The appeal was taken to the Court of Common Pleas, and comes here on exceptions. At the trial in the court below, the district put in the record of its proceedings and rested. The appellant moved to quash the proceedings, on the ground that they do not show a legal condemnation. The court granted the motion, because it appears by the record that the vote of the district to build the schoolhouse preceded the selection of the site by the school committee, the court being of opinion that the selection must precede the vote.

The statute, Pub. Stat. R. I. cap. 56, § 5, provides that "in case the school committee shall fix upon a location for a schoolhouse in any district, ... and the district shall have passed a vote to erect a schoolhouse," then, if the owner of the lot selected shall refuse to convey it, or cannot agree for the price of it with the district, the committee shall appoint appraisers who shall determine the price to be paid, and that upon tender or payment thereof the title of the lot shall vest in the district. The statute does not expressly provide that the selection of the site shall precede the vote to build, but only that the selection and vote shall both precede the steps next to be taken. In the former case between the parties to this proceeding the court remarked, "the statute contemplates that the selection of the site shall precede the vote to build." The remark was an inference from the order in which the two acts are mentioned, and from the supposition that a district, before voting to build a schoolhouse, would naturally like to know where it is to stand when built. We see no reason to retract the remark; but it does not follow, because it may be inferred that a particular order of procedure is contemplated, that it is therefore commanded; and unless we can find that the order is in effect commanded, we cannot hold that a deviation from it is fatal, so long as the statute is literally complied with. The question then is, not whether the statute contemplates, but whether it imperatively requires, that the selection of the site shall precede the vote to build. The General Assembly knew, of course, when the statute was enacted, that its execution would often devolve on plain men, unskilled in the kind of work which it imposes, and it is therefore reasonable to suppose that they intended to express their meaning so that it would be readily understood. But, if they had intended that the selection of the site should necessarily precede the vote to build, it would have been natural for them to add the word "thereon," or some equivalent expression, after the words "erect a schoolhouse." The word or expression may have been omitted because such was not their intention. We see nothing to warrant our making the addition by construction. Our conclusion is that the court below erred in quashing the proceeding for the reason assigned.

The appellant contends that the proceeding, if not void for the reason assigned by the court below, is void and ought to be quashed for other reasons, to wit: because it does not appear that the notices given of the district meeting were posted in such public places as the law requires, or that they conformed to the law; and because the record does not show at what hour the meeting was held. We do not discover any fault in the notice as recorded in point of form. It is in the form given in the Rhode Island School Manual. It states the time, place, and purpose of the meeting. It bears date six days before the meeting notified, and is signed by the trustee. It meets the requirement of the statute. Pub. Stat. R. I. cap. 52, §§ 3, 5. The record does not state specifically how or where the notices were posted, but states that the meeting "was duly notified by posting two notices of the time, place, and object of said meeting in the district for five days previous to the day of meeting." It may be questionable if this statement would be sufficient at common law, but our statute, Pub. Stat. R. I. cap. 58, § 11, provides, "The record of the district clerk that a meeting has been duly or legally notified shall be prima facie evidence that it has been notified as the law requires." We think the statement is prima facie sufficient under this provision. The record does not state in express terms at what hour the meeting was held, but it describes the meeting as that which was notified, and the notice appoints the hour. A meeting held at any different hour would not be the meeting which was notified. We do not think the record is fatally defective in this respect.

The appellant contends that the proceedings should be quashed because there is no record of any vote to build on the lot located by the school committee. This merely raises in another form the question which we have first decided. The statute does not require a vote to build on the lot located, but, as we have seen, only requires a location of the lot by the committee, and a vote to build a schoolhouse by the district, as a prerequisite to subsequent proceedings.

A motion to quash can be granted only for defects apparent on the record. We can know nothing of defects or errors which may be brought to light by the evidence. We do not think the proceeding should be quashed for any defect pointed out by the appellant.

THOMAS DURFEE, C. J. S. C.

1887.

See No. 8.

DECISION No. 19.

Edward W. Howland vs. School District No. 3, Little Compton.

When a school district attempted to condemn land under Pub. Stat. R. I. cap. 56, § 5, and the records of the district did not show that the "proprietor of the land refused to convey the same, or could not agree with the district for the price thereof" the proceedings must be quashed.

This is an appeal from the doings of school district No. 3, of the town of Little Compton, and of the school committee of said town, in condemning for school purposes a certain lot of land in said district belonging to the appellant. The appeal was taken to the Court of Common Pleas, and comes before us on exceptions after jury trial in that court.

At the trial, after the records of the proceedings of the district and committee had been put in evidence and verified, and other testimony had been introduced in support of condemnation, and the district had rested in its opening, the appellant moved that the proceedings of the district be quashed, because it did not appear that the appellant, owner of the land condemned, could not agree with the district for its price. The statute requires that, before condemnation, "the proprietor of the land shall refuse to convey the same, or cannot agree with the district for the price thereof." Pub. Stat. R. I. cap. 56, §5. The records of the district do not show that the district ever authorized any person to procure a conveyance, or to agree on its behalf with the appellant, but only show that at a meeting held three days after the school committee had selected the lot, the trustee of the district, who had been appointed to ask the school committee to select a lot, reported that he was unable to get any price on it. The records of the district are clearly defective in this particular, since a refusal to give the trustee a price cannot be held to be a refusal to give the district a price, and does not show that the appellant could not have agreed with the district, the trustee having no authority to represent the district. The counsel for the district contends that the acceptance of the trustee's report amounted to an adoption of his agency, and supplies the want of a prior appointment. We do not think the acceptance can have this effect, there being nothing to show that the appellant received the trustee as the representative of the district, and intended to have his refusal to treat with him regarded as a refusal to treat with the district. Nor do we think the defect is aided by the record of the school committee, since their record does not state or find it to be a fact that the district and the appellant could not agree, but only that the trustee so stated when he applied for the appointment of appraisers.

The trustee was called as a witness by the district, and testified that, "after the school committee located the site, I was directed to buy the land of Howland. I saw him and he would not sell, and I reported to the district." The counsel for the district contends that the defect is supplied by this testimony. The district and the school committee were acting in pursuance of a special jurisdiction, and according to the ordinary rule it was for them to show affirmatively that they acted within their authority, or the contrary will be presumed. The district and the school committee, in condemning land for school purposes, perform a public function judicial in its nature, and their records are the proper proof of their acts. We have come to the conclusion that the motion to quash ought to have been granted. The motion, however, was unreasonably delayed. It might have been made immediately after the proceeding was brought to the Court of Common Pleas on appeal, and, if then made, much trouble and expense would have been avoided.

We shall order the proceedings quashed without costs.

THOMAS DURFEE, C. J. S. C.

1888.

See No. 17.

DISTRICT MEETINGS.

DECISION No. 20.

In the election of a committee to purchase land for site of a schoolhouse which has been approved according to law and the price of which is known to the meeting at the time of making such appointment, and in the election of a building committee for the building of that which has been lawfully approved, the moderator may receive the vote of any resident of the district, who is at the time qualified to vote in town meeting for town officers.

HENRY BARNARD, C. P. S.

1848.

Approved. RICHARD W. GREENE, C. J. S. C.

See No. 9.

DECISION No. 21.

It is the duty of the moderator to put all questions to vote.

ELISHA R. POTTER, C. P. S.

1848.

DECISION No. 22.

School District No. 3, North Providence.

Omissions in the records of school officers may be supplied on proper evidence.

Evidence to correct or supply omissions in the records of school officers, I think may properly be admitted. In the case of clerks of districts, it seems absolutely necessary, as they are often unacquainted with the forms of doing business. In the case of a school committee, however, the presumption is stronger that they are competent men, and will be careful to see that their record is well kept. Yet even here great mischief might result from excluding all evidence other than the record. But it should be received with great caution, as after any considerable length of time parties might not recollect it alike.

ELISHA R. POTTER, C. P. S.

I approve of the above decision.

RICHARD W. GREENE, C. J. S. C.

1853.

See No. 14.
See No. 31.
See No. 45.
See No. 58.

DECISION No. 23.

School District No. 3, North Providence.

1. Qualifications of voters in district meetings.
2. Residence of voters.

The question turns upon the legality of the votes of Finigin and Heaton, which had been struck off by the school committee.

It appears in evidence that Finigin is a naturalized citizen, and a resident in said district; that he has owned real estate sufficient to qualify him to vote since September 4, 1850; that his naturalization papers are dated March 4, 1851, and that he is taxable in the town, and is liable to be taxed in the district for the house in which he lives. It was contended that, his name not being on the town voting list, he could not, for this reason, be allowed to vote in district meetings. The qualifications for voting in district meetings are identical with those for voting in town meetings, with the same proviso as to voting upon any question of taxation. But the restriction which forbids the moderator to receive the vote of any one whose name is not on the voting list, is not contained in the school laws as a restriction to voting in district meetings. A moderator is therefore bound to receive and count the vote of a person who is a citizen and a holder of real estate in a district, whenever he has resided in it a sufficient length of time, even if his name is not on the voting list. Such is the opinion of the late commissioner of public schools, in the case of Asa M. Allen.

In the case of Heaton, it is testified, that he became of age on the 28th of December, 1853, that he holds undivided real estate to a sufficient amount to qualify him to vote, and that he is a resident in said district. It is objected that, prior to August 17, 1854, he removed into Massachusetts, and thus lost his citizenship in Rhode Island. In opposition to this it was proved that he went into Massachusetts for a merely temporary purpose, and that he never intended to change his abode, and that his estate, his business, and his real home, remained in Rhode Island. It appears to me that the principles which ought to govern in deciding questions of domicile or residence, as laid down by Judge Story in his Conflict of Laws, and quoted in Appendix No. 9 to the Report of the Commissioner of Public Schools for 1854, would render Heaton still a citizen and a voter in district meetings in Rhode Island, since his intention of only temporary removal seems plain.

It is, therefore, my opinion that the votes of Finigin and Heaton ought to be counted as against said motion to rescind. The vote will then stand seventeen ayes, eighteen nays; and the motion is lost. The several votes of the district relating to building are therefore still unrescinded, and of the same force and validity as if such motion had not been made.

ROBERT ALLYN, C. P. S.

Approved.   GEORGE A. BRAYTON, A. J. S. C.

1854.

See No. 8.
See No. 25.
See No. 26.
See No. 27.
See No. 39.

DECISION No. 24.

School District No. 3, North Providence.

All business of special meetings of school districts must be specified in the notice of the meeting.

The commissioner is of opinion that an election of trustees at a special meeting, the notice whereof did not specify that business, cannot be considered valid. Section 29 of the school law enacts that notice of the time, place, and *object*, of every special meeting shall be given. The notice put up for a meeting to be held on the 6th, contained no specification concerning the election of a trustee; and as this meeting was adjourned, and another notice was posted up, it must be held that the meeting of the 15th was not competent to elect a trustee—an item of business not named in the original warrant. If it is said that a motion was made to accept the resignation of Trainer, and this being postponed to the next meeting was a sufficient notice of the intention to elect a trustee, it will be an ample reply to say that such postponement cannot be considered a notice according to the requirements of the law. For section 30 of the school law specifies the mode of notice, which is "by publishing in some newspaper, or by putting up notice, or in such manner as the school committee may require." The notice certainly was not given in any of these three ways. It may also be said, that if the law requires the business of every special meeting to be named in the warrant, trustees, if so disposed, might prevent action on any necessary matter by failing or refusing to insert it as an item in the warrant calling the meeting. But section twenty-seven of the school law provides against this by commanding the trustees to call a meeting to be held "within seven days, on the written request of any five qualified voters, stating the object for which they wish it called," and if the trustees neglect or refuse to call such meeting the school committee may call it and fix the time of holding it.

ROBERT ALLYN, C. P. S.

1856.

Approved.   GEORGE A. BRAYTON, A. J. S. C.

See No. 32.

DECISION No. 25.

School District No. 7, Burrillville.

1. No person to vote on any proposition to raise a tax, unless he is liable to pay a part of said tax.
2. To change a vote of a district it must be shown that enough illegal votes were cast to change the result.

The commissioner decides that the school law does imperatively prohibit any person from voting on any question concerning taxation, unless he has paid, or shall be liable to pay, a portion of such tax; and on examination of the names of persons who voted for and against said motion to pay the debts of the district with this money, he finds that no person so having paid a portion of said tax voted in the affirmative, and that five persons so having paid a portion of said tax voted in the negative. He, therefore, declares that the motion was lost.

ROBERT ALLYN, C. P. S.

1856.

See No. 8.
See No. 23.
See No. 26.
See No. 27.
See No. 30.

DECISION No. 26.

School District No. 2, Cranston.

Any resident of a school district, qualified at the time as a registered voter to vote in town meeting, is entitled to vote in the district meeting to assess a tax for the repair or improvement of the district schoolhouse, provided he be liable on account of his personal estate to contribute to the tax for which he votes, although he has never been assessed for such personal estate, and his name is not upon the last list of town voters.

Appeal to the commissioner of public schools, from the vote of a district meeting of school district No. 2, Cranston, ordering a tax of $500 to be assessed upon the ratable property of the district, for the purpose of repairing and improving the schoolhouse in said district.

By the statement of facts it appears a vote was passed at a district meeting held on the 21st of May, 1859, by eighteen affirmative, against sixteen negative, votes; and the appellants contested the validity of the order of assessment by impeaching the right to vote, at said meeting, of Horatio N. Randall and Charles O. Bennett, residents in said district, both of whom voted in the affirmative. It further appears from the statement that Randall was in September, 1858, assessed in the town of Cranston, for town taxes, the sum of $3.65 upon real estate valued at $1,200, which he paid to the town collector on the 8th day of March, 1859; and that having, in January or February, 1859, sold his real estate, he was in July of that year assessed, for town taxes in Cranston, the sum of $1.07½ upon personal estate valued at $500—the same estate for which he was assessed for his proportion of the tax in question. Bennett's name, though upon the registry, was not upon the list of voters of the town of Cranston, prepared for the April or June elections, 1859.

By § 8, cap. 62, of the Revised Statutes, every resident in a school district is entitled to vote in a district meeting, who is qualified at the time to vote in a town meeting, with this further restriction,—that to vote upon any question of taxation of property, or of expenditure of money raised thereby, he must either *have* paid, or *be liable* to pay, a portion of *the* tax. He need not, however, be upon the last list of town voters; since such lists are not prepared or made up for district, as they are for town, meetings; and there is, therefore, no mode provided by which he could get upon the list, however well qualified he might be at the time to vote.

In this view of the statute, it is plain, that Randall was entitled to vote for the tax ordered to be assessed by the district meeting of school district No. 2 of Cranston, held on the 21st day of May, 1859. Though not upon the town voting list made up for the April election, 1859, he was qualified, as a registered voter, to vote at the meeting in question, by the payment of a tax to the amount of a dollar, upon property valued at a sum exceeding one hundred and thirty-four dollars, assessed within the year next preceding, and more than four days prior to the time of his voting (Rev. Stat. cap. 22, § 1; cap. 23, § 14), and although he had parted with the real estate upon which *this* tax had been assessed, he was, on account of personal estate to the amount of $500, liable to contribute to, and therefore entitled to vote for, the school district tax in question.

SAMUEL AMES, C. J. S. C.

1859.

See No. 8.
See No. 23.
See No. 25.
See No. 27.
See No. 39.

DECISION No. 27.

I am satisfied no particular length of residence is necessary in a district to entitle a person to vote, provided it be *bona fide*. This was formerly held so, and I cannot see any good reason to doubt it.

ELISHA R. POTTER, A. J. S. C.

1872.

DECISION No. 28.

Right of a husband to vote on his wife's real estate.

1. Any husband who married his wife previous to December 2, 1872, and whose wife acquired the property on which he claims the right to vote previous to

December 2, 1872, is entitled to vote under Art. II, § 1, if he is otherwise qualified and if the property is a freehold estate of the value prescribed in the constitution, whether he has had children by his wife or not.

2. Any husband married since December 2, 1872, or whose wife has acquired the property on which he claims the right to vote since December 2, 1872, is entitled to vote under Art. II, § 1, if he is otherwise qualified and if the property is an estate of inheritance of the value prescribed in the constitution, provided he has had issue by his wife capable of inheriting it,—but otherwise, not.

THOMAS DURFEE,
WALTER S. BURGES,
ELISHA R. POTTER,
CHARLES MATTESON,
JOHN H. STINESS,
} *Supreme Court.*

1878.

DECISION No. 29.

Emma A. Frink vs. School Committee of Coventry.

1. District meeting held under but *one* notice is illegal, even though all the voters knew of the meeting.
2. Neglect of duty by a school officer renders him liable to a penalty. but does not invalidate a school.

This was a case where a trustee was elected at a meeting called by only one notice, whereupon objection was made and the old trustee called another meeting by posting two notices, at which meeting another party was elected trustee than at the first meeting. The trustee elected at the second meeting, hired the appellant, who proceeded to teach the summer term of school; the trustee elected at the first meeting having in the meantime surrendered possession of the schoolhouse. The school committee, however, from doubts as to the legality of the trustee's election, refused to recognize the school, though notified of its existence by the teacher according to their rules; and at the end of the term they refused to draw an order for the payment of her wages, though the proper return, duly signed, was presented.

It was decided, First, that an election held at a meeting called by but *one* notice was invalid, that verbal or parol notice cannot be accepted in place of the plain statutory requirement of *two* written notices. Second, that a failure of the school committee to recognize a school, which was otherwise legal, could not be construed into a condemnation of such school. Third, that the failure of a school officer to visit a school, or to give notice as required by law renders the *official* liable for neglect of duty, but does not destroy the legality of the school.

THOMAS B. STOCKWELL, C. P. S.
1875.

Appeal to Supreme Court and decision sustained.

ELISHA R. POTTER, A. J. S. C.
1881.

DECISION No. 30.

Annual Meeting of Joint School District No. 17, South Kingstown, and No. 4, Richmond.

Call for a record vote must be made before the voting begins.

From a careful examination and consideration of the testimony I find the following facts to be well established :—That the meeting was duly notified and organized, and that its proceedings were without contest till the election of trustee. When the moderator announced the election of trustee in order, R. P. Smith was nominated and his nomination seconded. Other nominations were called for by the moderator, but none were immediately made. A call was however made for a paper ballot and the moderator prepared his hat for a ballot box and the voting began. Very soon after it began A. E. Wilcox was nominated and his nomination seconded, and then a request was made that a record of the voters and how they voted be kept. This request the moderator did not heed, but allowed the ballot to go on till all present who wished to had voted. The votes were then counted and found to number 31, of which R. P. Smith had 17 and A. E. Wilcox and E. A. Wilcox (both forms of initials being used) had 14, and R. P. Smith was declared elected.

As to the point in question I do not see how it can affect the legality of the election. I think that there is no doubt about a call for a record of the votes being made, but it is just as clear that it was not made until after the voting had begun, and if that is so, I think that the moderator, not only was not obliged to stop the balloting and begin again, but had no right to do so. To acknowledge such a right on the part of the moderator would put it in his power to stop a ballot at any point, even after parties, who had voted, had left the meeting, and thus enable a minority to obtain control. If it be urged that the moderator allowed the balloting to begin too soon, without allowing time enough, it does not so appear from the records or the testimony. The impression made by both of those sources of information is that no undue haste was used. The time for a demand to have a record of the votes made was when the ballot was called for. It is not pretended that it was made until after the nomination of Wilcox which followed the call for a ballot.

In view, therefore, of all these facts the appeal is dismissed, and the election of R. P. Smith as trustee of said joint district is hereby confirmed and established.

THOMAS B. STOCKWELL, C. P. S.

1882.

See No. 35.
See No. 36.

DECISION No. 31.

Annual Meeting School Districts 3 and 4, North Kingstown.

1. It is not necessary that a district take a formal vote each year upon the question whether it will elect one trustee or three.
2. The fact that a clerk, duly elected, is subsequently found to be ineligible does not render invalid his records made previously.

In the matter of the appeal of W. C. Davis et als. from the election of Owen G. Gardiner as trustee of

Consolidated School Districts 3 and 4 of North Kingstown, at the annual district meeting held April 18, 1887.

The hearing was held at the district schoolhouse in Wickford, on May 28, 1887, at which time the following facts were adduced:—

That the annual meeting of said districts 3 and 4, North Kingstown, was called by the trustee of last year, Owen G. Gardiner, by three notices in proper form, posted, one each, at the Belleville depot, at the town clerk's office, and at the store of Potter and Page in the village of Wickford; that the hour for the meeting was 7 o'clock; that the meeting was organized by the choice of S. O. Myers, M. D., as moderator, and Chas. Stafford, the clerk of the previous year, as clerk; but as Mr. Stafford was absent at that time, one McDonald was elected clerk pro tem., who proves to be a minor; that no motion was made to fix the number of trustees, but that two candidates were nominated for the office of trustee, viz.—Owen G. Gardiner and George E. Gardiner, and a ballot taken, 73 ballots being cast, of which Owen G. Gardiner had a clear majority and was declared elected; that the other officers were elected in due form and no protest or claim of illegality was made at that time so far as appears in evidence; that Owen G. Gardiner has been duly engaged and has discharged the duties of the office since his election.

It is also in evidence that in past years it has been customary to post the notices for the district meetings in the post office, and in the store of George T. Cranston, and sometimes in the schoolhouse, and that the usual hour for the meeting has been $7\frac{1}{2}$ o'clock.

It further appears from the records of the district

that the clerk, Chas. Stafford, has made out the records of the meeting from the minutes taken by Mr. McDonald, the clerk pro tem., and signed them, first with McDonald's name and then with his own.

It also appears that prior to 1883, it was the custom of the district to elect three trustees, but that year a vote was passed to elect but one trustee, and since that time at each annual meeting, without any vote upon the question, a single trustee has been chosen.

After a consideration of the above facts, with the law involved in this case, I am of the opinion that the appeal is not sustained for the following reasons:

First. The first question to ask about any meeting whose legality is questioned is as to its warrant or notice. In this case we find that the number of notices was one in excess of the number required and that they were in proper form. The only question is as to whether they were posted in such public places as the law contemplates. As to the town clerk's office, there can be no question it would seem; it may not be as public as the post office, but still it would naturally be called, I think, a "public place" for such a purpose as this.

A second one was posted in one of the principal stores of the village, but in a different one from that where it has been the practice to post it. So far as I can see one place is just as public as the other, the only difference being that probably each place was a centre of resort for different bodies or sets of persons, and in case it was posted in either one the party represented by the other might complain, provided there was a just ground of complaint; but I hardly think there was. The third notice was at a railroad station in a different part of the district, which is of course a "public place," and while it was not where the majority of the district would see it or know of it, it certainly did give a section of the district notice, that otherwise would have had no probable opportunity of knowing of the meeting. In view of all these facts I fail to see wherein the notice of this meeting was not strictly legal in form. If we raise the question of the spirit of the proceedings it is incumbent on the appellant to show that the proceedings were actually or presumably so affected by the questionable acts as to prevent a fair expression of the will of the people, that they exercised a controlling influence in securing the result appealed from.

The two points presented by the appellants in this connection are the places where the notices were posted and the hour of the meeting. It may be said that such deviations from the usual practice of a community are not wise, and certainly lay a person open to suspicion, and had the attendance at the meeting been unusually small so that it was clear that a full "notice" had not been given, that the district had been trapped, then there would undoubtedly have been sufficient cause for overthrowing the proceedings. But the fact is that instead of being a small meeting it was one of the largest, if not the largest meeting, ever gathered in the district. That being the case it is difficult to see how the points complained of could have worked to the injury of the district and hence I do not believe that they constitute a sufficient ground upon which to vitiate the proceedings dependent upon them.

Second. As to the point that there was no decision by the district of the question whether they would elect one or three trustees, prior to the election, and hence that the election was void, I would say that the law does not make such a requirement. In the School Manual, among the remarks given for the guidance and assistance of school meetings and school officers, it is stated that "the decision as to one or three must be made before the election of any." This it is clear cannot have the force of the statute law. It is given, like many other of the directions, to point out, as nearly as possible, the absolutely safe way of procedure, but absolute compliance therewith cannot be exacted as in case of specific requirements of the law. If in this case the *advice* of the manual had been followed, this question at least could not have arisen. The question is now, is such a specific vote or decision an absolute requirement of the statute? It certainly is not required in specific terms. If required then at all it must be by inference, and in such a way as to make it impossible without it to carry out the intent of the law. If a district wishes to have three trustees, it is quite clear that it must so express itself at the beginning, in order that the electors may have the fact in mind in their election; and, as has been decided, when a district has elected *one* trustee, it cannot *then* decide to have three, and elect two more.

But where the desire or intent is to have but one trustee; it is the almost universal practice to proceed directly to the election of trustee, and *one* trustee is elected.

The question at once arises whether the nomination of a single person for *trustee* for the ensuing year and his election do not determine for all the purposes required that but *one* trustee shall be elected for that year. I certainly think so, and especially is this true in case of a district which, like the present one, has taken a definite vote at some previous meeting upon this question and since that time has acted uniformly in accordance therewith.

Third. We now come to the question of the clerk and the validity of his records. There can be no question as to his ineligibility.

It has always been held that *all school district* officers must be qualified voters. Does the fact then of his ineligibility render void his acts as clerk? By reference to a decision made in 1864 by School Commissioner Chapin and approved by Chief Justice Ames, it will be seen that in a similar case the office was considered as *voidable* only and not void; that the officer had a title to his office by *color of election* and that until his title was questioned his acts were valid. Moreover in this case, where the records have been accepted and certified to by the regular clerk, it would seem that they must be regarded as valid and binding beyond all question.

In view, therefore, of the aforesaid facts and reasons, I do decide that the annual school meeting of districts 3 and 4 of North Kingstown, held April 18, 1887, was a legal meeting and that its proceedings were valid and binding in law and that therefore this appeal should be dismissed.

THOMAS B. STOCKWELL, C. P. S.

1887.

Approved. CHARLES MATTESON, A. J. S. C.

See No. 14.
See No. 45.
See No. 58.
See No. 63.

DECISION No. 32.

Benjamin C. Seabury, Collector of Taxes, vs. Edward W. Howland.

1. The object of a school district meeting must be stated in the notice of a special meeting, but need not be stated in the notice of the statutory annual meeting.
2. Records of district meetings should state that the meeting "has been duly or legally notified," in order to be *prima facie* evidence of the fact.
3. Under Pub. Stat. R. I. cap 51, § 4, the amount of a school district tax may be approved by the school committee after the district has voted it, as well as before.
4. Objections to a district tax must be raised on an appeal to the commissioner of public schools, before being carried into court.
5. Notice of a special meeting to take "action in regard to the collection of the tax already assessed" was sufficiently explicit to warrant the election of a collector.

This is an action brought by the plaintiff, as collector of taxes of school district No. 3 of Little Compton, to recover a tax of $327.17 assessed for the district against the defendant. The action was brought in the Court of Common Pleas, and there tried to the court, jury trial being waived. At the trial the plaintiff put in evidence the records of district meetings held April 23, 1885, at which the tax was voted, and August 25, 1885, and by adjournment September 4, 1885, at which latter meeting the plaintiff was appointed collector; also the notices under which said meetings were held. The plaintiff further put in evidence the record of a meeting of the school committee of the town of Little Compton, at which the tax voted by the district was approved by the committee; and also a record of assessment by the assessors of taxes showing the amounts assessed against the defendant and others. The plaintiff also submitted oral testimony to show that the notices were given by the assessors of the assessments, and when and how they were given, and for other purposes. The defendant admitted that notices of the district meetings of April 23, August 25, and September 4 were posted in due time, and at the same places as the assessors' notices were posted. The defendant did not offer any testimony, but at the conclusion of the plaintiff's testimony asked the court to rule that the plaintiff was not entitled to recover, and to enter judgment for the defendant, because, besides other reasons specifically alleged, the evidence failed to show any legal tax in the district, or any cause of action against the defendant. The court refused so to rule, and entered judgment for the plaintiff. The defendant excepted.

The notice under which the meeting of April 23 was held stated that one of the objects of the meeting was "to decide what amount of money shall be raised by tax," but nothing more in regard to the tax. The defendant objects that the notice was defective, because it did not state what the tax was for. We do not think the objection is valid. The record shows that the meeting was an annual meeting, which is by statute a meeting held every year, in April, "for choice of officers and for the transaction of any other business relating to schools," of which no other notice is required than notice "of the time and place." It is only when the meeting is special that "the object" is required to be inserted in the notice. Pub. Stat. R. I. cap. 52, §§ 2, 5.

The records of the district meetings of April 23 and August 25 do not set forth how, when, and where the notices of the meeting were given, nor that the meetings were "duly or legally notified," which the statute declares shall be *prima facie* evidence that notices were given as the law requires. Pub. Stat. R. I. cap. 58, § 11. The records simply state that the meetings were held "according to notice."

This does not answer the requirement of the statute. But, as is before stated, the defendant admitted that the notices were posted in due time, and at the same places as the assessors' notices. The oral testimony goes to show that the assessors' notices were posted in three places in the district which were as public as any three places in the district, to wit, one on the schoolhouse, one on a building formerly used as a grain building, and the third on a board six feet long and ten inches wide, fastened in or against the roadside wall, facing the road, at the south end of the district. The defendant contends that the third notice was not posted in a "public place" within the meaning of the statute, cap. 52, § 5, because the place was not safe as well as public, inasmuch as the board being movable, might be thrown down or carried away, so that the notice was not likely to remain to be read for five days. We do not think we can so decide as a matter of law. A notice so posted in a quiet, rural district would seldom be disturbed.

The defendant contends that the tax is invalid under Pub. Stat. R. I. cap. 51, § 4, because it was voted April 23, 1885, and approved by the school committee of Little Compton, June 13, 1885, whereas the amount should have been approved before the district voted it. Section 4 reads as follows, to wit:—

"Every such district may raise money by tax on the ratable property of the district, to support public schools and to carry out the purposes given them by any of the provisions of this title: provided that the amount of the tax shall be approved by the school committee of the town."

In Holt's Appeal, 5 R. I. 603, decided in 1858, Chief Justice Ames expressed the opinion that the section requires that the amount of the tax "shall be first approved by the school committee as a condition of the right to raise it." In that case, however, the amount of tax had been increased after approval before it was voted, and as increased it had never been approved. The commissioner decided that it was invalid because as increased it had never been approved. The question on appeal was whether the decision of the commissioner was correct, and Chief Justice Ames, in expressing the opinion aforesaid, went farther than he needed to go. We are informed by the school commissioner that the opinion has not been followed, but that it has been the general practice, both before and since the opinion, for the school committee to give their approval after the tax has been voted. It will be observed that the appeal was not to the Supreme Court, but to Chief Justice Ames as a single justice, and it is therefore not entitled to the same weight as if it were the considerate judgment of the full bench. The opinion on this point was given without reasons, and without reference to other statutory provisions which seem to imply or assume that the approval may follow the vote, see cap. 54, § 4, and cap. 58, § 5, and apparently as a matter of first impression. We have come to the conclusion that the construction which has prevailed as a general practice is both reasonable and natural and supported by other provisions, and that it should be sustained.

We do not think the objection to the copy of the record of approval because not duly certified, or to the sufficiency of the vote of approval as too indefinite, can be sustained. The certificate appears to be in due form. The vote of approval was adopted June 13, 1885, and purports to approve "the tax of $750 on district No. 3," and $750 is the amount of the tax voted at the meeting of district No. 3, April 23, 1885.

The defendant contends that the tax is invalid because it does not appear that it was raised for the support of public schools, or to carry out the powers given the district. We think that the objection cannot be raised in this proceeding, but that, under cap. 58, § 5, the defendant having omitted to appeal, such an objection is no longer open.

The meeting of August 25 was a special meeting, and therefore a notice of the object of it was necessary. The notice given was that the meeting would be held for "the purpose of taking action in regard to the collection of the tax already assessed." The defendant contends that the notice was too inexplicit to warrant the election of a collector. We do not think so. The statute provides two modes for the collection of a tax. The district can either commit the collection to the collector of the town taxes, or elect a collector of its own as it shall deem best. The notice was so worded as to enable the district to proceed at once to determine the mode, and adopt the appropriate measures to carry it into effect. Doubtless the notice might with advantage have been more explicit, but it is not the policy of the law to be very exacting with such bodies. The language used by Chief Justice Parker in Welles v. Battelle, 11 Mass. 477, 481, is particularly apposite. "Too much strictness in subjects of this nature," he remarks, "would throw the whole body politic into confusion, for it cannot be expected that in all the corporations persons will be every year selected who are capable of performing their duty with the exactness which would be useful and convenient."

The trustee of district No. 3 had authority, in our opinion, to issue a warrant to the plaintiff as collector under Pub. Stat. R. I. cap. 55, § 4.

Our conclusion is that no error in law is shown to exist in the decision of the court below, and that the exceptions must therefore be overruled, and the judgment of said court affirmed with costs of this court.

THOMAS DURFEE, C. J. S. C.

1887.

See No. 24.

DECISION No. 33.

Special Meeting of School District No. 5, North Kingstown.

A call for the purpose of considering the expediency of building a new schoolhouse, or of enlarging the old one, will warrant action deciding to build and the appointment of a committee to carry out the will of the district, but it will not authorize the purchase of a new site, or the voting of a tax.

The clerk's record of the proceedings was submitted and agreed to by all parties as the statement of the facts in the case.

From said record it appears that, pursuant to a request from five legal voters made upon the trustee, he called a special meeting of the district on Dec. 23, 1887, for the following purpose, to wit: "for the purpose of considering the expediency of building a new schoolhouse, or to enlarge the present one."

A somewhat careful analysis of the proceedings of the district up to the present time divides them into three groups; one pertaining to the building of a new schoolhouse, another to the purchase of a new site, and the third to the assessment and collection of a tax.

The question then arises, how far these are provided for by the notice of the meeting of Dec. 23, 1887, which constitutes the sole warrant for all of the proceedings;—each meeting being an adjournment of its predecessor.

It is my opinion that all of the proceedings relating to the building of the house are covered by the notice and are therefore legal and valid; because it is very evident that in such a matter the crucial test is upon the question of building, and all subsequent questions are mere matters of detail; and to allow that a meeting, called as this was under a form that has been in vogue ever since the law was first passed, could vote to build a new house, but could not vote to appoint a committee to carry out that vote, would be absurd.

But if they could appoint a committee to carry out that vote, of course they could retain that power and exercise it themselves. I do therefore decide that all proceedings and votes relating simply to the building of the new schoolhouse are valid and binding.

As to the second group of votes, those relating to the purchase of a new site, I am of the opinion that they are not within the scope of the call. Certainly no one can claim that the question of building a new house necessarily involves the purchase of a new site. Of course it *may* do so, but I do not think under the ordinary rules of construction it could be so claimed. It is really a very different question, and one on which parties, who were perfectly agreed as to building, might differ widely. But even if the purchase of the lot could be considered as coming within the call, I do not think it could possibly carry with it the power to authorize the treasurer to give the note of the district. Such an act as that must be more specifically stated in the call, if it is a special meeting.

As to the third group of votes relating to the tax and the collection thereof, there is no question as to their illegality under such a call. A vote to levy a tax is legal only at an annual meeting, or at a special meeting when the subject has been specifically mentioned in the call, or notice.

I do therefore declare such of the proceedings and votes of said meeting of Dec. 23, 1887, and its several adjournments, as relate to the purchase of a new site and also to the levying and collection of a tax to be invalid, and hence null and void.

THOMAS B. STOCKWELL, C. P. S.

1888.

DECISION No. 34.

Special Meeting of District No. 1, Johnston.

1. In computing time *back* from a certain date, that date is not counted, but the day of posting or serving the notice is counted.
2. In reckoning days the law does not regard fractions of days.
3. A meeting to take additional steps in carrying out a previous vote of a district does not require the previous consent of the school committee.

In the matter of the appeal of George W. White from the proceedings of a special meeting of school district No. 1, of the town of Johnston, so far as they relate to the following vote then and there passed, viz., "*Resolved*, That the treasurer of this district be and hereby is authorized to hire a sum of money sufficient to grade said lot and to build and furnish said schoolhouse in accordance with the foregoing resolution, provided that said sum of money shall not exceed ten thousand dollars," and submitted to me for my decision by the commissioner of public schools upon an agreed statement of facts signed by the appellant, the treasurer of the district, and the chairman of the building committee.

I am of the opinion.

First. That the notice given was ample under the law. The law says that a notice for a meeting must be posted "for five days before holding the same."

In computing time back from a certain date, that date is not counted, but the day of posting or serving the notice is counted; and in this case, excluding the 14th day of November, the day on which the meeting was held, we have five days from the 13th back to the 9th, the day on which the notice was posted. The law does not regard fractions of a day in such a case.

Second. As to the point that the object of the above resolution was not included within the notice of the meeting, it is clear that it is covered by the last clause in the notice, to wit, "and to transact any other business that may pertain to the building of said schoolhouse."

Third. Upon the point that the meeting was "illegal because it was called without the consent of the school committee, as provided in Public Laws, cap. 445, § 1," I think the meeting did not come under the operation of the above provision of law. The meeting held Oct. 31, 1889, was for the purpose of building a new schoolhouse and appointing a building committee. This meeting was called "for the purpose of making appropriations, etc., of authorizing the building committee to make contracts and to transact any other business that may pertain to the building of said schoolhouse." I do not see how any one of the purposes named in the last notice can be construed to mean the same as either of those named in the first call. They are additional steps in the carrying out of the decision of the district as made at the first meeting, and in no way conflict with said decision. It is very clear that at said second meeting it would have been impossible for the district to have rescinded either of the votes of the first meeting, or in any way to have interfered with them, for they were in no way included within the scope of the second notice.

In view of the above reasons the appeal is dismissed.

CHARLES MATTESON, A. J. S. C.

1890.
See No. 43.
See No. 65.

DECISION No. 35.

Annual Meeting of Joint School District No. 13 of Lincoln and No. 15 of Cumberland.

Refusal of moderator to allow a record vote as provided by statute, and other informalities of proceedings. sufficient reason for rendering invalid entire proceedings of meeting.

It appears from the testimony that the meeting was properly notified, and called to order by Mr. Gregory, the moderator elected at the meeting in 1890. The records of the last meeting were read and approved, reports were made by the treasurer and the trustees for the past year, and received. The meeting then proceeded to the election of officers for the year ensuing, beginning with the moderator. Humphrey Gregory and Michael H. McCarthy were nominated for that office. Speeches were made by the two candidates, and then Mr. Charles H. Collins, a legal voter of the district, requested that a record vote be taken upon the election of moderator. The moderator, Mr. Gregory, said that he had come prepared to rule that in the circumstances he should not allow a record vote.

Immediately after this decision of the moderator a motion to adjourn the meeting was made and seconded and the question was put by the moderator and declared carried, and the meeting was adjourned without any further action.

There is a conflict of testimony as to the manner of putting the motion to adjourn; the moderator, clerk, and some others declaring that a call was made for all in favor to say "Aye," and then for those opposed to say "No," and that the ayes had it by an overwhelming majority. On the contrary the appellants testify that, although they were in some cases within a few feet of the moderator, they heard no call for the "Noes," and that the decision in favor of adjournment was made immediately upon the response to the call for the "Ayes."

While it is difficult to believe that the officers of the meeting would deliberately misstate the facts it is clear that the call for the "Noes" must have been made in a very hurried and indistinct manner, for we have the testimony of Mr. George Farnell, a stenographer, who was present and took down the entire proceedings, and who sat within five feet of the moderator, to the effect that he heard no call for the "Noes" whatever.

It is my opinion, therefore, that the question was not put before the meeting in such a way as to give the opponents of the motion "to adjourn" a proper opportunity to express their opinion.

It also appeared that quite a number of persons must have been present at the meeting who were not voters.

In view, therefore, of the facts, viz.: that the meeting was composed of both voters and non-voters, and that thereby the decision of any question by a *viva voce* vote must be very unreliable; that at the very beginning of the business of election of officers the moderator declared his positive purpose not to allow a record vote, so-called, to be taken, as provided for by section 7, chapter 52, of the Public Statutes; and that the motion to adjourn was so put that the opponents of the motion did not, and following the previous decision of the moderator could not, have a fair and just opportunity to express their opinion:—

I do give my opinion that the aforesaid annual meeting of joint school district No. 13 of Lincoln and No. 15 of Cumberland, held April 27, 1891, was not lawfully conducted, and that in consequence thereof its proceedings are null and void, and that the trustees of said district should at once issue a call for a special meeting for the election of officers for the current school year.

THOMAS B. STOCKWELL, C. P. S.

1891.

See No. 30.
See No. 36.

DECISION No. 36.

Annual Meeting Joint School District No. 7 of Richmond and No. 13 of Hopkinton.

1. A record vote to comply with statute must include not only *names* of persons voting, but *how* they vote.
2. Record vote may be demanded on election of officers as well as upon any other question.

From the records of the district it appears that the meeting was duly notified and held according to notice; that in the course of the proceedings, when they came to the election of trustee, it was voted to have one trustee, and Charles H. Brown and Albert L. Niles were duly nominated and seconded. Wm. F. Segar then, before any balloting or voting of any kind had begun, demanded a record vote according to the provisions of § 7, cap. 52, of the Public Statutes.

The moderator thereupon directed the clerk to record the names of the persons who voted, but not on which side of the question, or for which party. The clerk accordingly proceeded to so record the names of all persons who voted, thirty-one (31) in all, but did not make any record of how they voted. The ballot resulted as follows :—Whole number cast, 31; for Chas. H. Brown, 21 ; for Albert L. Niles, 9 ; and for George Langworthy, 1; and Chas. H. Brown was declared elected trustee.

Mr. Segar at once publicly in the meeting announced his purpose to test the legality of the election of Mr. Brown, upon the ground that the provisions of § 7, cap. 52, of the Public Statutes had not been complied with. Subsequently the appellant served a written notice upon both the trustee-elect, Mr. Brown, and the moderator, Mr. Fuller.

It was claimed by Mr. Fuller, that § 7, cap. 52, did not require a record of how each voter voted, except upon questions of taxation; that the election of officers was not included within the provisions of the section, and that a record of the names of the voters was enough to comply with the law; that to call upon a voter to announce the name of the party for whom he voted was an infringement upon the rights of the citizen.

The appellant held that the language of the statute was explicit and unmistakable in its terms, and that it recognized no distinction between the different kinds of "questions" which might come before a meeting to decide ; that the statute was not complied with unless the records showed for whom, or on which side of the question, the voter voted.

In this case there is no dispute as to the main facts

as they are set forth in the attested records of the meeting. The only dispute is over the meaning of § 7, cap. 52, of the Public Statutes, and practically over the word "question." Does that word include *every form* of question which may come before a school district meeting, or is it restricted to a particular class of questions?

The significance of this section may be understood better by reference to the section immediately preceding, that relating to the rights of voters in district meetings. From that section, as interpreted throughout the history of the school law, we see that any man may vote at a school district meeting who has at *that* time the necessary qualifications for voting in the town; that is, who would be entitled to be placed upon a voting list, provided the board of canvassers were to meet on that day. This renders it impossible to provide any check list or other guide for the use of a moderator in receiving votes, but practically throws the door quite wide open.

Now for the protection of the district and the legal voters thereof this section 7 was inserted, because under its provisions any voter can secure such a record of *any* vote taken by the district as shall enable him to contest its legality, if he has reason to think it was carried by illegal votes; since on appeal the right of each and every voter can be legally tested and determined, and the fact established whether or not the matter in question was carried by illegal votes.

With the law as it is with reference to the right to vote, I do not see how else than by such a provision as this of section 7 it is possible to protect the legal voters against illegal voting. No more do I see how the election of officers is any the less worthy of protection than the assessing of taxes or the voting of repairs upon the schoolhouse. Indeed the former may often be the more important action to be taken by the district.

That this section 7, as it has been interpreted, infringes upon any *rights* of the voter I do not believe, because the *"rights"* of voters are defined by the constitution, and it nowhere specifies the *right* of a secret ballot. On the other hand, the constitution expressly gives to the general assembly the power to prescribe the manner of conducting elections. Art. II, § 6.

Under that authority the State has from time to time prescribed various forms and methods of voting; —sometimes tending to the most open forms, and again in the direction of the secret ballot. The provisions referred to by the respondent are rendered obsolete by the new system of voting adopted two years ago. But previous to that time there was no uniformity in the matter, for while § 11, cap. 10, provided that the voter for certain officers might use an envelope or not at his option, § 17, cap. 37, expressly provides that in voting for mayor and other city officers *no* envelope shall be used. The method prescribed by this § 7, cap. 52, for voting is not only within the limits of the power lodged with the General Assembly, but it is perfectly reasonable and just, being as it is, the only defence against illegal voting.

It is, therefore, my opinion that owing to the failure of the clerk, under the direction of the moderator, to record, as requested by the appellant, the names of each voter and on which side of the question, or for which person, he voted, the election of Chas. H.

Brown as trustee of said joint district, No. 7 of Richmond and No. 13 of Hopkinton, was illegal and hence null and void, and I do hereby declare the office of trustee for said joint district in consequence thereof to be vacant.

THOMAS B. STOCKWELL, C. P. S.

1893.

Approved.   CHARLES MATTESON, C. J. S. C.

See No. 30.
See No. 35.

DECISION No. 37.

In re Plurality Amendment to the Constitution.

The plurality amendment to the Constitution does not apply to elections in school districts.

I am of the opinion that the word "district" as used in the amendment to the Constitution relates only to *voting* districts and does not include *school* districts.

This being so, I am further of the opinion that the amendment does not apply to the election of officers for school districts of the state, and that, consequently, at such elections a majority of the votes cast is still necessary to an election, as it was before the adoption of the amendment in question.

CHARLES MATTESON, C. J. S. C.

1894.

DECISION No. 38.

Joint District No. 13 of Lincoln and No. 15 of Cumberland.

A joint district is dissolved by the action of either town in abolishing its school districts.

STATEMENT TO THE COURT.

At some time prior to 1890, by the concurrent votes of the school committees of the towns of Lincoln and Cumberland, a joint school district was formed at the village of Berkeley, comprising territory in both towns.

The town of Lincoln at its April town meeting, 1891, voted to abolish the school districts therein; and since that time the schools of said town have been carried on by the school committee.

The schoolhouse is located in the town of Cumberland, and the said town of Cumberland still retains its school districts.

The question now arises whether voters residing in that part of the town of Lincoln which was included within the joint district as above established have the right to vote now in any district meeting which may be held in the Cumberland district; or in other words was the joint district dissolved by the action of the town of Lincoln in town meeting, or does the joint district continue to exist until it is dissolved by the concurrent acts of the two school committees.

OPINION.

I have to say that as the joint school district formed at Berkeley was composed in part of territory embraced in a school district or districts in the town of Lincoln, it necessarily follows that the joint district ceased to exist when any of the districts which went to make it up ceased to exist.

I am of the opinion, therefore, that the joint district referred to was dissolved by the vote of the town of Lincoln, at its April town meeting, 1891, to abolish the school districts in that town; and, consequently, that voters residing in that part of Lincoln included in said joint district as established prior to said vote have now no right to vote in any district meeting held in the Cumberland district which formed part of the joint district prior to its dissolution.

CHARLES MATTESON, C. J. S. C.

1894.

See No. 75.

DECISION No. 39.

Annual Meeting of School District No. 6, North Smithfield.

1. Moderator must vote *before* the poll is closed. He has no "casting vote."
2. The clerk should record proceedings as declared by the moderator.
3. A legal residence once acquired is retained until there is evident intention, through word or deed, to change.
4. A recognized resident of a town divided into school districts must have a residence in *one* of the districts.

The records were presented by the clerk from which it appeared that on the vote for trustee six (6) votes were for G. P. Lovell, the trustee of 1893, and five (5) votes for Fred M. Carpenter. But it appears from the unanimous testimony of all parties present, including the clerk himself, that the vote as declared by the moderator was a tie vote, six (6) votes for each candidate, and that therefore there was no election. The above discrepancy between the facts and the records seems to have grown out of a difference of opinion among the voters present as to the right of the moderator to vote. He voted in this instance at the same time with the other five who voted for Mr. Carpenter, thus making six (6) votes; but it was claimed upon the other side that the moderator had no right to vote except in case of a tie, and hence the record was made upon that basis.

It should be said here, that it is the duty of the clerk to record the proceedings as declared by the moderator. If they are wrong there is a legal remedy. In this instance, it may be said that the decision of the moderator was correct, for the *only* vote which a moderator can cast is that which he casts with the other voters and before any declaration of the vote is made. The moderator of a school district meeting has no " casting vote," as it is called.

It was claimed in the appeal that the meeting was illegally organized, but no evidence was presented to sustain that allegation, and I see nothing in the proceedings to warrant any such conclusion.

Then it was contended that two of the voters for Mr. Lovell were not legally qualified to vote for trustee in said school district No. 6, and hence that their votes should be thrown out, which would make the vote stand four (4) votes for Mr. Lovell and six (6) votes for Mr. Carpenter, and would give the election to the latter.

The two persons whose votes were thus contested were Mr. Joseph Bouley and Mr. Emor Bartlett. In the case of Mr. Bouley it was claimed that though he owned a house and land in the district, he was not a resident, having moved away over two years ago to Woonsocket, where he still lives, together with his wife. It was shown that he had not *lived* in his house during this time and that the house has stood empty for nearly the whole period, the windows being boarded up. But upon the other side Mr. Bouley swears that he has always, even during the brief time he let the house, retained one room in it where he has a bed and where he has stayed over night since he went to Woonsocket; that he visits his place frequently during the year; that he claims North Smithfield as the town of his residence, based upon his ownership of this real estate in school district No. 6; that he has exercised the right of voting in the town of North Smithfield upon the basis of that same real estate; that he has never claimed a residence or attempted to claim or to gain a residence in Woonsocket or in any other place; that he has refused to secure a residence in Woonsocket; that he has never kept house in Woonsocket but always boarded; that it is his intention to maintain his residence in said school district No. 6, of said town of North Smithfield.

In the case of Emor Bartlett it was shown that he is a single man, without really a permanent home; that within the past two years he had lived in at least one other school district of the town of North Smithfield, and also in Lincoln; that upon the town clerk's registry of voters for 1894 he was put down as living in school district No. 10; and while it was admitted that he had lived, for the most part at least, within school district No. 6 for the past six months, still it was claimed that he was not a bona fide resident of the district and hence could not vote. In behalf of Mr. Bartlett it was claimed that he went to work for, and lived with, Mr. Frederick Ballou about the first of October, 1893, and that he had lived with him ever since; that he has no other home or residence; that he is now and has been a registered voter in the town of North Smithfield; that the location given for his residence was kept the same as it was last year through his carelessness when he registered; and it was shown that since he registered last year he had surrendered the keys to the house he formerly occupied in district No. 10 to the owner thereof and that another party had occupied it.

It is my opinion that judged by the laws and customs of this State both Joseph Bouley and Emor Bartlett were residents, in the eye of the law, of school district No. 6, town of North Smithfield, on April 28, 1894, and hence were qualified to vote for trustee in the annual meeting of said school district.

The case of Joseph Bouley is not unlike that of very many cases which exist in nearly every town in the State. It is the universal rule in all of the cities and towns after a man has once acquired a legal residence, to allow him to maintain it upon his desire to do so expressly stated, and the maintenance therein of some token or basis of a domicile. It has always been held by the courts that, after a man had once acquired a residence, it was not necessary for him to maintain his home there in order to retain it, but that its continuance depended upon his intention not to change it, or to adopt any other. Judged by such principles it is clear that Mr. Bouley has never lost his residence in North Smithfield and hence in school district No. 6.

The case of Mr. Bartlett is different, as he is not a real estate voter and is a single man, without a settled home. But there is no question, as I understand, about the justice or legality of his registering as a legal voter within the town of North Smithfield. If he is a legal voter in said town he must have a residence therein, and that necesitates a residence in some school district. The question then arises in which school district did he reside on the 28th day of April, 1894. There is no doubt but that during a portion of the year 1893 he lived, or made his headquarters or home, in a house situated in school district No. 10; that since October, 1893, he has lived within the limits of school district No. 6. Just when he may be said to have legally changed his residence it is difficult to say, but I think from all the testimony given that it is clear that he is not now, and had not been for several months prior to April 28, 1894, entitled to claim his residence in district No. 10; and if he had no residence there, he must have secured one in some other district, and the only one in which it was possible for him to have secured it is district No. 6, within whose limits he has had his home since he gave up the one in district No. 10; and if he was a legal resident of said district of course he had the right to vote for the election of officers. This is the more clear from the fact that it has been decided that no specified length of residence in a district is necessary to qualify a person to vote therein. It is only necessary that it be a bona fide residence. In this case, as in the case of single men usually, it is not easy to determine what the person's *intention*, upon which so much depends, is, but it is impossible to see any other residence which he can claim, and as he must have one somewhere there is no alternative but to declare him a resident of district No. 6.

I do therefore decide that the votes of the said Joseph Bouley and Emor Bartlett were lawfully cast for G. P. Lovell, and that, as declared by the moderator, there was no election of trustee; and as the meeting adjourned without another ballot the old trustee holds over and there is no vacancy.

THOMAS B. STOCKWELL, C. P. S.

1894.

See No. 8.
See No. 23.
See No. 25.
See No. 26.
See No. 27.

DISTRICT TAXES.

DECISION No. 40.

The approval by the committee of a tax legally voted cannot be appealed from.

HENRY BARNARD, C. P. S.

1844.
Approved.   ELISHA R. POTTER, C. P. S.
1854.

See No. 54.

DECISION No. 41.

Committee may rescind their approval of a tax before contract has been entered into.

ELISHA R. POTTER, C. P. S.

· 1853.

See No. 7.

DECISION No. 42.

The bondsmen of a town collector are not liable for his acts as district collector.

ELISHA R. POTTER, C. P. S.

1854.

DECISION No. 43.

School District No. 14, Smithfield.

1. Votes as to times for assessing or collecting a tax are directory merely and do not prevent the action being taken subsequently.
2. Real and personal estates must be kept separate in all assessments of taxes.
3. It is sufficient if a tax is approved by the school committee before the warrant for collection is issued.

A direction to assess or collect a tax within a specified time is directory merely, and if, by accident or otherwise, it is not done within the time fixed, it may be done within a reasonable and convenient time afterwards.

The law positively requires real and personal estate to be assessed in separate columns, and any assessment made otherwise is illegal.

Although it is prudent to procure a tax to be approved by the school committee before any proceedings are had under the vote, yet it is sufficient if the tax be approved before the warrant is issued to collect it.

ELISHA R. POTTER, C. P. S.

Approved.   RICHARD W. GREENE, C. J. S. C.
1854.

See No. 34.

DECISION No. 44.

School District No. 7, Scituate.

A district tax cannot be paid to any other person than the collector.

Where Y's land had been levied upon and sold by a tax collector for nonpayment of a school district tax, and Y brought ejectment against the purchaser, alleging and offering to show that prior to the levy and sale he had paid his tax to the treasurer of the district. *Held* that the evidence to this effect was inadmissible; that the tax collector is the only officer authorized to collect a tax assessed by a town or school district; and that the levy and sale was valid.

It is by law made the duty of the district collector to collect the tax and pay it over to the treasurer or his successor in office. To him is delivered the tax bill and warrant for that purpose. He gives bond for the proper performance of that duty if a bond is required, and is entitled to the commission provided by law for his services in collecting the tax. He must collect the tax and pay it over to the treasurer within the time specified in his warrant. If he fails to do this he may be sued or prosecuted for his default. The treasurer has no authority to collect the tax; but only to receive it of the collector when collected, and disburse it according to law. He does not have the tax bill for the purpose; and payment to him is no more a legal payment than it would be if made to any other officer of the district, who is not authorized by law to collect the tax.

ALFRED BOSWORTH, A. J. S. C.

1855.

See No. 50.

DECISION No. 45.

Case of Edward S. Wilkinson, guardian, in appeal from tax in District No. 1, North Providence.

1. Imperfection of a district clerk's record does not render invalid a tax properly voted.
2. A vote to assess by percentage is not illegal.
3. The assessment of a tax will be legal if it is clear to whom and on what property it is assessed.

Upon the facts as presented and after considering the arguments of the parties, and after advising with Judge Brayton, of the Supreme Court, the commissioner is of opinion that the imperfection of the records of the clerk will not affect the legality of the tax. The proceedings, so far as the notice of the meeting and the form of the resolution are concerned, were undoubtedly legal and proper. As to the mode of levying the tax by percentage instead of by specific sum, the commissioner is not aware that this is contrary to the school law. It is evident that the school committee might approve a specific sum after the tax had been assessed by the trustees; and as there is no evidence to show that the committee did not approve some specific sum, it must be held that the failure to vote a specific sum does not render the whole tax invalid. Also in reference to the assessment of the tax to Edward S. Wilkinson for Nathan Lazelle, instead of to Edward S. Wilkinson, guardian for Nathan Lazelle, since it was shown that this had been the mode of assessing taxes on the said Nathan's personal property in the town of North Providence, and since it was not shown that the said Wilkinson had ever experienced any difficulty in the settlement of his accounts with the said Nathan's inheritance before the court of probate, the commissioner does not deem it to be proper for him to interfere, and solely on this account decree a forfeiture of the tax on the part of the district. This is a matter of technical law and he does not therefore attempt to settle the meaning and usage of that law. It is deemed just and best that in this case this tax should follow and be paid as other taxes have been paid.

ROBERT ALLYN, C. P. S.

1856.

See No. 22.
See No. 58.

DECISION No. 46.

School District No. 7, Warwick.

A district tax can be confided to a town collector when there is a district collector duly appointed and qualified.

I decide, that, according to the 37th section of the act relating to public schools, "Any district may vote to place the collection of any tax or rate bill in the hands of the collector of town taxes," notwithstanding there be a district collector; and I, having been satisfied by evidence that a vote to that effect has been passed at a regular district meeting of school district No. 7, of the town of Warwick, decide that the collection of the tax in question may be legally confided to the collector of town taxes of that town.

ROBERT ALLYN, C. P. S.

1856.

I approve of the above decision.

SAMUEL AMES, C. J. S. C.

DECISION No. 47.

Joseph Crandall vs. Trustees of School District No. 2, Exeter.

Where land lying in two districts is assessed in one parcel by town assessors, trustees of a school district have no right to assess its value, and must call on a town assessor.

The facts as ascertained by the commissioner are as follows, and they are reported to Hon. Chief Justice Ames for his opinion on them, at the joint request of the parties, namely:

On the 30th day of August, 1856, at a legal meeting of the voters of school district No. 2, town of Exeter, it was voted to assess a tax of $150 on the ratable property of the district. This tax was assessed during the month of November, 1856; and on the 7th of February, 1857, the trustees issued a warrant to collect it.

Among the persons taxed for real estate was Joseph Crandall, who is owner of two farms in Exeter, one called the "Rathbun farm," lying on the north side of the so-called "Ten-rod road," the other, called the "Hazard farm," lying adjacent to the Rathbun farm, but on the south side of the said road. This road divides the two districts No. 1 and No. 2,—the latter being on the north, and of course including only the Rathbun farm. It appears that part of the Hazard farm adjacent to the Rathbun land has for several years been rented with this Rathbun farm; and as the tenant was to pay road taxes, it has been by the town assessors taxed or valued in the same parcel with it.

The tax against which complaint is made was for this parcel of land, which on the assessors' book for 1855, the book by which the trustees were governed in their assessment, was called the "Rathbun land," and was valued at $900 under their rules. The sum assessed was $12.30. The appellant claims that this parcel of land, so valued at $900, includes a part of the Hazard farm, lying in another school district, and liable to a tax there; and that said tax cannot be legal, inasmuch as the trustees did not in making the assessment, proceed according to the requirements of section 45 of the act relating to public schools, which declares that, in case of property lying in two districts, and having no separate values on its respective parts, the trustees, if they cannot agree with the owners, shall call on a town assessor, who shall assess the value of the property so situated.

The only question, then, to be decided is a question of fact, as to whether the parcel of land named in the assessors' tax book of 1855, and in the trustees' warrant called the "Rathbun land," is situated wholly within the boundaries of school district No. 2, or partly also in No. 1.

From the testimony the commissioner cannot doubt that the aforenamed sum of $900, taxed as the value of the "Rathbun land," does include the value of a part of the "Hazard farm," which lies without the bounds of this district No. 2, and which, in his opinion, ought not to have been taxed.

As this is one of the cases specially provided for in section 45, above referred to, in which a town assessor ought to have been called in, to apportion the value of the land thus situated in two adjoining districts, and as the tax was assessed by the trustees without the assessor, contrary to the requirements of the statute, the commissioner is of the opinion that the tax appealed from was illegally assessed ; and the assessment is therefore hereby delared void.

ROBERT ALLYN, C. P. S.

1857.

Approved.   SAMUEL AMES, C. J. S. C.
See No. 55.

DECISION No. 48.

School District No. 11, Exeter.

1. A tax approved by the school committee, if subsequently increased, must be again approved.
2. A trustee not authorized to insure a schoolhouse without authority from the district.

Three points of objection can be sustained. The "notice" of the second meeting, the approval of the school committee, and the insurance. The "notice" and "insurance" may be reduced to one. The power to insure a schoolhouse is by § 3, cap. 61, school law, vested in the district and not in the trustee. Yet if the "notice" had specified insurance as one of the objects of the meeting, a vote of the district sanctioning the trustee would have been legal.

It is my opinion and decision that this tax is not legal, because the whole tax has not been approved by the school committee, and the notice was not sufficient to authorize the district to sanction the act of the trustee in procuring insurance on the house.

JOHN KINGSBURY, C. P. S.

1858.

Approved.   SAMUEL AMES, C. J. S. C.

DECISION No. 49.

The excess of a tax beyond the district's indebtedness does not affect the legality of tax.

JOSHUA B. CHAPIN, C. P. S.
1859.

DECISION No. 50.

If taxes are paid to the treasurer, the collector will have the same claim to his percentage as if the taxes had been paid to him originally.

JOSHUA B. CHAPIN, C. P. S.
1860.

See No. 44.

DECISION No. 51.

In the case of a person who resides in a district only a part of the time, the question of taxation of personal property must depend upon the time that said person resides in the district.

JOSHUA B. CHAPIN, C. P. S.
1860.

DECISION No. 52.

When there is only one tax-paying voter in the district his vote is sufficient to order a tax.

ELISHA R. POTTER, A. J. S. C.
1868.

DECISION No. 53.

School District No. 4, Middletown.

1. In any appeal where a district as such is an interested party, the district must be officially notified of the hearing.
2. Where a tax is assessed by assessors appointed by the commissioner they must give notice of their assessment and proceed to value the property independent of the town valuation.
3. A tax collector acting under an apparently legal warrant would not be liable for damages in case it was proved defective.

In this case the trustee made a contract with the teacher, and this contract was made known to the district meeting, and the vote of the district thereon (though invalid for other purposes) may well be held to be a ratification of it.

Subsequently, upon the district refusing to carry out the terms of the contract, the teacher, Coggeshall, and the trustee, Carpenter, united in an appeal which we may construe to mean that they applied, under the provisions of Rev. Stat. cap. 64, § 4, to the commissioner May 12, 1870, and he appointed the same day for a hearing; and it is alleged that "due and actual notice of such hearing before the commissioner was given, and both parties were present." It is not alleged to whom notice was given, or who were present; and by both parties, we must understand the two persons before named, no others being either directly or indirectly referred to. The district was the party against whom the contract was to be enforced, and of course a proper party to this proceeding, but as the plea does not allege that the district was notified, we must infer that it was not, and that omission was fatal.

It is also alleged that the commissioner, on July 9, 1870, decided that the tax voted by the district, "sufficient to pay the residue of the contract," should be assessed and collected in accordance with the power conferred by Revised Statutes, R. I. cap. 64, § 4; and issued a warrant to Messrs. Peckham, Carpenter, and the district clerk, to assess a tax "on the valuation of the town assessors of 1869-70," and appointed the district collector to collect it; that the district clerk declined to act as assessor, and notified the commissioner; and the commissioner (whether verbally or in writing is not said) directed the other two to proceed and assess the tax; and that they were legally appointed and qualified, and did assess a tax on said valuation, etc., etc.; that the commissioner approved it, and, August 30th, 1870, issued his warrant to said Wm. F. Peckham to collect it.

When a district trustee apportions a tax, he is to do it (Rev. Stat. cap. 64, § 2,) on a valuation made by the town assessors. But when a tax is to be collected under the commissioner's warrant, the assessors may use the town valuation as a guide; but they must, after all, assess it upon their own judgment. And it being an actual assessment, proper notice should have been given, which is nowhere alleged.

The collector, acting under an apparently legal warrant, would not be held liable as collector.

ELISHA R. POTTER, A. J. S. C.

1877.

DECISION No. 54.

School District No. 19, South Kingstown.

1. School commissioner has no power to order a tax in a district except in cases where the law specifically provides for such a case.

2. School commissioner cannot approve a district tax, hence there is no appeal to him in such matters, except as to questions of its formalities and illegalities.

In this case school district No. 19 of South Kingstown voted a tax for school purposes and the school committee of the town refused to approve of it. From that refusal an appeal was taken to the school commissioner, and on the hearing it was objected that the school commissioner had no jurisdiction to reverse the committee's vote and to approve of the tax himself and as requested by the party he has laid the case before one of the judges for his decision.

The right of appeal given by cap. 55, § 1, of the school law, is expressed in very general terms. Yet it is evident that it cannot be construed to authorize him to reverse the proceedings of the Board of Education, and so of some other officers who have duties to perform under the law. So if a district refuses to order a tax, *he* can only order a tax in the case provided for by law, where a contract has been made, etc. To hold otherwise would be to make the school commissioner the absolute dictator on questions of taxation.

We must be guided in deciding this question by the intention of the law so far as can be gathered from its language and history, and we may also resort in cases of doubt to the practical construction of it as settled by usage and previous decisions.

It is obvious that the commissioner may on appeal reverse a vote of a district or committee for informality or illegality in many cases where he would not have a right to make any further or new decision of his own. This would be carrying out the object of the law in giving the appeal, which has always been held to be the prevention of litigation, by furnishing a cheap and speedy mode of deciding on such informalities and illegalities.

The location of schoolhouses is one of those questions where the object of the law is to guard against the prevalence of mere local interests, to guard the interests of minorities and of non-resident owners of property; and in these cases the commissioner has always from the very beginning of the system, and with the presumed acquiescence of the legislature, exercised the right to make a new location on appeal; and so in many other cases, where it may be necessary to protect the rights of teachers and scholars from the consequences of local excitements and quarrels.

The principal difficulty in the present case grows out of the very different language used by the General Assembly in cap. 48, "Of the powers of school districts," §§ 3 and 4. The difference is too marked to be overlooked, and I must therefore conclude that while the commissioner may reverse, or refuse to reverse, a vote or decision of the committee in such a case as the present one for illegality or informality, he cannot make a decision approving the tax.

ELISHA R. POTTER, A. J. S. C.

1877.

See No. 91.
See No. 94.

DECISION No. 55.

School District No. 1, Richmond.

1. In case of assessing tax where a town assessor is to be called upon, the trustee before calling upon him must endeavor to agree with the parties as to their valuation.
2. The school committee's records, and not the town clerk's, are the ultimate authority as to a district's boundaries.
3. An assessment of a greater amount than that voted by the district is illegal, whether the excess be great or small.

In the matter of the appeal of the Wood River Branch Railroad against school district No. 1, of Richmond, it was claimed by the appellant that a certain tax assessed by the trustee of said district in accordance with a vote of the district, of November 3, 1878, was illegal and void. 1st. Because the trustee called upon a town assessor to value that portion of the railroad's property lying in the district, without trying first to secure an agreement with the corporation. 2d. Because the records of a district's boundaries as recorded in the town clerk's office are the legal bounds and the ultimate authority on that question, while in this case the trustee followed certain bounds which were furnished by the school committee. 3d. Because the vote to levy the tax only authorized a tax of $125, whereas the tax as assessed by the trustee amounted to $125.40.

Upon the first point raised by the appellant I am of the opinion that the trustee should, after the tax was voted, have endeavored to agree with the railroad corporation before calling upon the assessors for their aid. Such is the natural and only legitimate meaning of the proviso, " if unable to agree with the parties interested," which occurs in the section under which the action complained of was taken. Moreover, no such proviso existed in the school law of 1845; but it was subsequently inserted, evidently because it was found by experience that a change was necessary in that direction.

The second claim of the appellant I do not think is sustained by the law. In the section of the law which refers to the town clerk keeping the records of the district boundaries, nothing is said or implied which makes them the final authority. On the other hand, the school committee is explicitly given full power over this question of district boundaries.

In regard to the legality of an assessment where the total amount assessed is greater than the amount voted by the district, I think there can be no doubt that it is illegal. The right to exceed the prescribed amount at all implies the right to carry the excess to almost any amount, and hence, in fact, transfers the power of determining the amount of the tax from the district to the trustee.

THOMAS B. STOCKWELL, C. P. S.

1879.

I hereby confirm the above decision.

ELISHA R. POTTER, A. J. S. C.

See No. 47.

DECISION No. 56.

School District No. 4, West Greenwich.

1. Where school committee change territory from one district to another, with an agreement of the owners that they are willing to be set back when the committee think best, such agreement is a waiver of notice of such action by the committee.
2. Property that has never contributed to the erection of a schoolhouse ought not to be relieved from such responsibility.
3. Change of boundaries does not alter or destroy the identity of the district.
4. Property added to a district after a tax is voted is liable if it is in the district at time of assessment.

From the evidence submitted it appears that in February, 1876, the appellants being then located in district No. 4, West Greenwich, petitioned to be set off to district No. 10, because at that time there was no schoolhouse in district No. 4, and therefore their school privileges were very poor; and unless they belonged to district No. 10, if they availed themselves of the school there, they would be liable to pay for it.

They were accordingly set off to district No. 10 by the committee; upon the understanding as confessed by both parties, that whenever district No. 4 should build a schoolhouse this property should contribute its regular quota thereto, it never having been assessed for this purpose.

Matters continued thus till the spring of 1879 when the question of building a house was agitated in district No. 4, and finally at a meeting held March 24, 1879, the district voted to build and also to assess a tax of $350 to defray the expenses.

The house was constructed during the summer and fall of 1879, and in November, when the question of raising the money to pay for the building arose, the trustee before making the assessment of the tax applied to the school committee for a particular statement of the bounds of the district and for such a correction of the lines as would restore to the district the property previously transferred to district No. 10.

Accordingly a meeting of the committee was called for November 29, 1879, when the matter was discussed and finally laid upon the table till the next meeting, December 4.

One object of the postponement was to give notice to these two parties of the proposed action, but through some misunderstanding no such notice was given, and on said December 4 the committee met and passed the vote appealed from.

On the 5th of December the trustee made out his rate bill of the tax voted as above on the 24th of March, and delivered it to the town collector for collection.

After a careful examination into the facts I am of the opinion that the decision of the school committee in question should be confirmed for the following reasons:

First. The original boundaries of the districts are thus re-established. It is quite safe for us to assume that the original division into districts was the fairest distribution that could be made, so far as the rights of all were concerned.

For the transfer of this property from district No. 4 to district No. 10 to be made permanent, would be to the very manifest injury of district No. 4, and would require for its justification very strong reasons which I fail entirely to find.

Second. The acknowledged understanding between the appellants and the school committee at the time of the transfer from district No. 4 to district No. 10 constitutes a practical waiver of notice; the act complained of being virtually the second part of an agreement previously made.

Third. The property in question having never contributed to the erection of a schoolhouse should be so assessed, and it is very clear that district No. 4 is the district entitled to the benefit thereof.

Fourth. I am fully of the opinion that the best interests of the two farms in question will be full as well, if not better, promoted by their being joined to district No. 4, than if they were annexed to district No. 10.

The claim that the tax is not collectible of the appellants because it was voted before they were joined to the district and therefore a tax in which they had, and could have had, no voice, is not tenable, because the district which voted the tax and the district which assessed it were legally one and the same district, and all rights and powers which were vested in the one were of necessity vested in the other. If such were not the case, every time the bounds of a district were changed it would be necessary to re-elect officers and re-enact any votes passed previous thereto which were intended to have any farther force or validity. It is difficult to see, therefore, how the trustee when he came to assess the tax which had been voted by the district could do otherwise than assess *all* property which the district contained at the date of his assessment.

To the claim that such a decision violates the principle that one cannot be assessed for a tax which he had no voice in ordering, it is sufficient to say that protection against any injustice is secured by the provisions for an appeal, as in this case, on the question of merit in the change of bounds.

THOMAS B. STOCKWELL, C. P. S.

1881.

Approved. CHARLES MATTESON, A. J. S. C.

TRUSTEES.

DECISION No. 57.

The loss of the qualification as elector required to render a trustee eligible to the office would not cause a forfeiture of the office.

ELISHA R. POTTER, C. P. S.

1849.

See No. 9.

DECISION No. 58.

When no appeal from the manner of the election of trustees is taken within a reasonable time, if they act in this capacity during the year, their acts as such are valid, and they are the acting trustees of the district.

ELISHA R. POTTER, C. P. S.

1849.

See No. 14.
See No. 31.
See No. 45.

DECISION No. 59.

When, from neglect of trustees, the school committee assume the power of opening a school, the trustee is bound to respect their orders.

Elisha R. Potter, C. P. S.

1851.

DECISION No. 60.

School District No. 5, Little Compton.

A trustee of a school district can only be removed during his term of office for cause.

I am of opinion that a district having once legally made an election, of any of the officers required by law to be elected, would have no right to rescind it.

The case would be different, however, with persons who were merely appointed by the district as a committee for some particular purpose. Over such cases the district would have complete control, and might remove such agents at pleasure.

A trustee once elected and accepting could only be removed for good cause, and after notice and hearing. The contrary doctrine would lead to continual contests and confusion.

Elisha R. Potter, C. P. S.

1853.

See No. 16.
See No. 63.

DECISION No. 61.

School District No. 2, North Providence.

1. Trustees can hire at whatever wages they please.
2. The legal school year for the district begins May 1st, annually.
3. Trustees have no power to reduce a teacher's wages or to dismiss him during the term for which he is hired.

At the proper time of the year, and under the approbation of the school committee, the trustees have unlimited authority to employ a teacher at whatever wages they please. If they employ at very high wages, they may, by a vote of the district, assess and collect a tax to defray the extra expense. If they employ at cheap wages, the unexpended balance of their appropriation must be divided among the other districts. And if trustees choose to use only a part of their share of the "teachers' money" for their own district, and leave the remainder to other districts, thereby providing an inferior school for their own children and a better one for their neighbors, no power is known to prevent, provided they do it at the proper time. At such times as trustees may lawfully hire teachers for their schools, they may hire as cheaply as they can, provided the school committee will approbate those hired.

In reference to the time when the legal school year commences, there can be but one opinion. In absence of any vote of the district prescribing the time at which the teacher's contract shall terminate, and in the absence of any written or specific agreement between the trustees and teachers as to this time of terminating the contracts, and in such districts as have established permanent or yearly schools with fixed terms and vacations, the legal school year must be settled by the statute. Section 21 of the act relating to public schools makes it necessary for a district to keep a school not less than four months at some time during the year ending on the first of May, in order that it may be entitled to draw its portion of the "teachers' money" for the year thereafter ensuing; the commissioner is required by section 2, annually in May to apportion the money annually paid out of the general treasury for public schools among the several towns according to law, and his office annually expires on the second Tuesday of that month. Section 20 enacts, among other things, that the school committee "shall apportion as early as practicable in each year, among the districts, the money received from the State;" and section 21 further provides "that at the end of the school year any money which shall remain unexpended may be divided by the committee among the districts the following year;" and finally, section 26 makes it the imperative duty of a district to hold its annual meeting near this time, namely, in April or May. From all this and from the fact that the returns of the districts to the school committees and from the committees to the commissioner are made to this date, and the district officers are elected for the year ending at the annual meeting, when their terms of office expire unless continued by special statute, the commissioner must decide that the legal school year begins on the first of May annually, or by section 26, in cases there provided for, at the time of the annual district meeting.

As to the general power claimed by the trustees to reduce a teacher's wages, or in the alternative to dismiss him from their school, and that on a very brief notice, it should be remarked, that the school law manifestly intends that the State shall have some charge of all the schools which it in part supports. It therefore very properly forbids trustees to hire as teachers persons who do not possess certain moral and literary qualifications—and even those who possess these in an undoubted degree, unless they hold or can obtain a certificate in the required form and signed by the proper authorities. The law aims to prevent trustees from retaining a teacher who neglects his duty, and provides that the school committee may dismiss such an one. All these guards seem to be reared in order to prevent the trustees of a school district from doing two things which would necessarily tend to destroy or degrade their school;—from employing the immoral or incompetent, and thus poisoning or stinting the morals and the minds of the children; and from hastily dismissing the worthy teacher by reason of any private or personal pique, or in consequence of some temporary excitement. And as the state furnishes a portion of the money which supports the public school of every district, and gives that district all the right it has to exist and to collect taxes for the further support of its schools, it is but proper that it should step in by its officers and prevent the trustees from injuring the school, or from suddenly discharging or reducing the compensation of a teacher against whom no deficiencies are alleged. It is believed that such powers as are claimed would materially injure any school, and that under the school law they are not conferred upon the trustees.

ROBERT ALLYN, C. P. S.

1855.

See No. 62.
See No. 67.

DECISION No. 62.

School District No. 8, West Greenwich.

1. Districts have no power to hire teachers by vote.
2. District trustees must act as a board.

The commissioner decides that a district, at a meeting of its voters, has no power to hire a teacher even if the meeting is legally called, and such an item is inserted in the warrant. In sections 33-36, inclusive, of the act relating to public schools, which enumerate the powers of districts, no mention is made of the "power to employ" teachers; but, on the contrary, section 40 specially confers upon the trustees that power, and it is made "their duty" "to employ one or more qualified teachers for every fifty scholars in average daily attendance." It is, therefore, the plain duty of the trustees to employ all teachers, and a meeting of the voters of a district could only be advisory.

As to the mode in which the trustees shall discharge their duty, it ought to be a rule never to be departed from, that when the district appoints three trustees, as it may, the three should meet and confer upon all questions relating to their official duty. Many of their duties are deliberative, and, therefore, cannot be delegated to, or assumed by, any one of their number,—such as making contracts with teachers, for repairs, or fuel, and preparing tax lists; and these things, of course, require a meeting of the three, or at least of a majority after due notice given to the absent minority. And it is highly improper that any single one should, in any duty not strictly ministerial and prescribed to him by vote of the body at a meeting, act with the expectation that his colleagues will ratify what he shall have done.

The mode of notifying meetings of trustees is not specified by law, and is therefore left to be a matter of common agreement among them. Generally, as they are near each other, a verbal notice from the chairman will be sufficient.

ROBERT ALLYN, C. P. S.

1856.

Approved.   GEORGE A. BRAYTON, A. J. S. C.

See No. 61.
See No. 66.

DECISION No. 63.

School District No. 2, Cranston.

If a district elect one trustee at annual meeting, it cannot at a subsequent meeting elect two more.

My decision is that the vote and proceedings of the district at their meeting held May 7, 1859, are void.

At the annual meeting the district could elect one trustee or three trustees, as they might decide. They decided to elect, and did elect, but one,—Mr. Richardson. There was thus an election at the annual meeting, and the trusteeship of the district was full, according to the authorized decision of the district. There was, therefore, no election of trustees to be made at any subsequent meeting.

SAMUEL AMES, C. J. S. C.

1859.

See No. 16.
See No. 60.

DECISION No. 64.

William Tiffany in re Special Meeting of School District No. 4, Warwick.

1. A board of only two trustees is not a legal board. When one of three trustees elected declines to qualify there is no vacancy, but one of the old board holds over.
2. The order of the trustees is determined, in lack of other evidence, by the records of the meeting.

In the matter of Appeal of William Tiffany from proceedings of school district No. 4, town of Warwick, it appears that at the annual meeting of said school district No. 4, held April 2d, 1883, under a valid call, it was voted by the district to have three trustees and the following-named persons were elected as such trustees, one at a time, and in the order named, viz.: C. E. Luther, Edwin Millard, and O. P. Sarle. Messrs Sarle and Millard were engaged immediately after the meeting.

Mr. Luther declined in writing to qualify, and on the 7th of April Messrs Millard and Sarle called a special meeting for April 13th, "to elect a trustee in place of Chas. E. Luther who was elected at the annual meeting and who refuses to serve; to elect a district collector; and to raise a tax to pay the present indebtedness of the district and to authorize the trustees to enlarge the schoolhouse."

This notice was issued by Messrs Millard and Sarle without consulting, or recognizing, Mr. Tiffany as a trustee.

At this meeting of April 13th, Mr. J. W. Tibbitts was elected trustee and engaged. Mr. J. B. White was elected collector, and it was voted to assess a tax of six cents on each hundred dollars of the ratable property of the district, to pay the indebtedness of the district and to make any necessary repairs.

From the action of this meeting of April 13th, Mr. Tiffany appeals and claims that its proceedings may be declared illegal and null and void, on the ground that the notice under which it acted was not a legal notice.

He claims that in the first place there was no vacancy in the office of trustee to be filled, but that he held over in the event of Mr. Luther's refusal to serve; and hence no person elected under the call could legally act as trustee. In the second place, as to the issuing of the notice, he claims that it was not valid in that it was signed by only two trustees.

After a careful consideration of the issue involved in this case I am of the opinion that the notice of the special meeting for April 13th, issued April 7th, and signed by Messrs Millard and Sarle, was not a legal notice, because, First, It was signed by but two trustees, who were either the whole board, or a majority of the board. If they are called the whole board, I do not believe they were qualified to act, because the law only recognizes one trustee or three trustees; and as to the claim that the general provision of the statutes, that "all words purporting to give a joint authority to three or more officers or persons, shall be so construed as to give such authority to a majority of them" warrants the exercise of such power, it seems to me that that provision has no application here.

There is in this case a board of "two" trustees, and two only who have been elected and qualified, and to allow them the authority to issue notices for meetings and transact business in general for the district, is practically to nullify the explicit statute which says that a district may elect "one" or "three," but nowhere provides for but two. The practical effect of such a theory would be not to confer upon the majority of a board the power *to act for* the board, but *to be* the board, which is quite another thing.

If it be claimed, as the counsel for Mr. Tibbitts avers, that the two trustees signing the call of April 7th were a majority of a board of "three" and hence competent to act, it must be remembered that the action of the majority of any board, taken without the knowledge or consent of the minority, is always to be considered as contrary to law and not to be upheld. In this case there is no claim that Mr. Tiffany, or any party, was recognized, or consulted, as trustee by the two trustees who signed the call.

As to the question whether a vacancy in the office of trustee did actually exist on the date of April 7th, I am of the opinion that there was no such vacancy. The words of cap. 61, § 4, Public Statutes,

"Every school district officer elected or appointed under the provision of this title shall, without a new engagement, hold his office until the time of the next annual election or appointment for such office, and until his successor is elected or appointed and qualified," are very broad and explicit. They make no exceptions in favor of any officer; and in view of the fact that in the revision of 1872 the words "and qualified" were added to the section, they clearly indicate the purpose of the General Assembly to provide, first, that there shall be no interregnum or vacancy occurring by a lapse of authority; and second, that no person shall be considered as fully "elected or appointed" to any office, in any such sense as to take the place of another, until he has been "qualified."

In this case it is beyond dispute that Mr. Luther, one of the three persons elected as trustees on the 2d of April, 1883, did not qualify.

If he did not qualify, then by virtue of the provision of the statute above quoted, no other person's authority could have been terminated. There must then have resulted one of two conditions of affairs; either one of the old trustees held over, or, as we have already seen in the previous argument, the three old trustees held over.

There certainly is no place for but "two" newly elected trustees to become a legal board of trustees, and qualified to act in that function for the district. I am inclined to the opinion that one of the old trustees held over, making with the two elected and qualified at the annual meeting, the full board of three required by law.

Such an interpretation of the law seems to me the natural and legitimate meaning from the plain reading of the statute; and if so, I see no reason why it is not to be accepted, unless it be found practically impossible to carry it into effect. But I see no more trouble in ever determining the question of order in the election of trustees, than any other that may arise in district matters.

The clerk's record of the proceedings of the meetting, when approved by the district in open meeting, must of necessity determine an order, and such order, for such purposes as this, is all-sufficient.

In the case in question the original notes of the clerk, made at the meeting of April 3rd, 1882, and his record over his official signature, which was read and adopted in a subsequent district meeting, fix the order of the election of trustees in 1882 as follows, viz.: William Tiffany, Edwin Millard, and James Phillips.

Now as Mr. Luther, who declined to qualify, was elected first at the annual meeting in 1883, it is my opinion that Mr. Tiffany continued, and still continues, to be trustee, with full power to act as such in connection with Messrs. Millard and Sarle, the two who were elected and qualified at the annual meeting of 1883.

In view therefore of the above reasons, I hereby declare the meeting of school district No. 4, of the town of Warwick, held on April 13, 1883, to have been illegal, and all its acts null and void and of no effect.

THOMAS B. STOCKWELL, C. P. S.

1883.

Approved. CHARLES MATTESON, A. J. S. C.

DECISION No. 65.

In re Resignation of Trustee of District No. 1, Cranston.

Resignation of district officer may be withdrawn before district has accepted it, either by direct vote or by action filling the vacancy.

AGREED STATEMENT OF FACTS.

Lewis A. Walton was elected trustee at the annual meeting April 28th, and was duly engaged by the Town Clerk.

On Tuesday morning, Sept. 9, 1890, he posted notices for a special meeting to accept his resignation,—the meeting to be holden at the schoolhouse on Saturday evening, Sept. 13, at half-past seven o'clock P. M., that not giving the five days' notice required by the law.

The meeting was held according to the above call and it was voted to accept his resignation, but no one was elected in his place.

Some time early in November, Mr. Walton notified the clerk of the district in writing, withdrawing his resignation as no one had been qualified to succeed him, and he now claims to be the legal trustee and proposes to hold the office to the end of the year, or until his successor is qualified.

My decison is that he is trustee.

My reason for the decision is that his resignation has not been accepted by the district in any such definite and conclusive manner as the law would seem to require. The action of the meeting held on Sept. 13, 1890, cannot be held as legal on account of the illegal notice for the meeting. Had the notices been posted any time on Monday the meeting could have been held any time on Saturday.

No other action appears to have been taken by the district which can be in any way regarded or construed as an acceptance of the resignation. Had the district proceeded to the election of a trustee at any time, such election might have been considered as a virtual acceptance, sufficient at least to have barred the withdrawal of the resignation.

If there has been no valid or binding acceptance of the resignation, then the right to withdraw it must remain; and as Mr. Walton has so withdrawn it, matters stand as they did before he proffered his resignation, and he is trustee.

Thomas B. Stockwell, C. P. S.

1891.

See No. 16.

Powers and Duties of School Committee and Apportionment and Uses of School Money.

DECISION No. 66.

School District No. 5, Cumberland.

1. School teacher without a certificate cannot draw "public money."
2. No particular mode of notifying meetings of the school committee.

1st. No teacher can, under any circumstances, be entitled to demand any portion of the public money unless he has a certificate of qualification valid at the time he keeps the school.

2d. Although the committee may provide by by-law a mode of calling meetings of their body, such by-law would not exclude any other mode of calling meetings; and if a quorum be present, and all those who are capable of attending have had reasonable notice, and there is no charge of any unfair or improper proceedings, the meeting will be held to be a legal one; the committee being a body appointed by law for the performance of a trust, and the law itself prescribing no particular mode of calling such meeting.

ELISHA R. POTTER, C. P. S.

1849.

Approved.   RICHARD W. GREENE, C. J. S. C.

See No. 62.
See No. 82.

DECISION No. 67.

The school committee are the proper authority to dismiss a teacher who does not give satisfaction.

1852. ELISHA R. POTTER, C. P. S.

Approved. ROBERT ALLYN, C. P. S.
1855.

Approved. JOSHUA B. CHAPIN, C. P. S.
1861.

See No. 61.

DECISION No. 68.

School District No. 3, North Providence.

1. School committee may limit their certificates, but general certificates must be construed according to their plain purport.
2. School committee cannot delegate the power to annul a teacher's certificate.

On consideration I adhere to the decision formerly made upon this point, that although the committee have the power to limit their certificates to particular schools, yet if they see fit to give a certificate of general qualification, it must be construed according to its plain purport, and to allow the written certificate to be contradicted or varied by any understanding not expressed on the face of the certificate itself would be a dangerous practice, leading to continual misunderstanding and litigation.

The power of annulling certificates is an important one. It gives the committee control over the teacher, it authorizes them to pronounce a judgment against him for unfitness or misconduct, which may have the effect of ruining him in his profession, and of injuring materially his prospects for general success in life. If the construction was doubtful, these considerations would incline me to lean against the right claimed for the committee to delegate this power. But the construction appears to me to be plainly that the committee have not the right to delegate.

And if the sub-committee had not the power to annul the certificate, the subsequent recognition of it by the committee would not render it valid.

ELISHA R. POTTER, C. P. S.

1852.

See No. 69.
See No. 71.
See No. 85.

DECISION No. 69.

School District No. 3, North Providence.

1. School committee may not compel a gradation of schools.
   School committee have power to limit and explain their certificates.
3. School committee cannot delegate their general powers.
4. Committee have power to annul certificate for good cause.

1st. The school committee may promote by advice and recommendation, but have no power to compel, a gradation of schools by a district.

2d. The committee have the power to limit and explain their certificates. To construe the law to require perfection in the branches named in section 54 would be unreasonable, and, indeed, it is impossible to make a perfectly definite standard. If so, there is no reason why the certificate should not express the degree of qualification.

3d. The committee cannot delegate their general powers. The powers of visiting schools and examining teachers they are specially authorized to delegate.* There can be no objection, also, to a committee authorizing its officers to draw orders for payment of bills, upon the performance of certain conditions, as on making a return, etc. But to delegate a power which is supposed to imply the exercise of a discretion in the committee seems contrary to the intention of the law in giving such power to the committee.

4th. The committee have the undoubted right to annul a certificate, or dismiss a teacher, for good cause. No particular form is necesary for doing this. But the trustee should be plainly informed that the certificate is annulled, or the teacher dismissed. And the teacher should be notified, that he may have a chance to defend himself.

ELISHA R. POTTER, C. P. S.

1852.

See No. 68.
See No. 71.

*By the school law of 1851.

DECISION No. 70.

Appeal from School Committee of North Kingstown.

Scholars cannot be compelled to make fires for schoolhouses by either trustees or school committee.

The regulation No. 26, adopted by the school committee October 25, 1852, is in these words: "The trustee or trustees of each district, with the teacher, may cause the fires to be made in the schoolhouse, by directing the scholars of a suitable age to take turns in making the fires, or procure them to be made in any other way they may think proper."

In a private school the teacher has a right to prescribe his own terms. The parent who sends children to the school delegates to the teacher the right to govern them according to his own rules, and to punish to a reasonable extent for the violation of them. The remedy of the parent, if he does not like the school or its regulations, is in not sending to it.

To a public school every parent has a legal right to send his children. He sends them subject to the lawful authority of the teacher, and to the lawful regulations which may be prescribed for the discipline and studies of the school, but he has a right to insist that no regulations be made which the law does not authorize.

The right claimed, if it exists at all, must be derived from the general power of the committee to make regulations, or from the authority given to districts and trustees to make assessments on scholars and their parents. (§ 59, Law of 1851.) The latter, however, it is very evident, contemplates only assessments to be paid in money and not labor.

The power of the committee to make regulations is given by section 1, which authorizes them "to make and cause to be put up in each schoolhouse, or furnished to each teacher, a general system of rules and regulations for the admission and attendance of pupils, the classification, studies, books, discipline, and method of instruction in the public schools."

It seems to me very plain that the power to make a regulation of the character of the one in question is not given in this paragraph. We might as well infer a right to require the scholars to cut and saw the wood. And as I can find no other authority for it in the law, it must be considered as unauthorized by law, and accordingly null and void.

ELISHA R. POTTER, C. P. S.

1853.

See No. 84.

DECISION No. 71.

Case of Philip B. Stiness, Jr., vs. J. H. Willard, Clerk of School Committee, North Providence.

Clerk has no authority to perform of his own motion acts that are discretionary with the committee.

As to the point whether the clerk could legally order bills without the authority of the school committee, the commissioner is clearly of opinion, in accordance with a decision of the late commissioner, Hon. Elisha R. Potter, that the clerk has no power whatever to do any act that is discretionary with the committee to do or not to do. It is a well-settled principle that such a body as a school committee cannot delegate to any one of its servants any discretionary power. It may, and indeed will, often find it necessary to delegate ministerial powers, but it cannot go further than this in its acts of delegation. As these bills were under protest, and as it lay wholly in the discretion of the school committee to receive the schools and visit them and allow the teachers their bills for wages, in short, to make them legal, it must be held that any act of the clerk which would attempt to forestall the action of the committee in regard to that protest would be illegal and void.

ROBERT ALLYN, C. P. S.

1856.

See No. 68.
See No. 69.

DECISION No. 72.

A single estate may not be taken from one town to be united with a district in another town for the purpose of forming a joint district, especially when other estates are as favorably situated for the same purpose.

JOHN KINGSBURY, C. P. S.

1857.

DECISION No. 73.

Town money can be used for incidental expenses.

JOSHUA B. CHAPIN, C. P. S.

1860.

See No. 77.

DECISION No. 74.

The power to expel a pupil from school is in the hands of the committee.

JOSHUA B. CHAPIN, C. P. S.
1864.

DECISION No. 75.

Isaac M. Bull et al. vs. School Committee of the Town of Woonsocket.

1. The power to originally lay out or form school districts is vested in the school committee.
2. School committee have the power to discontinue one district, even against its will, and join it to another.

This is an appeal from the decision and doings of the school committee of Woonsocket, the effect of which was to discontinue district No. 10 and to enlarge No. 9, so as to include the territory previously within No. 10.

The commissioner of public schools lays before us a statement of the facts of the case, agreed to both by the appellants and appellees, for our decision. These facts are: "1. The three villages of Globe, Bernon, and Hamlet were originally parts of the town of Smithfield, and were each organized as independent school districts. 2. When these districts were set off from Smithfield and annexed to Woonsocket, they retained their original district organization, suffering no change except that of name, the Globe District henceforth being known as No. 8, Bernon as No. 9, and Hamlet as No. 10. 3. At a legal meeting of the school committee of Woonsocket held June 6, 1873, it was voted, that district No. 10 at Hamlet be and it is discontinued; also that the boundaries of district No. 9 be established so as to include what formerly belonged to both Nos. 9 and 10."

The question raised upon these facts by the appeal is, did the school committee have power to discontinue district No. 10 and to alter the boundaries of district No. 9 so as to include the territory previously within No. 10, the voters in these districts having never voted to consolidate them?

Section 3, cap. 53, of the General Statutes provides, that "The school committee may alter and discontinue school districts, and shall settle their boundaries when undefined or disputed; but no new district shall be formed with less than forty children between the ages of four and sixteen, unless with the approbation of the commissioner of public schools." The school committee rely upon this section as authority for their action. It certainly seems sufficient.

The appellants, however, contend that such a construction of the section above quoted is inconsistent with other provisions of the statutes relating to public schools. They refer to § 2, cap. 47, of the General Statutes, "Of the powers and duties of towns . . . relative to public schools," which is, "Any town may be divided by a vote thereof into school districts," and argue that under the construction claimed, it would be possible for a school commitee to nullify the action of the voters of a town. They also refer to § 5, cap. 50, of the General Statutes, "Of joint school districts," by which "any two or more adjoining school districts in the same town may by concurrent vote, with the approbation of the school committee, unite and be consolidated into one district, for the purpose of supporting public schools, and such consolidated district shall have all the powers of a single district," and contend that the construction claimed renders this section practically useless, since if a school committee may first discontinue a district and then enlarge an adjoining district so as to include the one discontinued, a consolidation of the two may be effected by the action of the school committee alone, *without the concurrent votes of the districts;* and a result may thus be accomplished *indirectly* in a manner different from that provided for accomplishing the same result *directly.*

The appellants also refer to cap. 48, of the General Statutes, "Of the powers of school districts," by which school districts are made bodies corporate and vested with certain powers necessary for the discharge of their duties.

The appellants assert that § 3, cap. 53, of the General Statutes should be so construed as to harmonize with these several sections to which they refer, and suggest that all the General Assembly intended was, that school committees should alter and establish the boundaries of school districts when undefined or disputed, and form new districts from parts of districts, when from any cause it should become desirable to sub-divide existing districts, and should only wholly discontinue or abolish a district with its consent.

Doubtless all these provisions of the statutes are to be so construed as to make them consistent and to give effect to all. But is the construction claimed for § 3, cap. 53, really inconsistent with the proper construction of the other sections of the statutes to which our attention has been directed? We think not.

The language of the first of these—§ 2, cap. 47—is, "Any town *may be divided,* by a vote thereof, into school districts." This may mean either that the town may divide itself by its vote, or that it may be divided, if it shall so vote. We think that the true construction is the latter. When a town has voted that it be divided into school districts its power has ceased. It then becomes the duty of the school committee to lay off the districts and define their limits, the only limitation upon their power being, that "no new district shall be formed with less than forty children between the ages of four and sixteen, unless with the approbation of the commissioner of public schools." It is true that in the present statute no express authority is given to school committees to *form* districts, but we think it is necessarily implied by the language of this limitation. Some of the obvious reasons for this construction of § 2, cap. 47, are,—

1. The form of the expression is the passive *"may be divided."*

2. If the other construction be adopted, there is no limitation upon the power of towns in the formation of districts as to the number of children which such districts shall contain.

3. The districts can be laid off and their limits defined much more intelligently by a body like a school committee than by a town.

4. Our construction is more consonant with the policy of the school laws, which vest the ultimate control and direction of school affairs, subject to appeal to the commissioner of public schools, in the school committees.

A review of the legislation upon the subject of

forming school districts confirms the construction which we have adopted.

The second provision of the statutes to which the appellants have directed our attention as inconsistent with the construction claimed for § 3, cap. 53, is § 5, cap. 50. The purpose of this latter section was to enable adjoining districts in the same town, where the compactness and number of the population would warrant, to unite for the purpose of maintaining public schools,—the advantages of which are too apparent to be dwelt upon,—and as an inducement to so unite, § 6 provides that such consolidated district shall be entitled to receive the same proportion of public money as the districts composing it would receive if not united ; but they are not permitted to unite except with the approbation of the school committee, or, on appeal, of the commissioner of public schools. We do not think that this power of voluntary consolidation conferred upon adjoining districts was intended to prevent the school committees from consolidating two or more districts, if in their opinion the interests of the schools or the judicious use of the public money required it, even though it should be against the wishes of the districts. The right of appeal to the commissioner of public schools would restrain and afford a remedy against the arbitary exercise of such power by a school committee.

The third ground of objection urged by the appellants to the construction of § 3, cap. 53, claimed by the appellees, is that under that construction school committees have power to discontinue school districts without their consent. We do not deem this a valid objection.

By the school laws of Massachusetts, cap. 23, § 24,

of the Revised Statutes as construed in *Richards* v. *Daggett*, 4 Mass. 534, and *Allen* v. *School District No. 2 in Westport*, 15 Pick. 35, towns had power, from time to time, to form new districts and to divide or alter the limits of old ones. School districts were also corporations, with powers similar to those of our own. In *School District No. 1 in Stoneham* v. *Richardson*, 23 Pick. 62, Morton, J., in the opinion of the court, says: "But school districts are corporations not only very limited in their powers, but also of precarious existence. They may not only be varied and modified in the extent of their territorial limits, but also annihilated by a body over which they have no control." Again, on page 69, he says: "The power of towns to form new districts at their discretion necessarily implies the power of abolishing the old ones. And as these corporations are brought into existence without the volition of their members, embracing every one within their limits, *nolens volens*, so they may be abolished without the consent and against the wish of all the members."

We think the school committee were authorized to take the action appealed from, and that the appeal should be dismissed.

CHARLES MATTESON, A. J. S. C.

1875.

See No. 38.

DECISION No. 76.

Nathan T. Verry vs. School Committee of the Town of Woonsocket.

For general laws to modify special laws affecting particular towns, the modifying intention of the legislature must be clear.

The town council of Woonsocket, June 12, 1878, elected Mr. Verry superintendent of public schools. Afterwards the school committee claimed the right to elect the superintendent, and June 24, 1878, elected Mr. White. From this vote Mr. Verry appealed to one of the justices of the Supreme Court.

On account of the importance of the question involved, the case was, by request of the justice to whom it was presented, heard before the full court and argued by counsel.

By the act incorporating Woonsocket, Pub. Laws, cap. 666, January 31, 1867, it is provided that the council shall elect so many town officers as by the laws of the State are or shall be required, excepting only a few whose election had been before provided for in the act. It seems to have been the intention of the act to vest in the council, with these exceptions, all the powers of the town in regard to those matters.

The election of superintendent of schools has been at several times regulated by general law. See Revised Stat. R. I. cap. 60, § 5; Pub. Laws, cap. 923, March 24, 1871. And by Gen. Stat. R. I. cap. 47, § 5, 1872, now in force, any town may elect, and if it fails, the committee shall elect one. It is compulsory that the town shall have a superintendent, but the committee are to elect if the town does not.

By Gen. Stat. R. I. cap. 31, § 8, it was enacted that "every town . . . shall have and exercise all the powers and privileges . . . . conferred upon it by its charter or by the several acts of the General Assembly specially relating to it, until the same shall expire by their own limitation or shall be revoked or repealed."

The present case involves the question how far special laws affecting particular towns are to be deemed to be repealed or altered by general laws, without express mention.

Such cases are not without their difficulties; but while the power of the legislature is undoubted, the intention should be plain. It is obvious that if the legislature should grant to a town a right to do some particular thing, and should afterward enact by general law that no town should do it, there would be no doubt as to the construction. See cases in Dillon Municip. Corp. § 54, 2d ed.; Sedgwick Stat. & Constit. Law, 2d ed. 99.

In the present case, under the special act, the powers of the town as a corporation in this respect were to be exercised, not in town meeting, but in town council, and the general law merely enacts that if the town, which does not necessarily imply town meeting, fails to elect, the school committee should elect. On this view there is really no repugnance between the general and special acts.

The town here did through its council elect, and the election by the school committee was therefore illegal, and this vote must be reversed.

As there is nothing in any of the special acts to which our attention has been called prescribing the number or mode of classifying the committee, there can, of course, be no question but that these subjects must be regulated by the General Statutes of the State.

ELISHA R. POTTER, A. J. S. C.

1879.

DECISION No. 77.

Uses of the Public Money.

1. Public money may be used for current expenses of the schools.
2. Public money cannot be used for repairs or fixtures to schoolhouses.

As to the law concerning the uses which may be made of the money raised by the town for school purposes, there is no section or clause which specifically sets forth such uses. A careful comparison, however, of two or three different sections of the law will at once convince one of the fact that the law makes a broad distinction between the "support of schools" and the "providing of schoolhouses, etc." See §§ 1 and 3 of cap. 50 and §§ 3 and 4, cap. 51, of the Public Statutes.

But lest there might be some question, we have had at least two decisions from the highest authority, covering this point.

In 1851, Judge Potter, then commissioner of public schools, decided that no portion of the school money, either State, or raised by town tax for the "support of schools," could be used for the building, furnishing or repairing of schoolhouses where the district system prevailed.

In 1858, John Kingsbury, commissioner, wrote as

follows: "After consulting Chief Justice Ames I must decide that the phrase 'other expenses' in cap. 64, § 9, Revised School Laws, applies to expenses for things similar to books, fuel, etc., and which do not come under the name of fixtures. I must therefore further decide that window curtains are fixtures."

If reference is made to the law above quoted it will be found to refer to the old rate bill and the uses to be made of the proceeds thereof. Now since the increased appropriation for the support of schools, which the towns were obliged to make when the rate bill was abolished, was clearly intended to supply the deficiency created by the absence of the rate bill, it is equally clear that one purpose for which this increased appropriation was designed must be identical with those for which the former fund was raised.

On the other hand it has always been held, whenever the question has been raised, that, in any town where the property was owned by the districts, no part of the appropriation for the support of schools could be used in payment for such district property or any part thereof.

THOMAS B. STOCKWELL, C. P. S.

1880.

See No. 73.

DECISION No. 78.

School District No. 3, South Kingstown.

1. The motive or reason which prompts a gift of land or money to a district not a subject of inquiry or appeal.
2. A gift of land or money to a district not contrary to law.
3. The location of a schoolhouse adjacent to one's territory not a grievance within the view of the law.

In the appeal case of C. W. Wilcox from the action of the school committee of South Kingstown whereby they fixed a new location for a schoolhouse in district No. 3 of said town, the following is a statement of the main facts. After several meetings of the district for the purpose of considering the question of repairing the old house and building a new one, at a meeting held September 5th, an offer was received from W. H. Potter to give the district $500, if they would use it to buy a lot, called the Hazard lot, about fifty rods farther north on the same road as the old site. His offer was accepted and the district, by a vote of 25 to 10, decided to take that lot and build a new house. The action of the district was reported to the school committee, who met, examined all the sites proposed, heard all parties interested, and finally voted unanimously to locate the new house on the Hazard lot.

The appellant resists the location of the schoolhouse on the new lot because it abuts directly upon his premises and he regards the schoolhouse so near him as an injury, and its location there will entail expense upon him. He also claims, in common with some others, that sufficient reasons do not exist for a change of site, and that, even if they did exist, the proposed site is not a suitable one.

During the hearing the appellant offered evidence as to the character of the motive or purpose which prompted Mr. W. H. Potter to make his offer of $500 to the district, but it was ruled out by the commissioner on the ground that the result of the act, as affecting the interests of the district, and not the motive or cause for it, was the subject of inquiry.

Upon the question of personal inconvenience raised by the appellant, I do not regard the alleged grievance as coming within the scope of the provisions of the law, and it must therefore be set aside.

As to the claim that the gift of Mr. Potter was of the nature of a bribe and so contrary to law, and the subsequent action of the district, growing out of it, void, I do not so understand either the law or the practice under it. From the beginning of the school system, private parties have continually donated lands and money to towns and districts for school purposes and with specific provisions and conditions, and I have never known it to be held that such gifts were contrary either to the letter or the spirit of the law.

Upon the claim that sufficient reasons do not exist for a change of site and that the proposed site is an unsuitable one, I am of the opinion that a change is needed, and that the Hazard lot is, under the circumstances, a fit and suitable lot and one that will tend to promote the best interests of the district. I do therefore approve of the action of the school committee, and confirm their vote whereby they located the proposed new schoolhouse on the so-called Hazard lot; and the appeal is dismissed.

THOMAS B. STOCKWELL, C. P. S.
1881.
Approved.   CHARLES MATTESON, A. J. S. C.

DECISION No. 79.

Case of Appeal of John Nevins vs. School Committee of Cranston.

1. A change from one edition of a text-book to another edition of the same book not a "change" of text-books.
2. The notice of the proposed "change" required by law does not include a specification of the particular book to be introduced. It is enough to state the *kind* it is proposed to change.
3. Notice must be given at a regular meeting of the committee, but action may be taken on the question at any subsequent meeting, provided proper time has elapsed since the notice.

The facts appear to be as follows: In 1880 the agent of Warren's geographies visited the several members of the school committee of Cranston with reference to the introduction into the schools of their revised, or N. E., edition, as it is called. After interviews with all of the committee, the chairman of the committee ordered of the publishers, Messrs. Cowperthwait & Co., a lot of the N. E. edition, which were sent to him with authority to put them into the schools at what are called exchange or introduction rates. No minute however appears on the records of the committee of any action by them relative to this matter.

After the receipt of these books, the chairman notified part of the schools, and possibly all, that the pupils could change their geographies in accordance with the terms as given to him. But in no case were the pupils compelled to make this change; it was left optional with them and the teacher.

At the regular meeting of the school committee, January 9, 1882, the following written notice of a proposed change in geographies was given by Mr. J. A. Latham, one of the committee: "Notice is hereby given the school committee that the matter of changing the text-books upon geography be considered at some future meeting." Upon the records of a special meeting, held February 4, 1882, the following minute appears: "The notice in relation to Harper & Bros'. geography was brought forward and action thereon deferred till next meeting."

At the adjournment of this meeting, February 11th, the following action on this subject was taken.

Voted, "That it is advisable to adopt Harper & Bros'. geographies for the use of the public schools of this town."

It is from this vote of the school committee that the appeal is taken.

I am of the opinion: First. That no change in text-books was made by the committee in 1880. It is certain that no legal change was made, as no record exists of any such action, nor is there any claim that the committee ever took action as a body on that question. But it is claimed that there was a *de facto* change, and that the law was framed to protect the people from actual changes. Without deciding how far there may be a *de facto* change, which is not a *de jure* change, I am quite clear in this case, there was no such mandatory and general change as would justify any one in claiming that a change in text-books had been made. Again it is claimed by the respondents, and I think justly, that the substitution of one edition of the same book for another edition, even if the second is fuller and in many respects better than the first, is not a change as contemplated by the law. In such cases the two books are not different books, but different forms of the same book. The only case where such a claim could be maintained, would be where the book had been re-written and made so entirely unlike the old one that the two could not be used together.

Second. I am of the opinion that the notice given January 9th was a legal notice. The law requires that a "notice of the proposed change" shall be given in writing at "a previous regular meeting." The notice in question was given in writing by a member of the committee and constitutes a part of the record of the meeting of January 9th, which was a regular meeting of the committee, so that there can be no question either as to the fact of its having been in writing, or as to the time when it was given. As to the character of the notice I do not think that the words "proposed change" cover more than the specification of the *kind* of text-book which it is designed to change.

It is also claimed that the notice lacks definiteness because it refers to *some* future meeting. But the law says that the notice must be given at *a* previous regular meeting, which certainly allows some latitude. It could not have been intended that it must be given at the *preceding* regular meeting, for in that case the law would have used that word, so that I see no deficiency in this particular.

Third. I am of the opinion that the meeting of February 11th was clothed with the power to consider the question of making a change of text-books in geography, because the fact that the law does *not* specify that the changes shall be made at a *regular* meeting, while it does so specify with regard to the "notice," is conclusive evidence that it was not intended to apply the same restriction in both cases.

THOMAS B. STOCKWELL, C. P. S.

1882.

Approved.   CHARLES MATTESON, A. J. S. C.

DECISION NO. 80.

Stephen C. Arnold vs. School Committee of Scituate.

1. School committee have no jurisdiction in case where "unlawful and aggravated assault" is charged upon a teacher.
2. No appeal lies to the commissioner from the failure of a school committee to sustain the charges made in a matter brought before them.

In the matter of the appeal of S. C. Arnold from a certain decision of the school committee of the town of Scituate, made by them on the 4th day of February, 1882, in which they declared that a certain charge of "unlawful and aggravated assault," preferred by said Arnold against Miss Elizabeth J. Smith, teacher in school district No. 5 of said town of Scituate, "was not sustained," the appeal is dismissed for the following reasons:

First. I am of the opinion the school committee had no jurisdiction over the complaint made to them, and therefore no appeal can lie to the commissioner.

Second. If the doings of the committee, which are complained of, related to a charge which could be properly investigated by them, I do not think that their failure to sustain said charges can be regarded as a cause of grievance under our statutes. By such a decision they neither violate any right of any party, nor deny him anything which is guaranteed him by the laws; they simply exercise a discretionary power which is lodged in their hands by the statutes, and over which neither commissioner nor court has any control.

For the above reasons, therefore, I do hereby declare said appeal to be dismissed.

THOMAS B. STOCKWELL, C. P. S.

1882.

Approved. CHARLES MATTESON, A. J. S. C.

DECISION No. 81.

Appeal of A. W. Kenyon vs. School Committee of Richmond.

The *school*, and not the *district*, is now made the basis of the apportionment of the school money.

AGREED STATEMENT OF FACTS.

In the matter of the appeal of A. W. Kenyon, trustee of joint district No. 4 of Richmond and No. 17 of South Kingstown, from the action of the school committee of Richmond in dividing the public money for the year 1888-89 the following statement of facts was agreed upon by the appellant and Charles J. Greene, clerk of the school committee:

That school district No. 4 of Richmond is united with school district No. 17 of South Kingstown to form a joint district, so called, under the provisions of § 8, cap. 53 of the Public Statutes, with the schoolhouse located in South Kingstown.

That during the year ending April 30, 1888, there was an average attendance of eleven scholars from district No. 4 of Richmond.

That on the second day of July, 1888, the school committee of Richmond met and passed the following vote, to wit: *Voted,* To divide the public school funds for the year 1888-9 among the several districts by allowing for each school $172, and for each pupil per yearly average $6.50, and that the remainder be reserved for tuition and printing after allowing district No. 4 $50 additional.

The appellant claims:—That school district No. 4 of Richmond, being a whole district, duly formed and created in accordance with law, is, as such, entitled to the same recognition in the matter of the apportionment of the public money as any other district in the town.

That according to the report of the school committee and in the eye of the law the district maintained a school and still maintains it, and hence is entitled to its just share and proportion of the public money under the law.

That the fact that said district No. 4 is joined with district No. 17 of South Kingstown does not in the least degree interfere with, or destroy, its claims upon the public money.

That by virtue of §§ 8 to 11 inclusive, cap. 53 of the Public Statutes, said district No. 4 is entitled to the same recognition by the school committee of Richmond as if it were an independent district, and maintained a school within its own territorial limits.

That under the provision contained in cap. 689 of the Public Laws, said district No. 4 is entitled to at least one hundred and eighty dollars.

Charles J. Greene, for the school committee, claims that as there is but one school in the joint district, and that is located and maintained in district No. 17, South Kingstown, said school cannot be at the same time maintained in district No. 4, Richmond.

That district No. 4, Richmond, does not at all maintain a school in the sense recognized by the law, and hence that the committee were not obliged, under the provision of cap. 689 of the Public Laws, to apportion to said district the minimum amount specified in said chapter; but that the amount to be allotted for the pupils residing in said district was within the discretion of the committee.

That the provision at the end of said cap. 689, by its very terms, making the *school* and not the district the basis of the division, precludes the claim of the district as such.

OPINION.

Under Public Laws R. I. cap. 689, the *school*, and not the *district*, is made the basis of apportionment of the school money. The town's proportion of the $120,000, received from the state, and the one-fourth at least of the town's appropriation for the support of schools is to be apportioned by the school committee among the districts equally, *according to the number of schools maintained in each*, the remainder of the town's appropriation, moneys received from registry and dog taxes, from school funds and other sources is to be divided into two equal parts, one of which is to be apportioned to the several districts *according to the average attendance of the schools therein* for the year preceding, and the other is to be apportioned at the discretion of the committee.

The proviso of § 1 of the chapter is that the total apportionment for each *school* shall not be less than $180.

I am of the opinion, therefore, that inasmuch as no *school* is maintained *in* district No. 4, Richmond, that district is not entitled as of right to any portion of the school money, but only to such sum as the committee in the proper exercise of its discretion shall allow.

Public Statutes R. I. cap. 53, § 11, relied upon by the appellant in support of his claim, being inconsistent with Public Laws cap. 689, was repealed by § 2 of said cap. 689.

CHARLES MATTESON, A. J. S. C.

1888.

TEACHERS.

DECISION No. 82.

Case of Layton E. Seamans vs. School Committee of Coventry.

1. Committee have a legal right to refuse to examine a teacher as to literary qualifications if they are dissatisfied with his moral character.
2. A teacher, having been dismissed, cannot draw teachers' money.

Layton E. Seamans applied to the school committee of Coventry for examination as a teacher of a public school. The committee, however, as they had a legal right, and as they thought upon their oaths they were bound to do, refused to examine him as to his literary qualifications, on the ground that they considered his moral qualifications insufficient for the requirements of the law. Mr. Seamans then succeeded in obtaining a county certificate (under Law of 1851) from a county inspector in Providence county, and also obtained the counter signature of the commissioner of public schools ; both of these gentlemen supposing that no objections had ever been made to Seamans' moral character. With this certificate thus countersigned, Mr. Seamans entered the school in district No. 5, Coventry, as a teacher. He gave no notice of beginning to the school committee, neither did he in any way conform, or show a disposition to conform, to the rules of the said committee for the government or instruction of the schools of their town.

On the 26th of January, 1855, the committee formally dismissed him from his school, on account, as they alleged, of his having fraudulently procured the above-named county certificate, and non-compliance with their regulations.

Mr. Seamans, however, continued his school to the close of his term, when the school committee granted him an order for the money to pay his wages for the time previous to January 26th, 1855, and refused to grant an order for the time subsequent. It was from this refusal that the appeal was taken.

The commissioner is of opinion that the vote of the school committee, by which Mr. Seamans was dismissed, was a legal and proper vote, and in accordance with the 56th section of the act relating to public schools, which gives to a school committee the power to dismiss a teacher, by whomsoever examined, for just cause. The cause which they alleged appears to be a just and sufficient one. They had after this dismissal no right, according to the 21st section of the act above referred to, to grant any order to Mr. Seamans for services performed as a school teacher in any of the schools of the town, subsequent to the time when he was informed of the act of the school committee by which he was dismissed. The vote of the school committee is therefore affirmed.

ROBERT ALLYN, C. P. S.
1855.
See No. 66.
See No. 67.
See No. 68.
See No. 69.

DECISION No. 83.

Case of Emor Smith vs. School Committee of Smithfield.

1. The act of one member of a committee not the act of the committee.
2. Notice to a teacher that he is on trial is sufficient to proceed with annulment, after the trial.
3. Possession of a certificate entitles teacher to a trial before annulling.
4. Failure to properly instruct and govern, good cause for annulling.

In this case a certificate was legally issued to the appellant, and subsequently the clerk of the committee visited his school and not being satisfied therewith immediately sent a note to the trustee that he had annulled the certificate, but sent no notice to the teacher. Another teacher, however, was hired by the trustee. Smith appealed to the commissioner of public schools, and a partial hearing took place on the 27th of January; and on the 31st, the committee failing to appear, the act of Holmes, the clerk, was decided to be void, since in fact no annulment had been made, nothing but a notice having been sent to the trustee that such annulment was made.

The school committee of Smithfield, however, met on the 29th of January, and by a unanimous vote proceeded to annul the certificate of said Smith, given him by Harvey Holmes and dated December 16, 1854, "for deficiency and want of qualification." It is from this vote that the appeal is taken, and in reference to this that the following decisions are made.

The first point made by the appellant was that the decision reversing the act of Holmes, made on the 31st of January, was necessarily conclusive in this, and reversed it also. That, however, was clearly an illegal act done by a single member of the committee, to whom no such power to annul was ever delegated,—in fact, there is no evidence to show that Holmes ever wrote an annulment. He undoubtedly supposed that he had annulled the certificate of Smith, but the contrary is clear; and therefore the committee were at liberty to take original action in the case. It is their act that is to be examined on its own merits. And this can only be justified where it is shown that the circumstances of the case actually called for this course on their part.

A second point made for the appellant was, that he had no notice of the intention of the committee to annul his certificate, and therefore he had no opportunity for trial and defence. It is believed on this point, that the conversation which passed between him and the examiner was notification enough that he was to have four weeks for trial and practical demonstration of his ability to teach and to govern in the schoolroom. And this is a better form and mode of trial than can be had elsewhere. It is therefore decided that such a trial is sufficient, especially as the teacher always has an appeal, where it can be examined whether the trial in the school was fair and sufficient.

The points made by the committee were two:

1. That Smith was not qualified in literary attainments for the office of teacher.
2. That he failed to comply with the regulations for the schools of Smithfield made by the school committee, and that he failed to impart instruction and to govern his school in a proper manner.

On the first of these points, the commissioner does

not feel bound to go back of the certificate of the committee. They, or their clerk, gave him a certificate in proper form, under their oath, after due examination and consideration of the circumstances. It must therefore be held that he was qualified, at least, to make a trial of his skill in the schoolroom.

The case then must turn wholly on the questions, whether or not Smith did comply with the regulations of the school committee, and whether he did really properly instruct and govern his school. The testimony on this point was large in amount and conflicting in character.

From the facts in the case, as they appear to the commissioner of public schools, it seems to him that the school committee of Smithfield only discharged the duty imposed upon them by the law and by their oath of office, and their act of annulling the certificate of the said Smith ought to be sustained.

ROBERT ALLYN, C. P. S.

1855.

Approved. WILLIAM R. STAPLES, C. J. S. C.

See No. 68.
See No. 69.
See No. 71.

DECISION No. 84.

A teacher cannot be required to make fires in a schoolroom.

ROBERT ALLYN, C. P. S.

1855.

See No. 70.

DECISION No. 85.

Appeal of L. A. Freeman & R. E. Budlong vs. School Committee of Cranston.

1. In towns without districts school committees are not obliged to issue a certificate of qualification before engaging a teacher.
2. School committee may determine qualifications of a teacher by other means than examination.
3. After a formal vote to appoint, and notice of same to teacher, school committee have no right to interpose an examination or other condition.

In this case it appears that the school committee of Cranston, on July 8th, "appointed Miss Jeanette H. Ramage to teach in grades 4 and 5 in district No. 4, at a salary of eleven dollars per week, *for one term*," and on the following day notice of her appointment was sent to her through the mail by the clerk of the committee, and her acceptance was received by him in due time. The last of August Miss Ramage was notified by the superintendent that she would be expected to appear for an examination the week before the schools were to be open.

As Miss Ramage was sick she could not be present at that time, and it was not until the first of October that she was able to take up her duties. On Monday, Oct. 7, she reported for duty at the school to which she had been appointed, but was met there by the superintendent who forbade her teaching until she had taken the examination, which was required by the rule of the committee. After some discussion an arrangement was effected whereby Miss Ramage was to take the examination Monday night and Tuesday, which she did. At the close of the examination, on asking if she was to take charge of the school the next day, the superintendent told her that she was not to teach until she heard from him. On Thursday morning she received a letter from him announcing that the average of her examination fell below the percentage required by him, and that he must refuse to give her permission to teach.

In consequence thereof Miss Ramage, though ready and waiting, was unable to fulfill her engagement.

The question at issue here is, was the school committee of Cranston authorized in the circumstances to refuse Miss Ramage permission to teach in the school in the Edgewood district to which she had been appointed.

There is no dispute over the terms of the formal action of the committee on July 8th, and of the official notification thereof to Miss Ramage. It remains to consider what was the nature of that action and whether the school committee were authorized under the law to take it. It would certainly seem that the vote of the committee was an explicit and definite appointment to teach a given school for one term, without any condition or qualification. And the notice sent her by the clerk seems to be capable of no other construction or interpretation.

That it was so considered by Miss Ramage is shown by the nature and tenor of her reply, and her immediate resignation of the position held by her in Shenandoah, Pa.

We now come to consider whether the school committee had the authority to make such an appointment. Under the original organization the schools of Cranston were carried on under the district system and the teachers were hired by the trustees, but in 1892 the town voted to abolish the school districts and, by virtue of § 3 of cap. 447 of the Public Laws, the school committee became clothed, among other powers and duties, with that of hiring all of the teachers. The sections of the law bearing upon the powers and duties of the school committee in this connection were very evidently drafted with reference to the management of the schools under the district system, that being the almost universal form of management when the law was first framed. About the only change in any of the sections is the one made in § 1, cap. 57, where the words, "by any trustee," were inserted in the law in the revision of 1882, which clearly shows that it was intended to relieve the school committee, in cases where they hired the teacher, from the formality of issuing certificates to those whom they had decided to hire. Section 7, chapter 56, says "The school committee *may* examine" etc, but the word "may" is used instead of "shall," as in the next two sections with reference to other duties, showing that, even when they were required to give certificates, they were allowed to use other means than an examination, if they saw fit, to determine the teacher's qualifications.

In this case I do not see any exercise of power on the part of the committee, which they were not fully authorized to make and also justified in making. The person proposed, or recommended, for the vacancy was known to be possessed of diplomas from a high school and a State Normal School, which, while by no means conclusive evidence, are certainly credible evidence of literary ability, and the personal testimony of one of their own number as to the candidate's success in teaching would certainly be regarded as worthy of respect. It is my opinion that any school committee would be justified in appointing for "one term" at least, as a trial, any person coming before them with such credentials. Of course I do not mean that such testimony is absolute, but it does afford suitable basis for a trial engagement, if it seems best to the committee.

I must conclude, therefore, that the action of the committee on July 8th, as formally conveyed in writing by the clerk to Miss Ramage, and her formal acceptance in writing, constitute a legal contract, which is binding upon both parties, according to the terms thereof.

The question now arises was the school committee authorized in refusing Miss Ramage the opportunity to fulfill her part of the contract, upon the ground set up by them, viz.: the failure of Miss Ramage to pass a satisfactory examination.

I do not think so, for the reason that no such condition entered into the contract or agreement which they had made with Miss Ramage.

The only ground upon which such a condition could have been introduced would have been the fact that it was required by State law, over which, of course, they could have no control. But no such law exists. If the original law remained, it would not have absolutely demanded an examination, but that she should have had a certificate before she began to teach. As it is, the only thing that can be claimed to give a basis for the insistence on the examination is a vote of the school committee, passed in 1893. But that vote, like any other vote or action of the school committee, was subject to the control of the committee, and by the passage of a vote like that appointing Miss Ramage was waived or repealed in that particular case.

There is no question as to the authority of the school committee to require every candidate for a position as teacher under their jurisdiction to pass as thorough an examination as they may deem best, but it must *precede* the appointment, or the appointment must be made *upon that condition*.

In view, therefore, of the above, I do declare the action of the school committee of the town of Cranston in refusing Miss Jeanette H. Ramage permission to teach in grades 4 and 5, of the Edgewood district, to have been contrary to law, and that Miss Ramage was entitled under the terms of her appointment to teach in said position from the date of her reporting for service, for the balance of the period for which she was hired.

THOMAS B. STOCKWELL, C. P. S.

1895.

I concur in the opinion of the commissioner on the questions of law discussed.

CHARLES MATTESON, C. J. S. C.

LEGAL PROCEEDINGS.

DECISION No. 86.

School commissioner has power to define the bounds of a district, when appealed to from vote of committee.

HENRY BARNARD, C. P. S.

1848.

Approved. ELISHA R. POTTER, C. P. S.

1852.

Approved. JOSHUA B. CHAPIN, C. P. S.

1864.

See No. 88.

DECISION No. 87.

School District No. 7, Burrillville.

I am of opinion that the decision of the committee, though not involving the merits of the question, is such as may be appealed from, and that on such appeal the whole merits of the case may be examined and decided.

ELISHA R. POTTER, C. P. S.

1850.

Approved. LEVI HAILE, A. J. S. C.

DECISION No. 88.

Upon the refusal of the committee, the commissioner may fix the district boundary.

ELISHA R. POTTER, C. P. S.

1851.

See No. 86.

DECISION No. 89.

School District No. 3, North Providence.

Where express power is not conferred on commissioner, he can, on appeal, simply remand the matter with his decision, and if the official interested will not acquiesce, the remedy is a mandamus from the Supreme Court.

The difficulty which the court experiences in this case results from the 21st section of "the act to revise and amend the law regulating public schools," which defines the duties of the town committee. This section provides that the town committee shall draw orders upon the treasurer for the payment of money due, in conformity with the law : *Provided*, "that the committee shall not be obliged to give any order until they are satisfied the services have actually been performed for which the money is to be paid." They are to decide when money is due, and, having so decided, to draw an order for its payment. And the 23d section of the same act prescribes that "the town treasurer shall receive the money due from the State treasury, and shall keep a separate account of all money appropriated by the State, or town, or otherwise, for public schools, and *shall pay the same to the order of the school committee."* These two sections are exceedingly significant. The first prescribes who shall draw the orders, and the other what orders the town treasurer shall be bound to pay. The 65th section of the school act gives an appeal from the decision of the school committee to the commissioner, whose decision is to be final. But the commissioner, by this section, has only authority to affirm or reverse the decisions of the town committee, but has no authority to draw orders; and any orders drawn by him are not obligatory upon the town treasurer. We think the proper course for him is to adjudicate upon the appeal, and certify his decision to the town committee, requesting them to draw the order required, and, if they refuse, a mandamus may be granted to compel them to draw the order.

RICHARD W. GREENE, C. J. S. C.

1852.
See No. 54.
See No. 91.
See No. 93.
See No. 94.
See No. 96.
See No. 99.

DECISION No. 90.

School District No. 3, North Providence.

I am of opinion that the commissioner has a right to allow a rehearing for good cause, in his discretion; but it is not in the power of the commissioner to dispense with the teacher's having a legal certificate.

ELISHA R. POTTER, C. P. S.

1852.
Approved.   RICHARD W. GREENE, C. J. S. C.
See No. 93.

DECISION No. 91.

School District No. 8, North Providence.

Commissioner cannot compel trustees to grant a warrant for the collection of a tax, and must not interfere to perform their duties.

A tax was voted, assessed, and partly collected; and the commissioner is now asked to appoint a collector and to issue a warrant to collect the balance.

Counsel for a taxpayer in said district opposed to the granting the petition raised a question of jurisdiction, and moved that the petition be dismissed because the commissioner had not power to grant the relief prayed for.

After consideration, the commissioner submits the following as his decision on the question of jurisdiction:

It is seriously doubted whether, under the forty-sixth section of the school law,—the section cited as giving all the authority over the case,—the commissioner has power to order and enforce the collection of the balance of a tax legally voted, approved, assessed, and partly collected by a district under the rightful authority of their trustees. The case contemplated by that section appears to be one in which there is no power in the district to collect taxes and thus satisfy any just claims which creditors may have against it, and not one in which the power has already been exercised to a certain extent, and the officers of the district are simply indisposed to proceed. The petition does not allege any errors in the assessment nor any want of power to collect, but only asks the commissioner to perform a duty legally devolving upon their officers, but very repugnant to their feelings; or, in other words, it is but asking one officer of the State to undertake a duty where his authority is at least doubtful, and discharge it for another where the latter's power is far more clear.

Besides, it seems that, according to the sixty-sixth section of the school law, the trustees of the district have a right to presume that the tax was a legal one, and that it is, therefore, properly and lawfully due, inasmuch as there appears to have been no exception taken to the vote by which it was ordered, nor to the act by which it was assessed.

It is a principle which must govern the commissioner, that he will not encroach upon the powers, prerogatives, or duties of any officer below him elected by the people themselves. And as the trustees of the district were elected for this very purpose of collecting all lawful taxes, and as they have ample powers and securities, the petition is therefore dismissed.

ROBERT ALLYN, C. P. S.

1855.

See No. 54.
See No. 89.
See No. 93.
See No. 94.
See No. 96.
See No. 99.

DECISION No. 92.

Transfer of land does not make another appraisal of a lot necessary, and the failure from sickness to make an appeal invalidates the claim to make another, without special legislation.

JOHN KINGSBURY, C. P. S.
1856.

Approved.   ELISHA R. POTTER, A. J. S. C.

See No. 95.

DECISION No. 93.

Petition of Emor Smith for Rehearing.

1. Rehearing not possible after approval by a judge of the Supreme Court.
2. Commissioner to make up a statement of facts from the evidence, but not to submit the evidence as such to the judge.
3. Jurisdiction of the commissioner.

In the matter of the decision of the commissioner of public schools in case of the appeal of Emor Smith from a vote of the school committee of Smithfield, annulling the certificate of said Smith as a teacher in said town.

This is a motion or petition for a reconsideration, by the commissioner and the judge, of the above decision, on the ground that the decision of the commissioner reported to the Hon. William R. Staples, late Chief Justice of the Supreme Court, on the 24th day of August, 1855, and approved on the 26th day of September, 1855, is not valid and binding, because the commissioner did not report a statement of the facts as they were sworn to or admitted, but instead thereof reported *as facts* his own conclusions upon the testimony; it appearing from the petition of said Smith that "he insists that there can be no final or binding decision, until a *statement of the evidence* shall be made to the judge," for reasons by him in his petition set forth.

The 65th section of the "act to revise and amend the laws regulating public schools," provides "that the commissioner may (and if requested on the hearing of either party shall) lay a statement of the facts of the case before some one of the judges of the Supreme Court, whose approval of such decision shall be final." If then, in the matter of this decision, upon such request, a statement of the facts of this case, in the sense of the statute, has been laid before one of the judges of the Supreme Court, and the decision of the commissioner has been by him approved, this "approval" is, by the very words of the statute, made final, irrespective of the merits of the decision approved. The "appeal" in other words, in the civil law sense of the term, and as it is used in our statutes,—that is, a rehearing of the whole cause, matter of fact as well as law, after it has been decided by a competent tribunal,—is expressly given, by the first words of the section of the school act above referred to, to the commissioner; and the section provides that his decision upon such appeal shall be final, if the commissioner, upon the request of either party, shall "lay a statement of the facts of the case" before one of the judges of the Supreme Court, and he shall approve the decision. The purpose of this last provision was, undoubtedly, to give to the commissioner and the parties the aid of such a judicial officer in matters of law, and to secure as far as conveniently practicable, by an uniform construction of the act, an uniform system of legislation upon so important and interesting a subject as the discipline and government of our public schools.

The document entitled "Decision of commissioner of public schools in case of appeal of E. Smith from a vote of the school committee of Smithfield annulling the certificate of Smith as teacher in said town," signed by Robert Allyn, commissioner of public schools, is, in my judgment, "*a statement of facts*" by the commissioner in the sense of the 65th section of the school act, although it is not, as it is averred by the petitioner that it is not, a statement of the testimony or evidence by means of which the commissioner ascertained the facts which he states in it. "A statement of facts" from testimony or evidence must, from its very nature, be the conclusions of the officer entitled to make it, from the testimony or evidence which he has heard ; and the distinction between such a statement, and a statement of the evidence or testimony on which it is based, is too well settled in legal practice and parlance to require illustration. Whether the conclusions drawn from the evidence or testimony by the commissioner were legitimate or not, is a matter which the law does not, in my judgment, confide to the judge, but solely to the commissioner, who alone hears the appeal, listens to the witnesses, examines the evidence, and arrives at the conclusion of what are "*the facts of the case.*" No power, no means, are, in my judgment, given to the judge to examine into these facts. It is the duty of the commissioner, under the law, to decide what the facts are, and to lay a statement of them before the judge, with his decision upon them, and the sole office and jurisdiction of the judge is, upon such statement, to approve or disapprove the decision of the commissioner. This is not only plain from the words of the act, but is to be inferred from the nature of the facts to be ascertained,—the good or ill discipline of schools, the fitness or unfitness of teachers to instruct or discipline scholars, and the like facts, peculiarly fitted to be ascertained from evidence by the commissioner, but which the judge would ordinarily have no such peculiar qualifications to ascertain.

The jurisdiction of the school commissioner under the public school act, by way of appeal from the decisions or doings of school committees, district meetings, trustees and county inspectors, is, looking to the subject, nature, and manner of its exercise, rather a visitatorial power than that of an ordinary legal tribunal, and the power of the judge of the Supreme Court in the matter of such an appeal is limited, precisely as might have been anticipated from the universal course in such cases, to the mere approval of the decision of the commissioner upon his statement of the facts.

It being admitted by the petitioner in his said petition that the decision and statement of facts of the commissioner in the matter of this appeal was laid by the commissioner before Chief Justice Staples on the 24th of August, 1855, and that the said decision was, by said Chief Justice Staples, then one of the judges of the Supreme Court, approved,—and it appearing to me that the statement of facts submitted to said judge was such a statement of facts as is required by the statutes, and that his approval thereupon of the decision of the commissioner is final,— I therefore approve the decision of the commissioner that this motion or petition for reconsideration must be by him dismissed for want of any jurisdiction in him alone, or in him conjointly with a judge of the Supreme Court, to rehear or reconsider the decision so approved.

After such a decision and approval made, neither the commissioner nor Judge Staples, if the latter were still in office, could rehear or reconsider the matter of the same, no matter how erroneous such decision and approval might be. Much less can the commissioner, with another judge of the Supreme Court, or subject to approval of such judge, whether then in office or succeeding to the office of Judge Staples, reconsider and rejudge his approval.

SAMUEL AMES, C. J. S. C.
1856.

See No. 54.
See No. 89.
See No. 90.
See No. 91.
See No. 94.
See No. 96.
See No. 99.

DECISION No. 94.

School District No. 10, North Providence.

The school commissioner has no jurisdiction in an appeal from a vote of a school district to enforce a claim against the collector of a district.

The appellant, tax collector of school district No. 10, North Providence, has suffered no grievance at the hands of the district, of which he can complain to the school commissioner. He has collected money which the district demands of him, as they have the right. His answer is, that he has paid it to the treasurer; but as the treasurer denies this, and the evidence of payment produced by the collector is not satisfactory, the district very properly persist in their demand. The appellant's admission charges him with the money, and he produces no sufficient evidence, as it would seem, in his discharge. A mere demand of money as due, though unfounded, is no ground of legal complaint, and this demand, under the circumstances was natural and proper.

Besides, a money claim of this sort, made by a school district against its collector or treasurer, seems to be wholly without the jurisdiction of the commissioner. He can issue no execution to enforce it, nor can he enjoin any suit commenced upon it. It must necessarily be adjusted by the ordinary tribunals of law, which are clothed with powers to aid the right, in the way both of pursuit and defence. The school law, by enabling school districts to require bonds of their clerks, collectors, and treasurers, points to the ordinary legal remedies against such officers in case they do not faithfully account for moneys received by them, or damages are sought against them for other breach of official duty.

The school commissioner in my judgment was right in dismissing this appeal.

SAMUEL AMES, C. J. S. C.

1861.

See No. 54.
See No. 89.
See No. 91.
See No. 93.
See No. 96.
See No. 99.

DECISION No. 95.

School District No. 7, North Providence.

An award of appraisers is void, unless both the owner of the land and the representatives of the district are heard at one and the same hearing.

In a suit against a school district, on an award of appraisers of the value of a lot taken for a schoolhouse under cap. 66, as amended by cap. 323, of the Revised Statutes, it appearing, that at the meeting of the district clerk and of the plaintiff, upon notice before the appraisers for hearing upon the matter of the valuation of the lot, the plaintiff, when going with the appraisers upon the land, with coarse and violent language forbade the clerk to accompany them, who thereupon remained behind, and the plaintiff in the absence of the clerk was heard by the appraisers; *it was held*, that the award thus made by the appraisers was void, and could confer no right of action in favor of the plaintiff against the district.

It was the right of the defendants to be present at all times during the hearing, that they might know and hear whatever was offered to the referees, either by way of evidence or argument, by the plaintiff; that they might know what was necessary to be answered by proof or by argument, and, especially, that they might see that no improper communication was made, or illegal evidence offered, to the referees. . . . .

We are of the opinion that the award obtained should be held void.

GEORGE A. BRAYTON, A. J. S. C.
1863.

See No. 91.

DECISION No. 96.

School District No. 19, South Kingstown.

Appeals may be made from decisions of committees in locating schoolhouses.

Objection is made to the decision of the commissioner in this case, that it is not a case where the law gives any right of appeal, and that therefore the decision of the school committee was final and conclusive, as was decided in the case of John H. Gardner, reported in 4 R. I. 602.

The grounds of the argument against the right of appeal in this case could not, of course, be more ably stated than they are in the decision to which the counsel refers us.

And they are, First. That a grievance implies a wrong growing out of some infraction of law; a litigated question of right. The present case involves no question of violated right and therefore the appellant is not a party aggrieved. Second. That the discretion is with the school committee; they have the power to decide it, and no wrong is done to any one, and no one has a right to complain, or correct them. Third. That a contrary construction would throw every discretionary power into the hands of the commissioner and the Supreme Court, which latter might be utterly unfit to exercise it.

First. Is the appellant a party aggrieved? He is a property holder in the district. The owners of that property have or may have children entitled to the privileges of the school. The distance of the location from his dwelling may seriously affect, not only the convenience of sending to school, but the value of his property hereafter. If the money was a gift from some one to found a school, he might dictate the site and the conditions of his bounty, and no one could legally complain. Here the whole money, as well what comes from the State and town treasuries to pay the teacher, as the money to build the house, is derived from taxation, of which the appellant, it is presumed, pays his fair proportion. Some hundreds of years ago, perhaps, a deprivation of school privileges might not be considered a grievance; hardly so now. The appellant pays his proportion of the whole expenditure, and has a very material interest in the proper application of it.

Second. Does the fact that the school committee exercise a discretion in the choice of a site prevent an appeal?

To apply such a doctrine to the school law would almost nullify the provisions for appeal.

There is hardly an exercise of power by the school committee or trustees which does not imply the exercise of discretion. The mere giving an order for payment of wages may, perhaps, be an exception; but the examining, and, in some cases, employing teachers, annulling of certificates, forming and changing school districts, supervision of taxes and building of houses, and the general regulation of the schools, all imply discretion. So with trustees; and so, in many cases, with the powers vested in school districts. If, because they have the power to decide in the first place, and because they exercise a discretion in doing it, there can be no appeal, there would be hardly a case left for the exercise of such a right.

And yet the language of the provision is very broad, and it would seem difficult, without a great deal of verbiage, to make it more comprehensive.

If there was any doubt as to the meaning of the law, there is another principle of decision which might be resorted to for aid. When a law admits of different constructions, it is well settled that the usage under it, and the practical construction of it for a series of years, is entitled to great weight, and sometimes may be decisive.

In the present case the practice was uniform. The first two commissioners under the law were constantly engaged in examining appeals of this very sort, sometimes confirming and sometimes altering, or wholly revising, decisions of committees as to sites of schoolhouses. The re-districting, which the law rendered necessary in most of the towns, led to frequent dissension. And the practice was continued under their successors, and does not seem to have even been questioned until 1858.

It would no doubt make the office of commissioner easier and more pleasant to take away this power. The decision of such cases leads frequently to enmities, or charges of being subject to improper influence.

School committees, however honest, may be subject to local influence; and the very knowledge that their determination was likely to be reviewed by a disinterested person, might, in many cases, prevent an improper decision. And a commissioner would seldom revise a decision of a committee, unless he was satisfied that the public good or justice to individuals required it.

And for the purpose of securing uniformity in the administration of the law, this provision is very important.

Third. The third objection is that the allowance of appeals would refer everything to the discretion of the commissioner and judge,—the latter, probably, not much acquainted with the subject, and unfitted for the exercise of this power.

It was deemed essential to the success of a comparatively new system to prevent litigation, if possible. A quarrel or a lawsuit in a school district is generally not long confined to the original parties. It spreads among all the families; it goes into the selection of teachers, and impairs the discipline of the schools; and, if the difficulty once takes the shape of a lawsuit, and the parties have expended money as well as temper upon it, it is still more difficult to settle. Hence the provision for a cheap and speedy decision, avoiding the delay and expense of a lawsuit; and as the commissioner would, probably, very often not be a lawyer, it was provided that he might resort to a judge for an opinion upon points of law.

The practical construction of the law from the beginning has been that the judge has nothing to do with deciding the facts in the case. (See "School Law," edition of 1857, remarks page 56; and see, also, decision of Judge Ames, in case of Emor Smith. R. I. Reports, vol. iv., 590, 592, 594.) The judge would not reverse the decision of a commissioner, unless there appeared to be a legal objection to its validity.

ELISHA R. POTTER, A. J. S. C.

1873.

See No. 54.
See No. 89.
See No. 91.
See No. 93.
See No. 99.

DECISION No. 97.

D. P. Spencer vs. School District No. 17, of Warwick.

In towns where the district system prevails neither town nor town treasurer is liable for teacher's wages, at least until an order has been given therefor by the school committee.

This case was submitted to the Supreme Court for Kent county on the following agreed statement of facts:

"1. School District No. 17, of the town of Warwick, is indebted to the plaintiff in the sum of $125,— due to said plaintiff as a teacher of the public school in said district.

"2. On or about the   day of   , A. D. 1876, suit was begun against the plaintiff in the Justice Court of the town of Warwick by one Oliver P.

Matteson, upon a writ of attachment, which directed, among other things, that the officer should trustee or attach moneys in the hands and possession of the town of Warwick due said plaintiff.

"3. The said attachment was intended to reach the moneys earned by said plaintiff as teacher in the school district No. 17, he being employed by the trustees of said district as teacher, in said town, and that a copy of said writ was served upon the town treasurer of said town for that purpose, there being no command in said writ to serve, nor was any copy in fact served, upon any officer of said district No. 17.

"4. That there were no moneys due from said town of Warwick to the plaintiff, nor any moneys of his in the hands of said town either directly or indirectly, except such as were supposed to go to said plaintiff for his services as teacher of the public school in said district.

"5. Said Matteson obtained final judgment against said plaintiff in the suit commenced in the Justice Court as aforesaid.

"6. There was no debt or demand of any kind laid by the plaintiff against said town other than the supposed claim mentioned in section 4 above.

"7. It is hereby agreed that jury trial be waived."

(*Per Curiam.*) The statute provides that moneys appropriated to, and raised by, the several towns for schools shall be kept by their respective treasurers, subject to the order of their respective school committees. Gen. Stat. R. I. cap. 47, § 6. A school committee may give its order either in favor of the trustees or treasurer of a school district, or directly in favor of a teacher. Cap. 53, § 17. Teachers, where towns are districted, are employed by the trustees of the districts; cap. 52, § 1; and neither town nor town treasurer is made liable for their wages otherwise than upon the order of the school committee. We think, therefore, that where a town is districted neither town nor town treasurer is liable to garnishment in respect of any teachers' wages, until at least an order has been given in favor of such teacher by the school committee of the town. This does not appear to have been done in the case at bar. The judgment, agreeably to the agreement, must be for the plaintiff for the full amount of his claim.

1877.

See No. 100.

DECISION No. 98.

George B. Carpenter vs. School Trustees of Joint School District 2 and 4, Hopkinton, and 8, Westerly.

Gen. Stat. R. I. cap. 58, § 13, which opens "all the public schools in the State to the children of officers and soldiers," etc., "without any cost or expense for taxes, or other charges imposed for purposes of public education," does not exempt the estate of such officer or soldier from taxes levied for school purposes.

This is an appeal to the commissioner of public schools from a decision of the trustees of the joint school district composed of districts two and four of Hopkinton, and eight of Westerly. The commissioner has laid before me a statement of facts assented to by both parties, and of the question raised thereby, for my decision.

From this statement it appears that the district has voted that a tax of twenty-eight cents upon each and every hundred dollars of the ratable property in the district be assessed for school purposes, for the year 1877; that the appellant resides in the district and has children who attend its schools; that he is the owner of estate, within the district, valued in the assessment at two thousand dollars; that in September, 1861, he belonged to the State of Rhode Island, and was mustered into the service of the United States in the war of the late rebellion, as a member of the 4th regiment of Rhode Island volunteers, and remained in such service till July 30, 1864, when he was discharged therefrom, in consequence of the loss of his right arm, in the battle known as the explosion of the mine in front of Petersburg. Upon these facts he claims that his estate is exempt under Gen. Stat. R. I. cap. 58, § 13, from the tax in question, and from all taxes that the district can impose. The trustees, on the other hand, insist that the appellant's estate is subject to assessment for the tax in question.

Gen. Stat. R. I. cap. 58, § 13, is as follows : "All the public schools in the State, including the State Normal School, shall be open to children of officers and soldiers belonging to the State, mustered into the service of the United States, and of those persons belonging to the State, and serving in the navy of the United States, and who died in said service during the late rebellion against the authority of the United States, or who were discharged from said service in consequence of wounds or disease contracted in said service, or who were killed in battle, without any cost or expense or taxes, or other charges imposed for purposes of public education."

The provisions of this section were originally contained in Pub. Laws R. I. cap. 547, § 1, January 18, 1865, entitled "an act for free education of children of disabled and deceased officers, soldiers and other persons belonging to Rhode Island in the army and navy of the United States." The two sections are substantially the same, except that the original section contained in the last clause the word "rates," so that it read, "without any cost or expense for taxes, rates, or other charges," etc. At the date of the passage of the original section, school districts had power to fix, or to authorize their trustees to fix, subject to the approval of the school committee of the town, a rate of tuition to be paid by the persons attending school, or their parents, employers, or guardians, to be used in addition to the moneys received from state appropriations in defraying the cost of fuel, books, and other expenses incident to the support of public schools. Rev. Stat. R. I. cap. 64, § 9. In towns not organized into districts, the school committee were authorized to fix the rate of tuition. Rev. Stat. R. I. cap. 64, § 11.

Payment of these rate bills might be required in advance, or collected by the town or district collector in the same manner as town taxes. Rev. Stat. R. I. cap. 64, § 13. No scholar could, as a matter of right, attend any other than the public school in the district to which he belonged, if the town was divided into districts, or if not so divided, any other than the nearest public school.

I am of the opinion, that the intention of the General Assembly, in the passage of Public Laws R. I. cap. 547, § 1, January 18, 1865, was to relieve the children of the classes of persons named, their parents and guardians, from the payment of rate bills which, as we have seen, under the provisions of law then existing, were liable to be, and were in fact, assessed upon scholars attending public schools, and from the payment of all other taxes and charges which might thereafter be imposed by law upon scholars personally as a condition of attending public schools, and also at the same time to confer upon such children the right to attend, not only the schools of their own districts, or the nearest public school in towns where there were no districts, but also any public school in the State. The language of the section, "All the public schools of the State . . . . shall be open . . . . without cost," &c., favors this view."

By Public Laws R. I. cap. 762, § 3, March 27, 1868, the power of school districts to impose rate bills for tuition upon scholars, or their parents, or guardians, was repealed; and hence, the word "rates" was omitted from Gen. Stat. R. I. cap. 58, § 13, which was doubtless intended as a reënactment of the law existing previously to its taking effect.

Had the General Assembly intended to exempt the property of the classes of persons named from taxation for the purposes of education, as contended by the appellant, they could easily have chosen words more apt. Some of the objections to such a construction, which suggest themselves, may be stated. 1. There is no limitation as to the amount of property which a person of the classes named may hold exempt from taxation. 2. There might be two persons living in a district, owning estates of equal value, the one having children to attend school and the other not, whose claims to exemption from taxation in every other respect might be equally strong.

Under the construction in question, the property of the one having children would be exempt, while the property of the other would be subject to taxation. Can it be supposed that the General Assembly intended such a discrimination? 3. If the construction contended for were to prevail, it may well be doubted whether any portion of the money appropriated by towns, for the support of public schools, derived from taxes assessed in the ordinary way, that is, upon all ratable property, including the property of the classes of persons named, could be properly appropriated for that purpose, and whether it would not be necessary for the towns to order a special tax for the support of public schools, in the assessment of which the property of the persons named should not be included. Such a mode of proceeding has never been considered necessary.

My decision is, that the appellant is not entitled to the exemption claimed, and that the appeal be dismissed.

CHARLES MATTESON, A. J. S. C.

1878.

DECISION No. 99.

Stephen C. Arnold vs. School Committee of Scituate.

Commissioner has no jurisdiction over the records of a school committee, to alter or amend them.

Mr. Arnold presents another appeal from the same action of the school committee which was involved in his appeal of 1882, and claims that the record of the finding and vote of the committee "shall be expunged from the records of said committee;" because, first, it was "decided, Feb. 16, 1882, that said committee had no jurisdiction over the complaint made to them which occasioned said record; second, that said committee exceeded its lawful powers in passing the final vote above named."·

I do not see how in this case, any more than in the former appeal, the commissioner has any jurisdiction. The records of the school committee are subject to their control, and to theirs alone.

The decision of the legality or illegality of any vote does not affect the record of the vote. That remains as it was, and is subject only to the action of the same body which originally made it.

The appeal is therefore dismissed for lack of jurisdiction.

THOMAS B. STOCKWELL, C. P. S.

1883.

See No. 54.
See No. 89.
See No. 91.
See No. 93.
See No. 94.
See No. 96.

DECISION No. 100.

Fred E. Hovey vs. The Town of East Providence.

In Rhode Island a mechanic's lien cannot be enforced against a building and lot held by a town for the uses of a public school.

This is a petition for the enforcement of a mechanic's lien against a lot of land belonging to the defendant town, and all the buildings and improvements thereon, for materials furnished for, and used in the erection of, a schoolhouse thereon, the materials having been furnished to the contractor. The question is raised whether such a lien is enforceable against a house and lot held by a town for the uses of a public school. In 2 Jones on Liens, 577, the law is stated to be as follows, to wit:

" On grounds of public policy the mechanic's lien laws do not, in the absence of express provisions, apply to public buildings erected by states, counties, and towns for public uses. Schoolhouses erected for the use of public schools come within this exemption; such buildings are exempt from attachment and from sale upon execution, and for the same reason are exempt from liens which might result in an adverse sale."

It is easy to see what detriment might follow if lands and buildings held for public uses,—as for instance for parks, courthouses, jails, town halls, or common schools,—could be sold to satisfy the debts or defaults of municipal corporations having the legal title. The public uses would be thereby annihilated. Courts have presumed that this could not have been intended and accordingly have decided, as a matter of public policy, that lands or buildings so held are not subject to mechanics' liens. We see no satisfactory reason why we should not follow these precedents. Our statutes recognize that there is property which is exempt from seizure on execution by public policy, Pub. Stat. R. I. cap. 209, § 4, clause 14. Our statutes do not permit executions to run against the property of towns, but provide other modes in which judgments against towns, or against the town treasurers representing them, may be satisfied.

We decide that the petition must be dismissed.

THOMAS DURFEE, C. J. S. C.

1890.

See No. 97.

DECISION No. 101.

Josephine E. Douglass vs. George F. Barber.

1. The interruption or disturbance of a school in violation of Pub. Stat. R. I. cap. 241, § 7, is a breach of the public peace, for which an offender may be arrested by an officer without a warrant when committed in his presence.
2. The interruption or disturbance of a school within the meaning of the statute includes not only acts which disturb the school while in session but also those which prevent the school from assembling.
3. Where an officer arrests a person without a warrant for an offence committed in his presence, the law requires him to make a complaint for the offence, but does not require him, in order to justify such arrest, to procure a complaint and warrant for the offence so committed.
4. If he makes the complaint, the fact that the magistrate does not issue a complaint and warrant thereon cannot make the officer a trespasser.

This is an action of trespass for an alleged illegal arrest, which the defendant justifies in a special plea setting forth that the plaintiff, at the time of the supposed trespass, had entered a schoolhouse in the town of Exeter, locked the door from the inside, and was detaining possession of said schoolhouse, thereby preventing the teacher and scholars of said school from entering therein; and the defendant, being an officer of the law, to wit, a constable, thereupon arrested the plaintiff and took her before the justice of the

District Court, where a warrant was issued, upon which she was arraigned and committed. The case is before us on exceptions to the refusal of the judge to charge the jury as requested at the trial.

The first request was to charge the jury that if the plaintiff took possession of the schoolhouse and was ejected before the school was called to order and before school time, she was not guilty of a misdemeanor. The third request may also be considered with the first.

It was this: "If the complainant took peaceable possession of the schoolhouse and locked the doors, so as to keep the teacher and scholars out, and stayed inside, making no threats and using no violence to retain possession, then the defendant had no right to arrest her and carry her to Wickford, but did have a right to remove her from the schoolhouse property, and that only."

Pub. Stat. R. I. cap. 241, § 7, provides a punishment by fine or imprisonment for persons who willfully interrupt or disturb any public or private school. From the nature of the offence, which violates public order and interferes with public and personal rights, as well as the specification of the offence in the statutes under the head of "Offences against the public peace and property," it is clear that the interruption or disturbance of a public school is a breach of the public peace, for which an offender may be arrested by an officer without a warrant when the act is done in his view.

The requests to charge are based upon the claim that the acts of the plaintiff in this case amounted only to a trespass or forcible entry and detainer. But we think that they were more, and that they amounted to a violation of the statute. To interrupt and disturb a school necessarily includes not only acts which disturb the school while in session, but also those which prevent the school from assembling. A school is as much interrupted or disturbed by preventing the assembly, as by breaking it up after it has assembled. The statute is aimed at the protection and peaceable conduct of schools. The fact of calling to order, therefore, is without significance. It would be a very narrow construction of the statute, which could neither be justified by its purpose or language, to say that a disorderly act after a school had been called to order would be an interruption or disturbance of the school and an offence; but one which prevented both the holding and calling to order of the school would not be an interruption or disturbance and so no offence at all. Accordingly we find that similar statutes relating to religious meetings have been held to extend protection " to the assemblage when it is in the act of gathering together at the place appointed for worship; while the exercises are in progress; and until there is a dispersion of the persons who have come together, and they cease to be an assemblage or congregation."

In State v. Gager, 28 Conn. 232, cited by the plaintiff, the statute provided only for the disturbance of a school "while the same is in session," and the court followed the language of the statute. Of course it is not to be understood that disorderly conduct in a schoolhouse, so long a time before or after school hours as not to interfere with the assembly or session of the school, would be a violation of the statute. But that is not this case. It appears from the record that near school time the teacher and a number of scholars arrived; the teacher tried to enter the schoolhouse, but the plaintiff prevented her, and then she was obliged to send for help. The defendant came, who, after a demand of entrance by him and refusal by the plaintiff, was obliged to break open the door. Not only might all this take enough time to go beyond the usual hour, but it was sufficient to show an interruption and disturbance in the assembling of the school. The requests to charge, therefore, were too broad and were rightly refused.

The second request was to charge that an officer arresting a person without a warrant for a crime committed in his presence must, in order to justify such arrest, procure a complaint and warrant for the identical offence so committed. It appears that the plaintiff had been guilty of disturbing the school while in session, on the day before her arrest; that the defendant took her before the judge of the District Court and made complaint for the same offence which he had seen that morning, and for which he had arrested her. The district judge, not sure that locking the teachers and scholars out of the schoolhouse was a breach of the peace, thought it best to make out a complaint and warrant for the disturbance on the previous day, and did so. Undoubtedly the law requires an officer who makes an arrest without a warrant to make a complaint for the offence, and this the officer did. He has no control over the magistrate, and having made the complaint, he can do no more. If he was justified in the arrest, the action of the magistrate cannot make him a trespasser, and we know of no decision which goes to that extent. We think, therefore, that the failure of the officer to procure a complaint and warrant for the offence committed in his presence was not decisive of his justification in the arrest, and that the request so to charge was rightly refused.

JOHN H. STINESS, A. J. S. C.

1894.

DECISION No. 102.

In the Matter of the Vote of the town of Johnston to Abolish School Districts.

Registry, as well as taxpaying, voters are entitled to vote upon the question of abolishing the school districts of a town.

At a town meeting of the town of Johnston, held on the first Monday of June, 1895, it was voted to abolish school districts in said town. By the agreed statement of facts, it appears that the meeting was regularly and legally called and that notice of the subject was inserted in the warrant for said meeting, pursuant to the provisions of Public Laws, chapter 447. It also appears that both registry and taxpaying voters were allowed to vote upon the subject, and that a majority of the taxpaying voters did not vote in favor of the proposition. A taxpaying voter of the town objects to the legality of the action taken and raises the following questions:

"Does a registry voter, under the provisions of chapter 447 of the Public Laws, have a right to vote on the question of abolishing school districts?

"If said chapter 447 confers such right, is said

chapter constitutional, so far as it provides for the vesting of school property in the town, for the assessment and remission of taxes for the payment of the same, and for the adjustment of differences in the value of school property, upon a vote to abolish?"

Under the provisions of the Constitution, registered voters have the right to vote on all questions in all legally organized town meetings, excepting the election of the city council of any city or upon any proposition to impose a tax or for the expenditure of money.

The proposition to abolish school districts is not a proposition to impose a tax or to expend money. It is a question of the management of schools, by a school committee or by trustees, in which registry voters are liable to be as much interested and affected as taxpayers. But it is said that this is practically a vote to impose a tax, because, under the law, a tax equal to the amount of the appraisal of the school property is to follow. While this is true, it is, nevertheless, quite different from an ordinary tax. None of the amount so assessed goes to the town, but is all remitted to the taxpayers of the several districts in proportion to the value of the district property taken by the town, for the purpose of equalizing the contributions thus made. It is a scheme for equalization rather than a tax.

It does not follow that a registry voter is disqualified because the ultimate result of action taken may affect taxation.

For example, dividing a school district would affect the expense of maintenance and the area of taxation. In 1854 a question arose whether registry voters could vote upon this question.

The Commissioner, Hon. Elisha R. Potter, afterwards one of the justices of this court, held that they could, and the decision was approved by Chief Justice Greene.

While the decision rests upon the fact that the vote was merely a recommendation, the concluding sentence assumes the right to vote upon all questions except those of taxing and expending money. We think that this is correct. The right to vote should not be curtailed except by the clear provisions of the Constitution; and where the limitation is not clear the Constitution should be liberally construed, especially in matters relating to public schools. When, in the opinion of the voters of a town, the schools can be better managed by the school committee than by districts, the law vests all the school property in the town and provides for the equalization of values by the tax referred to.

Education being a public duty, the legislature has the power to do this, and it is done by force of the law rather than by the action of the town. The vote of the town is the thing which sets in motion the operation of the law. Our conclusion is that Public Laws, chapter 447, was intended to give the right to vote to all voters in town meeting assembled; that the question submitted is not included in the proviso of Article VII, section 1, of amendments to the Constitution, and hence that the act and the action under it are not in conflict with the provisions of the Constitution in this respect.

The remaining question, whether the act is in other respects constitutional, is, so far as any objections have been called to our attention, sufficiently answered in Town Council of Cranston, Petitioner, Index N. N. 44.

JOHN H. STINESS, A. J. S. C.

1895.

See No. 8.
See No. 8.

REMARKS.

BOARD OF EDUCATION.

The State Board of Education is composed of the Governor and Lieutenant Governor, *ex-officiis*, and six members elected by the General Assembly.

In addition to the general supervision and control of the schools of the State, which the statutes confer on the Board of Education, the following specific duties are devolved upon them:—The election of the commissioner of public schools; the care and oversight of the free public libraries and distribution of the annual State appropriation for the same; the apportionment of the annual State appropriation for evening schools, and the supervision of their work; the supervision of the education of deaf, blind, and imbecile children; the provision of blanks for returns from all public educational institutions and all private schools; participation through two of their number in the management of the R. I. School of Design; the decision of all cases of remission of fines, penalties, and forfeitures arising under the school laws; and the presentation of an annual report to the General Assembly. The Board of Education, together with the commissioner of public schools, constitute the Trustees of the State Normal school, and are vested with the entire control and management of the same, subject, in the matter of expenditures, to the amount appropriated for the school by the General Assembly. The regular meetings of the Board occur monthly on the first Saturday of the month.

THE COMMISSIONER OF PUBLIC SCHOOLS.

The commissioner is secretary of the Board of Education, and its executive officer in the administration of the duties devolved upon them by the laws. His other duties are to advise with school officers, teachers, and others, in all matters relating to education ; to visit and inspect the schools of the State as often as practicable ; to deliver addresses in the several towns on subjects relating to the progress of the schools ; to arrange and conduct teachers' institutes in various parts of the State, as the several localities may demand ; to recommend and secure, as far as is desirable, a local uniformity of text-books ; to assist in the establishment of, and the selection of books for, school libraries ; to apportion the State appropriations for day schools and school apparatus ; to prepare and publish annually a programme for the use of the schools on Arbor Day ; to establish all forms of registers and returns and furnish the same to the school authorities ; to collect and collate the statistics relating to public schools, and to present an annual report to the Board of Education upon the state of the schools, with plans and suggestions for their improvement.

The commissioner is also a judicial adviser on all questions arising under the administration of the school laws, and is required to hear and decide all cases presented by appeal or otherwise, free of expense to the parties. In the words of the late Chief Justice Ames, the commissioner is " in legal idea, the visitor of the public schools of the State—a domestic judge—whose short and noiseless method of settling disputes arising between the different officers and members of this academic body is intended to preserve that peace and harmony which are so essential to its well-being."

TOWNS.

Each town is required to maintain a system of schools, and to appropriate for their maintenance a sum at least equal to that received from the State, under the provision of chapter 53. Any town which shall fail or refuse to raise for schools the above sum forfeits its proportion of the State appropriation for the benefit of the school fund of the State, but is not relieved from its obligation to maintain schools. The character and extent of the education furnished in any town is determined practically by the people in the making of the appropriation, either in town or district meetings. The State has established no standard.

The schools are carried on under either the town, or the district, system. Where the former prevails, the schools are wholly in charge of the school committee of the town. Under the district system the trustee has the superintendence of the school property of the district, and contracts with the teachers, while the school committee exercise all other authority over the schools. In all cases the schools are subject to the supervision of the commissioner of public schools.

The simplicity, unity, and economy of the town system are in favor of its universal adoption; and any town may, by a vote at the annual town meeting, so far relinquish the district system as to place the entire management of the schools in the hands of the school committee of the town, notice of the proposed change having been inserted in the warrant for the town meeting; but the school property will still remain in the control of the districts. Any town may also at any town meeting, the subject having been duly inserted in the warrant for said meeting, abolish all the school districts therein, whereupon all care and control of the schools and school property devolve upon the school committee.

Towns are authorized to establish and maintain free public libraries and are permitted to assess a tax, not exceeding twenty-five cents on each hundred dollars of ratable property, for the founding of such libraries, and an annual tax, not exceeding twenty cents on each one thousand dollars of ratable property, for the support and increase thereof.

TOWN CLERKS.

It is the duty of the several town clerks, or of some person appointed by the town council, to take the school census annually and make return thereof, as required by law, to the school committee; they are also to distribute to the persons designated all such school blanks and other documents as may be sent to them. In those cases where the town is divided into school districts the town clerk is required to keep a record of the district boundaries and of all changes therein; and he should provide a special book for that purpose.

TOWN TREASURERS.

The town treasurer, as soon as the town has voted the annual appropriation for public schools, or before the first of July in each year, should make his return to the commissioner as required by law. This return must contain a statement of the amount expended by the town for all school purposes, and the sources from which it was derived; and also a statement of the amount appropriated for public schools for the next year. Failure to make such return will prevent the payment of the town's share of the public money.

He is to keep a separate account of all school moneys, and is, before the first day of July in each year, to furnish the school committee with a particular account of all moneys applicable to the support of public schools for the current school year, specifying the sources of the same. He can only pay out the school moneys, whether derived from the State, town, dog or poll tax, upon orders signed by the chairman or clerk of the school committee, and if he should pay it out or appropriate it otherwise, he would be liable to the penalty of the law.

Special attention is now called to the fact that the law requires that the amount of money received from poll taxes shall be kept out of the school fund till the first Monday in May of each year, when the whole amount received during the year is to be credited to the school account. It is desirable that this provision of the law, as also a similar one in reference to the dog taxes, should be strictly obeyed, as it will aid very much in securing correct reports each year.

It is very desirable that the town treasurer's return to the commissioner should be made, as the law requires, on or before July 1st, because failure to do so is very vexatious, and will delay, if not stop, the payment of the town's share of the State money. It is also very necessary that the return of the treasurer shall cover the same period of time as that covered by the return of the school committee. The object of the law requiring returns from each source is that they may be used to verify each other and thus secure freedom from mistakes. But this cannot be done if they are made out for different periods of time.

SCHOOL COMMITTEES.

Great care should be taken by the several towns in the selection and election of the best *men and women* to this office. No political issues should hinder the election of competent persons to this most responsible office of the town. The interests of the children are too valuable to be entrusted to those who know nothing about them, and care not for their future welfare.

The law allows competent women, as well as men, to be elected to this office, and experience shows that some women have most faithfully, conscientiously, and successfully fulfilled its duties. Their time, interest, sympathies, and benevolent purposes eminently qualify them for the duties, and a portion of each school board may well be constituted of active and efficient women. The one condition imposed by law upon membership is residence in the town. The one disqualification is a pecuniary interest in any school text-book used in the town.

It is believed that in all cases it will be better to have the town's committee small rather than large.

Their duties are to examine teachers, visit the schools, and have supervision over them. There is danger that a large committee will not meet often, and that they will attempt to perform too many of their duties by small sub-committees of one or more. The delegation of the power to manage some particular district to each member has always been a great cause of the inefficiency of our system. The whole committee should have some knowledge of *all* of the schools, and the persons appointed to visit particular schools should always make specific reports to the whole board at their monthly or quarterly sessions. In this way alone can the committee act wisely and intelligently for all the schools under their care. Special attention to the duties of examination of schools alone can fit the committee to make such annual communication to the people of the town on the subject of their schools as shall be of the greatest service to them. *This annual report should by all means be printed and circulated among all the citizens of the town, as the law provides.* The mothers and sisters of the scholars should see it as well as the fathers and brothers, and the only way in which they can all enjoy this privilege is to have it printed, and at least one copy furnished to each family in the town. It is then easy to make all citizens acquainted with the workings of our school system, and to induce them, both to make ample provisions for its support, and to guard carefully the expenditures made for the common benefit.

ORGANIZATION.

At the first regular meeting of the committee, after the annual election of members of the school commit-

tee, the certificates of election of the new members
should be presented, together with the certificates of
their engagement, and these should be either spread
upon the records in full, or the record should state
the facts clearly, and the original papers should be
filed with the documents of the committee.

The committee should organize by choosing a chairman and a clerk, who are removable by the committee, during the year for which they are elected, only
for cause and after a hearing. At this meeting also
the committee should elect the superintendent of
schools.

Where the town system prevails it is usually best
for the committee to be divided into sub-committees having special charge of certain specific departments of the work, such as teachers, supplies, buildings and other school property, truancy, etc.

The extent of the authority of these sub-committees will always be determined by the rules and regulations of the full committee.

The number of the school committee in each town
is now fixed by statute law at the number constituting
the committee on the first day of February, 1896, and
cannot be changed except by special act of the General
Assembly. If the town fails to elect the requisite
number at the annual town meeting, the town council must elect them at its *next* meeting. Any town
may vote to delegate to the council the entire power
of appointing the committee.

Vacancies.—If any member of the committee resigns, removes, or dies, the vacancy must be supplied
by the town council until the next annual town meeting, which then fills the vacancy for the unexpired

term, or refers it to the council, which proceeds to do the same.

Meetings.—The school committee must hold at least four meetings in each year. The times for these regular meetings should be fixed by a by-law of the committee, in order that people having business to do before the committee may know when to attend. But as a general rule the schools cannot prosper unless meetings are held as often as once a month. In towns divided into school districts it would be well for committees to obtain a knowledge of the situation of the different districts,—the amount of taxable property in each, and the number of children, etc.; and this sort of information should be preserved, as it is absolutely necessary to enable them and their successors to discharge well their duties.

All acts of the school committee to be valid must be done at a *meeting* of the committee. Giving their assent to any measure separately, and without meeting, would be held illegal.

The manner of calling special meetings of the committee should be regulated by by-law for the sake of order and regularity. If there be no by-law, the chairman or clerk should call them, and should give every member notice.

The clerk should *make a full* record of all transactions of the committee, including the motions negatived, as well as those adopted, as parties may be interested in, and have a right to appeal in many cases from, a negative vote as well as an affirmative one. In cases of notices of proposed changes in text-books it would be well in all cases to copy them upon the records.

All changes in the boundaries of the districts must be immediately reported to the town clerk by the clerk of the committee.

When it can be conveniently done, the minutes of the proceedings, as drawn out by the clerk, should be read in open meeting, or at the next meeting, for correction if necessary. Misunderstandings may thus be prevented.

The clerk should always record the names of the members of the committee present at each meeting. He should also keep copies of all abstracts, and all reports made to the commissioner, so that the committee may have them for future reference and comparison.

If no special place is provided for the use of the committee for the safe keeping of their documents, the more important ones, such as completed record books, should be lodged with the town clerk.

Before the first day of July in each year, the school committee are entitled to receive from the town treasurer a report of all school moneys in his hands, or to be received, which will be applicable for the support of public schools for the current school year, specifying particularly the sources whence derived.

Laying off Districts.—In towns divided into school districts the whole power of making new districts, altering old ones, and of settling disputed boundaries is vested by law in the school committee, subject to an appeal to the commissioner. Notice must be given in all cases by posting on the schoolhouses, and sending to the trustees, of the districts liable to be affected, notice of the meeting and of the proposed changes, for at least five days previous thereto.

In laying off districts, regard should be had to the convenience of attending school, the number of scholars, the valuation of property, and ability to provide schoolhouses, etc. It will be always expedient to bound them by rivers, roads, or other natural or well-known boundaries, when practicable. When the lines can, without inconvenience, be so drawn as to include all of a person's farm in the same district where his dwelling-house is, it will save a great deal of trouble and expense in assessing taxes, but in all cases the lines must be continuous.

Districts must be set off by bounds including certain land. It is not sufficient to declare that a district shall be composed of such and such *persons*. The Supreme Court of Massachusetts has declared such districts to be invalid. [7 Pick. 106, and 12 Pick. 206.]

When a district which has built a schoolhouse is divided, or its bounds altered so as to take off any portion of it, the joint property is to be equitably apportioned among the several parts. If the district owes any debts, they should of course be considered in the apportionment. In some cases this can be done by a division of the property itself. In other cases the rent or income may be apportioned, according to the peculiar circumstances. The school committee must decide such cases, subject, of course, to the appeal provided by the law.

Where it is much more convenient for a person belonging to one district or town to send to a school in another district or town the policy of both school committees and trustees should be to extend the advantages of the schools as freely as the circumstances will permit. The State is now so large a contributor to the support of the great majority of the schools that the advantages thereof ought to be made as available as possible. The school committee have now the power to send a child into an adjoining town and pay for the tuition from the school money. The authority to admit or send from one district to another in the same town is now in the school committee, and not in the trustee. If the pupils come from outside of the town, the trustees have the authority to admit them, subject to the approval of the school committee.

As a rule district lines should not be changed, except for good and sufficient reasons. Frequent changes of boundary lines tend to confusion and error in the assessment of taxes and other business. In every town where the district system prevails it would be well to have a description of the districts *printed* for general information and circulation, one copy of which should be affixed to the record book of *each* district.

The provision of the law that the town clerk shall keep a record of the district boundaries is of great importance, and school committees should be very particular to report to the town clerk immediately all their actions relating thereto.

The power of forming *joint* districts on the borders of the different towns is also confided to the school committees. Many of the manufacturing villages are on streams which are the boundaries of towns, and are partly in both towns. In such situations the school committees should encourage the union of the adjoining districts, as both together will probably be able to establish a graded school, or at least to maintain a better and a longer school than either one alone.

In similar cases where the schools are managed under the town system the committees are recommended to unite in maintaining *one* graded school, instead of *two* ungraded schools, as it will secure a better quality of instruction at less cost.

In assigning to a district or portion thereof, which forms part of a joint district, its proportion of the public money, the committee of the town in which the school is located will assign to it on the same basis as to all of the other schools in the town, while the committee of the other town will assign to it its proportional share according to the number of pupils only.

Location, Plans, etc.—The school committee are to locate all schoolhouses. In towns divided into school districts the school committee must approve of all plans and specifications for building or repairing schoolhouses, and all district taxes for whatever purpose. When the district is unanimous, and the location on the whole unobjectionable, the committee should defer to their wishes; but in cases of dispute they should endeavor to select such a site as will best accommodate the greater portion of the district, and at the same time fulfill the conditions of a good site. In this connection it should be said that the size of the schoolhouse lot is of great importance, and the committee may not unlikely find it necessary sometimes to condemn a location on account of its unsuitable size. If a district is unable to secure by purchase a lot acceptable to the committee, the committee are authorized to proceed and select a lot and appoint three disinterested persons to appraise its value, and upon tender of said sum to the owner of the land the title is vested in the district. If the owner is aggrieved he may appeal within six months from said tender to the common pleas division of the supreme court for the county in which the district is located for such relief as the court may decide, according to the provisions made for relief from over-assessment of taxes.

The provision that all taxes which any district may order must be approved by the school committee was intended to operate as a salutary check against the improper exercise of the power given to school districts. In some districts there may be but few legal voters; in others, the majority of voters may be persons not interested in the property in the district; and various other cases may happen where a minority should be protected against abuse of taxation. And for this purpose the law requires the approbation of the school committee, the majority of whom will probably belong to other parts of the town, and have no private or personal interest in the local controversies and disputes of the district.

For the same and other reasons the law requires the plan of building to be approved by the committee. The committee should therefore investigate this subject, and visit and examine the best schoolhouses, and consult the best authorities on heating, ventilation, lighting, etc., so as to be prepared to act when called on. Moreover, the committee should not always wait till called upon, before acting in reference to the condition of the school buildings. The responsibility for seeing that the buildings used for school purposes are suitable rests with the committee, and they should not hesitate to act accordingly.

Granting Certificates.—In towns acting under the district system no person can be employed by any trustee as a teacher who does not hold a certificate of qualification from the school committee.

The granting of such certificates of qualification and the annulling of the same for cause are among the most important duties devolving on the school committee, and on their faithful performance the efficiency of the law largely depends.

In towns without districts, where the authority to hire teachers is vested in the school committee, no formal certificate of qualification is required, as it is not perceived how such a step affords any safeguard to the teacher's office. So long as there is no fixed standard of attainment, but each school committee is at liberty to make its own, the issuing of a certificate to those teachers whom they proposed to engage would be an act of pure formality.

But the fact that the committee is not obliged to grant formal certificates in such cases does not at all relieve them from the obligation of carefully determining the qualification of all teachers before engaging them.

The inefficiency of the school system in most of the towns may be traced to the fact that the duties of examining teachers and visiting the schools are too generally neglected or ill-performed.

The law gives the committee the power to appoint a sub-committee for the purpose of examining teachers, or they may impose the duty upon the superintendent. But it is respectfully suggested that where the whole committee can meet for this purpose it is most advisable. It will have a better effect upon the teachers themselves, and incompetent persons will be less likely to present themselves. It is certain that the authority to grant certificates, or determine qualifications, should never be vested by a committee in two bodies or persons at the same time. Such a division of responsibility is always attended with disastrous results. Where the duty of examining and certificating teachers is imposed upon the superintendent or a sub-committee, the action of such sub-committee or superintendent should be final. To allow an appeal to the committee is to weaken the force and value of the authority, opinions, and decisions of the examiner.

In making such examinations, whether by the whole board or by the sub-committee, they should inquire:

First, as to moral character. On this point the committee should be *entirely* satisfied before proceeding further. Some opinion can be formed from the general deportment and language of the applicant; but the safest course will be, with regard to those who are strangers to the committee, to insist on the written testimony of persons whose character and responsibility are known to the committee. In case of doubt the committee would be justified in declining to proceed with the examination.

While a committee should not endeavor to inquire into the peculiar religious or sectarian opinions of a teacher, and should not entertain any preferences or prejudices founded on any such grounds, they ought, without hesitation to reject every person who is in the habit of ridiculing, deriding, or scoffing at religion.

Second, as to literary attainments. The lowest

grade of attainments demands a thorough knowledge of the common branches of English education. Every teacher should prove, either by examination, or by previous experience which must have come to the personal knowledge of the committee, his ability to teach the English language, including reading and spelling, arithmetic, penmanship, geography, history, and physiology with special reference to the effects of stimulants and narcotics. An examination as to the attainments of a teacher in these branches should be so conducted as to test his capacity to teach them in any grade of schools. And in granting certificates some reference should be had to the condition and wants of the particular schools for which the candidates are presented. But no person should be considered qualified to teach any school, who cannot speak and write the English language, if not elegantly, at least correctly. He should be a good reader, and be able to make the hearer understand and feel all that the author intended. He should be able to give the analysis, as well as explain the meaning of the words, of the sentence, and explain all dates, names, and allusions. He should be a good speller ; and to test this, as well as his knowledge of punctuation, the use of capitals, etc., he should be required to write out his answers to some of the questions of the committee. He should understand practically the first principles of English grammar, as illustrated in his own writing and conversation. He should be able to write a good hand, and to teach others how to do so. He should show his knowledge of geography by applying his definitions of the elementary principles to the geography of his own town, State, and country, and by questions on the map and globe. He should be able to answer promptly all questions relating to the leading events of the history of the United States, and of his own State. In arithmetic, he should be well versed in some treatise on mental arithmetic, and have a clear and definite knowledge of the principles of written arithmetic, and be able to work out before the committee, on the blackboard or slate, such questions as will test his ability to teach accurately and successfully the topics prescribed for the class of schools in which he will be engaged. He should possess at least an elementary knowledge of physiology and the laws of health. Such knowledge is necessary to comply with the laws of the State, and is furthermore indispensable to the proper regulation of the air, temperature, and light of the schoolroom, and also to that care of the children which should be given to them daily if they are to do their best work at the school, or are to grow up to lives of vigorous manhood and womanhood.

A knowledge also of English literature, sufficient to enable the teacher to give to the selections of the reading-book more attractions and also to guide the pupils in their reading outside of school hours is very desirable and should be insisted upon so far as possible. And in addition to the above, some familiarity with the elements of natural history, freehand drawing, and music, will be found of great advantage both to teacher and school. Of course, for the upper grammar and high schools, the standard of qualifications of the teachers will be set by the course of studies adopted by the committee.

Third, as to ability to instruct. This ability includes aptness to teach, a power of simplifying difficult processes, a skill in imparting knowledge, and of inducing pupils to try, and to try in such a way that they will derive encouragement as they go along; all of which must be given by nature, but may be cultivated by observation and practice. An examination into the literary qualifications of a candidate as ordinarily conducted, and even when conducted by an experienced committee, or even by a teacher, will not always determine whether this ability is possessed at all, or possessed in a very eminent degree. Hence it is desirable for the committee to ascertain what success the candidate has had in other places, if he has taught before; and if this evidence cannot be had, whether he has received any instruction in the art of teaching, in either a normal or training school, and has visited good schools. The determination, if it is possible, of the candidate's ability to *teach* well is of the first importance.

In cases where satisfactory evidence as to the candidate's ability to teach cannot be had it may be well to grant a certificate for one term only, during which the question can be very clearly settled.

Fourth, ability to govern. This is an important qualification, insisted upon by the law, and indispensable to the success of the schools. On this point the committee should call for the evidence of former experience, wherever the candidate has taught before, and when this cannot be had, the examination should elicit the plans of the teacher as to making children comfortable, keeping them all usefully employed and interested in their studies, *his* systems of rewards and punishments and methods of securing order and attention, and all other information pertaining to the good order and government of a school. In this connection, the age, manners, bearing, knowledge of the world, love and knowledge of children, etc., of the applicant, will deserve attention.

If the teacher adds to his other qualifications a knowledge of the art of singing, it will be an additional recommendation of him with those who desire to have a good school. Singing in school serves as a recreation and an amusement, especially for the smaller scholars. It exercises and strengthens their voices and lungs, and, by its influence on the disposition and morals, enables a teacher to govern his school with comparative ease.

In addition to these qualifications, the address and personal manners and habits of the applicant may well be inquired into, for these will determine, in a great measure, the manners and habits of the children whom he will be called upon to teach.

The school committee must remember that on the thoroughness and fidelity with which this duty is performed depends, in a great measure, the success or failure of the school system. The whole machinery moves to bring good teachers into the schools, and to keep them as long, and under as favorable circumstances, as possible.

The committee should exercise a sound discretion in the whole matter, for the sole resposibility rests upon them in determining who shall, and who shall not, teach in our schools. No appeal can be taken to the commissioner from the refusal of a committee to grant a certificate.

If a person has been before examined by them, and the committee know him to be a good teacher, the law allows them to give him a certificate, founded on this experience. A committee would also have the right under the law to grant a certificate for one term at least, without an examination, to a person having a diploma from an accredited normal school or college.

Annulling certificates and dimissing teachers. As a teacher's qualifications depend not merely upon his learning (of which a committee can judge from examination), but upon his moral character, his disposition and temper, and his capacity to impart information and to govern a school, in regard to all of which the committee may be deceived or not fully informed, the law gives the committee the power to annul any certificate they may have given, if, on trial, the teacher proves unqualified. A teacher may also refuse to adopt the proper books, may introduce improper books, may refuse to adopt what the committee deem the best methods of instruction or discipline, or may violate other regulations of the committee, in which cases the committee have full power to dismiss the teacher. In case of all annulments of certificates of teachers or dismission, the school committee, who are the only authority in the matter, must give at least five days' notice in writing of such intention, and a hearing.

Visiting schools. There is no duty of the school committee more generally neglected than that of visiting schools.

The law makes it the *express duty* of committees and trustees to visit the schools often. Without personal visits to the schools, either by themselves or by the superintendent, the committee can know nothing about the teacher's capacity to impart information, or about his methods of instruction and government, or the progress of the pupils; neither can they know the state of the register and the general condition of the school.

Visiting the schools also has the effect of encouraging the teacher in the performance of his duties; and if the teacher is visited and treated with proper respect by the committee, trustees, and parents, it materially aids to secure to him respectful treatment from the scholars, and enables him to govern his school and preserve order with ease, and without resorting to severe punishments.

But the greatest influence is on the pupils themselves. School is too apt to be considered by many of them as a place of punishment. But if their parents and others visit them often, and take an interest in their studies and progress, it gives a new character at once to the school and the schoolroom, and they contemplate it with pleasure instead of dread.

It will also tend to accustom the pupils to recite before strangers, and help them to get rid of that timidity and reserve which, if not early removed, may prove a serious hindrance to their success in many pursuits in after life.

While it will be advisable to assign one or more schools to each member of the committee for the purpose of visiting and general supervision, it is very desirable that all the schools should be visited at least once a term by the *same* person or persons, so that a comparison can be instituted between the different teachers and schools, and the official reports and returns be made out more understandingly.

In visiting schools, whether by the whole board, sub-committee, or individually, the following are among the objects which deserve attention :

The condition of the schoolhouse and apurtenances;—its location; size and condition of yard and outbuildings; size, outward appearance, and state of repair of building; condition and size of entries and cloakrooms, and whether furnished with scraper, mat, hooks and shelves for hats and outer garments, water pail, cup, broom, duster, etc.; dimensions of schoolroom and its condition as to light, whether too much or too little ; as to the air, pure or impure ; as to temperature, whether too high or too low; modes of ventilation, whether by lowering or raising upper or lower sash, by opening into attic, by flue or otherwise ; whether heated by close or open stove, furnace, or steam; construction and arrangement of seats and desks ; whether all the scholars, and especially the younger ones, are comfortably seated, with backs to lean against, and with their feet resting on the floor, and all facing the teacher ; whether there is a place to arrange the classes for recitation, and accommodations for visitors, etc.

The school register should be called for to see if it is properly kept ; and such particulars as the number and names of the scholars, their age, parents, attendance and studies, should be gleaned as will give to the visitor a good idea of the character of the school. An inspection of the register will oftentimes inform the committee what children are not connected with the school, and a kind and timely call, a word with the parents or guardian, may save such children from ignorance, and the community from its consequences.

In this connection a word should be said in reference to the school census. As soon as the census returns are delivered to the committee, they should be examined with a view to finding out who are the regular absentees from school and where they live. Effort should then be made by the committee to secure their attendance. So far as it is possible a careful comparison should be made of the school register and these census returns, so that each may correct the other and thus the committee become possessed of reliable information in regard to the matter of attendance.

The committee should inquire into the number of classes, and the studies they pursue. Such exercises should be called for as will exhibit the proficiency of the pupils, and the methods of instruction adopted by the teacher, and will also enable the committee to judge of the tact of the teacher in imparting information. The teacher, in justice to himself and his pupils, should be allowed to conduct some of the exercises himself, and in his usual manner, as the scholars (if not used to being visited by strangers) will be less timid when examined by him, and the committee will have a better opportunity to see his mode of instruction. But the committee should also ask questions, and, in some cases, take the conduct of the class into their own hands.

Regular examinations should be had in order to determine the proficiency of the pupils, or the extent of their progress, and it will be well to place in the hands of the more advanced scholars questions to be answered in writing, while the examination of other classes is going forward. And the same or similar questions should be asked in every school visited, and the answers will be, to some extent, an unexceptionable standard of comparison for both the teachers and the schools.

Such inquiries should be made as will show how far the rules and regulations of the school committee as to teachers, books, the cleanliness and preservation of the schoolhouse, the manners of the pupils, etc., are observed.

The two distinct purposes of visiting,—inspection and examination,—should be kept constantly in mind, and as far as possible the two should not be allowed to be mingled. The best results will be secured by keeping them well separated, since the methods and means adapted to the one are seldom fitted for the other.

Great care should be taken in all cases not to wound unnecessarily the feelings of teacher or pupils, and commendation should be bestowed wherever it is deserved. It is better to err on the side of praise rather than on that of censure.

Selecting text-books. The schools have heretofore suffered much from the great variety of text-books used, even in the same schools. It has rendered classification impossible, and whenever a scholar changed his district or his school a new set of books was to be purchased, or a new element of confusion was introduced.

Under the new law providing for free text-books there is no reason why most difficulties connected with text-books should not be removed. In the first place the question of a change or of the introduction of a new book will not be affected by the expense imposed upon parents. Secondly, as the books are now owned by the towns, exchanges can be effected much more rapidly than before; and, when it is deemed desirable, an extra, or additional, set can be supplied. Uniformity should be established in the schools of a town. But no rule which a committee may adopt as to the books to be used should be so framed or construed as to prevent a teacher from using explanations or illustrations to be found in other books upon any particular subject, or to interfere with the use of all proper reference books by both teacher and pupils.

No book containing any passage or matter reflecting in the least degree upon any religious sect, or which any religious sect would be likely to consider offensive, should be introduced into any public school by the committee.

In all cases where a change in text-books is contemplated, a written notice to that effect must be given at a regular meeting of the committee, before the action is taken. The vote may be taken at any meeting thereafter, provided suitable time has intervened. Where a book has been adopted for introduction on or after a certain date, the vote can be rescinded any time before that date, but not otherwise.

Rules and Regulations. The school committee should prescribe a system of rules and regulations respecting the age, admission, attendance, classification, studies, discipline, and instruction of pupils in all the schools; the examination and duties of teachers; the kind of books to be used, etc. No town should be without such rules.

The age for admission should be uniform in all the

districts of a town, as otherwise some districts may have the advantage over others in the apportionment of the public money.

While the school census age, five to fifteen, may be said to practically fix the age of admission at five, it is within the discretion of the committee to admit at an earlier period, and where there are kindergartens children should be encouraged to enter at three or four. In this connection it should be noted that the law expressly forbids any person from being *excluded* from school for being *over* fifteen years of age.

In the matter of classification, number and kind of studies, and gradation, the schools need, and to accomplish anything must have, the guidance and care of the committee. The law establishes no minimum range of studies, hence, unless the committee acts, there is no authority to decide what shall be, or what shall not be, taught. It is therefore a very important duty for each committee to decide what studies shall be introduced and to what extent they shall be pursued. Only as this duty is thoroughly performed will our schools be capable of making any permanent progress. Even the ungraded schools are capable of great improvement in this direction, and a course of study if used as a general guide, rather than as an absolute rule, will do more than any other one thing to give efficiency to the schools. While the law plainly gives to the committee absolute power to determine the studies to be pursued, still the committee should be ever ready to heed all reasonable requests of parents and guardians for such deviations therefrom as the best interests of their children seem to require. What shall be adopted? how far the school shall go? is wholly within the province of the committee, who will doubtless seek to be governed in that matter by the dominant sentiment of their constituents. Practically the law allows each community to provide just such facilities for the education of its children as it desires.

In the matter of discipline it is suggested that the regulations of the committee should provide clearly for the exercise by the teacher of all proper authority over the pupil, not only during school hours, but whenever he is on school premises. While he is on his way to and from school, as he is under the concurrent jurisdiction of parent and teacher, the latter should be held responsible only for such matters as pertain directly to the school.

The attention of the teachers and pupils should be regularly called to the rules and regulations, and violations thereof should not only not be winked at, but made a matter of serious treatment.

The question of what holidays shall be observed by the schools, and of closing the schools for the purpose of allowing teachers to attend institutes and visit other schools, is one that belongs to the committee under this general provision of the law; and the committee should attend to it. Of course on all holidays established by State law the schools should not be kept. For all other cases the rule must be the voice of the committee.

Apportioning Money. The committee, having ascertained what amount they can depend upon from the State treasury, the town, poll and other taxes, and having reserved an amount sufficient to defray the expense of printing their report and other necessary contingent expenses, must apportion it on or before the first Monday in July in each year, according to law, and give immediate notice of the amounts of said apportionment to the several trustees. But they are not authorized to pay out or give an order to any district which has not maintained a school for at least six months during the year preceding, except in cases where the school was suspended by the committee for want of pupils. The law makes a district's complying with this provision for one year a prerequisite to its receiving any money the next year.

Where a school is suspended for lack of the requisite number of pupils, it will usually be found best the first year to set apart for such district a portion of the amount usually allotted, out of which can be paid the expenses incurred in providing school privileges for the children of that district. After the first year the matter will be determined by the facts as they shall appear. In cases of these districts the committee have full power either to send the children to other districts, which they can do without any payment of tuition, or to another town and pay tuition. They are also authorized to pay for their transportation to and from school, if their judgment so dictates.

The committee are not to give orders on the school fund any faster than they are satisfied that it is actually expended, and it is suggested that no payments be made for fuel and other incidental expenses except upon presentation of the vouchers therefor.

There is danger that trustees will endeavor to secure payment from the public money of bills that belong to the district, and the plan above mentioned will enable the committee to prevent such misuse of the public money. The times and manner of payment, with the above restrictions, are at the discretion of the committee.

Attention is specially called to the absolute requirement of the law that the committee shall not allow districts to carry forward unexpended balances from one year to another; nor is it legal, under the district organization, for the committee to give orders in payment of bills of the previous year.

Where the town system prevails there will be no necessity for any such apportionment as above, but such allotment to the several schools, or division of the funds, should be made as shall provide for all of the schools equal advantages and facilities, so far as it is possible. A committee, however, has no right to expend more than the amount appropriated by the town, and the town treasurer would not be authorized to honor the order of the committee for any amount in excess of the funds set apart, either by law or by direct vote of the town, for the support of schools.

The committee should always keep a regular set of accounts. A separate account should be opened with each school district, in which the district should be each year credited with the money apportioned to it, and then charged with the orders which have been given to it.

Under the town system an account should be kept either with each school, or school building, so that there may be some basis of comparison of cost between different schools. A separate account with each teacher is also of great value in keeping a check upon the expenditures.

Another account should be kept by entering all the

sums of money appropriated to schools on one side, and all orders given on the other, which will show at any time the balance under the committee's control.

Returns. By the Public Statutes, chapter 59, section 5, trustees are to make returns to the school committee at such time and in such form as the committee or commissioner may prescribe. These returns must be made in season to enable the committee to digest them, and prepare their return to the commissioner by July 1st, for which returns the commissioner will furnish forms. The attention of committees is particularly directed to this part of the law, for experience has shown that the incompleteness and inaccuracy of our statistics are due primarily to the failure of the committees to secure proper returns from the trustees and teachers. There is no excuse for such neglect, and every trustee and teacher should be firmly held to a strict compliance with this requirement. The committee are also, at the annual town meeting, to make a written or printed report to the town, of all their doings, the condition of the schools, plans for their improvement, etc. Until the above return, correctly filled out, and three or more copies of the above report are sent to the commissioner, the town's share of the State appropriation is withheld in accordance with the provisions of the law.

The committee are authorized to reserve enough (not exceeding $40) out of the school money to print their reports, and no action or vote of the town can take away this authority from the committee. It is believed that no part of the school expenditure will do more good and tend more to keep up an interest in the schools than this, and it is hoped that every committee will always make its report in print.

The committee must aid in organizing districts by giving the notice for the first meeting. When there are no trustees or clerk, or when these officers neglect to call meetings, the committee must call them, in the same manner and for the same purposes as the trustee would have called them. The notice may be signed by either the chairman or clerk of the committee, the same as in the case of other official documents issued by the committee.

Any district may vote to devolve upon the committee, with their consent, the whole management of its schools; and in that case, the committee will exercise in that district all the powers which the trustee might exercise;—have the custody of the schoolhouse, hire the teacher, etc.

Gradation of schools. The school committee cannot compel a district to establish graded schools, but they can promote a gradation of schools, or a separation of the younger and the older scholars, or the primary and advanced studies, into distinct schools or departments. By such a separation of pupils and instruction a great saving of time and expense is secured, while great benefits are derived by the children. Such a policy should be adopted, as a rule, in preference to the division of a district, where the children have become too numerous for one school.

Where the schools are so divided or graded, the determination of the grades and the promotions from one grade to another are in the hands of the committee.

The union of two or more adjacent districts, where

there are sufficient pupils for the purpose of establishing a secondary or grammar school for the older and more advanced pupils of each district, can be secured to advantage in many towns, and this phase of the subject should receive the attention of the committees, as it is to them that the people naturally look for suggestions in these matters.

Whenever the schools of a town are managed independent of districts, a sufficient number of schools of different grades should be established by the committee, at convenient locations, varying the studies pursued according to the circumstances of the population.

In towns where there are compact villages or communities evening schools should receive the attention of the committee, and efforts should be made to secure from the town specific appropriations for their support. In manufacturing centres they are a necessary factor in any system of public instruction, and the State now makes an annual appropriation for their support. In all evening schools supported wholly or in part by the public money, whether district, town, or State, the question of the qualification of the teachers is in the hands of the school committee.

SCHOOL SUPERINTENDENTS.

The school committee must elect a superintendent of schools each year at their first regular meeting.

The superintendent is not a civil officer, and hence he need not be a voter or even a resident; and a woman is as eligible as a man. He is simply the agent of the school committee, and subject wholly to their direction and control. Under the law he is vested with no powers or duties, but is expressly directed to "perform such duties and exercise such powers as the committee may assign."

While great good may be accomplished by the appointment of some qualified person especially to supervise the schools, it was not intended that the creation of the office of town superintendent should relieve the members of the school board from an active participation in this work. The school law renders this duty obligatory upon all the members of the school committee, and for their services they should receive a proper compensation. Each member of the committee should be to some extent familiar with all the schools of the town; but this he cannot be if he delegates the whole duty of visiting and supervision to some other person. In those towns where the school committee and superintendent exercise this mutual oversight, there is a natural and necessary concurrence of opinion as to the merits or demerits of school operations, and the most thorough harmony of sentiment with respect to methods of improvement. Hence school committees are urged to an increase, rather than a diminution, of personal attention to each school, even where the town enjoys the full labors of an efficient town superintendent.

The law provides that the town shall fix the salary of the superintendent, but justice and propriety both seem to demand that the body which determines the amount and character of the labor should also determine the salary; and if the towns would refer this matter to their committees, it is believed an increased efficiency in the service would be the result.

The following suggestions are submitted concerning town superintendents :

1. Each town should have a good superintendent of schools, elected by the school committee.

2. Where one town is not able to secure such an officer, two or more contiguous towns should unite in electing the same officer; his salary to be fixed by the school committees of the towns uniting, and paid by them jointly.

3. This officer should be paid such a salary as will enable him to devote the whole of his time to the work.

4. He should visit and inspect the schools, examine the pupils, make promotions, suggest improvements in instruction and government, hold teachers' meetings and public meetings in the different sections of the town, and in every way foster and encourage the work of public education.

5. He should examine the teachers,—in connection with the school committee if possible.

6. He should allow no text-books to be used in schools except such as are approved by the school board of the town.

7. He should see that the rules and regulations of the school committee are honored and enforced, and should make a written report on the condition of the schools and school property to the school committee at each quarterly meeting or oftener,—such report to be embodied in the report of the school committee, to be printed and distributed annually among the citizens and families of the town.

BRIEF SYNOPSIS OF DUTIES OF SCHOOL COMMITTEES.

1. The holding of at least four meetings in each year.

2. The appointment of a town superintendent of schools.

3. The examination of teachers.

4. The granting of certificates to teachers and the power to annul the same.

5. The visiting of the schools.

6. The adoption of all rules and regulations relating to the management of schools.

7. The suspension of pupils from schools.

8. The adoption of new text-books by a vote of two-thirds of the whole school board.

9. The supply of all needful text-books and other materials.

10. The apportionment of the public money to the several school districts.

11. The drawing of all orders on the town treasurer for school money.

12. The location of all schoolhouses.

13. The formation of all new school districts, the alteration or discontinuing of school districts, and the approval of the formation of associate, joint, and consolidated districts.

14. The written approval of all district taxes and of all plans for building and repairing schoolhouses.

15. The calling of district meetings in certain cases.

16. The contracting with teachers and the management of all school affairs, when so authorized by the town.

17. The enforcement of the truant and absentee law.

18. An annual report to the town, to be read in open town meeting, or printed for distribution.

19. A statistical return to the commissioner of public schools, on or before the first day of July in each year, including one copy of the above report if written, or three copies if printed.

DISTRICTS.

There are three provisions made in the law for uniting districts. Any two or more districts may form a partial union for the purpose of supporting a school for the older and more advanced children. Such a union is call an associate district.

Any contiguous districts in adjoining towns may be united by the school committees, and such a union is called a joint district. Adjoining districts in the same town may consolidate themselves, subject to the approval of the committee, and such a union is called a consolidated district. When united they constitute a single district, and their affairs must be managed in the same way as if originally one district.

A district cannot vote to dissolve itself. Such a vote will be wholly null and void. It can be dissolved by the school committee alone, who also have the sole power to create new districts and change the boundaries of those already existing.

Moderator. The moderator of a district meeting is now an annual officer and is to be elected with the other officers at the annual meeting. He need not be engaged. He will preside at all district meetings, both annual and special. If he is absent, a moderator *pro tem.* should be chosen. It is the business of the moderator to preside over the meeting, guide its business, and preserve order. While he will usually be justified in obeying common parliamentary rules in the exercise of his duties, still the meeting is superior to any rules, and if an appeal from any of his rulings is taken, it must be allowed, and, if sustained, the will of the meeting obeyed. The moderator is entitled to vote only as any other voter may vote. He has no casting vote. In receiving votes for any officer or on any question, the moderator has no right to reject any man's vote. He is in no sense a judge of a voter's qualification if he claims a legal right to vote, but he can insist upon knowing how he votes, and have his name and vote recorded by the clerk, so that, if a question arises, it can be settled by the proper authorities. In any case of doubtful legality, or of contested elections, a moderator would do well to have such a record of the voters and their votes made as the law provides for. The moderator has power to administer the oath of office to all the other officers, either at the meeting, or afterwards.

It is the moderator's duty to maintain order in a meeting, and in case persons present refuse to conduct themselves properly he should order them to leave the meeting. Provision is made in the law whereby town constables, upon the tender of the required fee, are obliged to be present at any school or other lawfully assembled meeting, and they are authorized to arrest without a warrant, and detain for six hours, any person found unlawfully disturbing such meeting.

Clerk. The district clerk should be engaged by the moderator and make a record of it. If not present at the time of his election so as to be engaged in open meeting, he should be engaged before entering upon the duties of his office. A clerk *pro tem.* should be engaged before he enters upon the duties the same as the regular clerk. When engaged, the clerk may engage all other district officers, and should enter all such cases in his record book.

When a trustee, treasurer, etc., is elected, the clerk should make out and sign and seal a warrant or certificate of his election, upon which he may be engaged. [See forms.]

The clerk should, at the request of any person interested, record a motion which is negatived, as well as a motion passed, as in many cases a person may be entitled to an appeal. And on *any* question which may come before the meeting he should record the number and names of the voters on request of any qualified voter; and in general he should endeavor to make his minutes as full as possible, so that they may give the whole history of the meeting.

In the record of every meeting the clerk should

state how the meeting was notified, and when and by whom the notices were posted. In many cases, at some distance of time, it might be important to know how the meeting was notified, and the evidence of it should not be left to depend upon mere recollection. The record of the clerk that a "meeting was duly notified" is made *prima facie* evidence that it was notified as the law requires, and inhabitants of the district can be admitted to prove the notice. But it would be easy and best to preserve one of the original notices themselves, especially in case of a special meeting.

It would be well also for the clerk, at the close of every meeting, to read aloud the minutes he has made of the proceedings, so that any mistake may be corrected at the time. Errors in the record may be subsequently corrected and the true record established by proper evidence.

The clerk is to procure a bound record book at the expense of the district. For any willful neglect or refusal to perform any duty, he is liable to indictment, and the Supreme Court would, probably, upon application, compel him by writ of mandamus to perform such duty.

District Treasurer. The treasurer should have a certificate of his election [see form] and be engaged. He need not give bond unless required by vote of the district. But if the district requires him to give bond it should run to the district, and the district should fix the sum and approve of the surety or sureties. [see form.]

His duties are very simple: to keep the district's money if they have any, pay it out to order, and keep proper accounts of it, and exhibit them to the trustees or district when required. He should always make a report at the annual meeting, and a copy of it should be given to the trustees, in order that they may make up their return to the school committee. In case the district hires money the treasurer is the one to sign the note. [See form.]

District Collector. The collector should always be engaged before beginning his duties. Like the treasurer he is not obliged to give bond except upon vote of the district. If the district requires him to give bond, the district should fix the sum, and, as in case of treasurer's bond, it should run to the district; and the district should approve of the surety or sureties. If, however, the district votes to have the town collector act, he is to give bond to the district, satisfactory to the school committee.

If no compensation is agreed upon before the collector is elected, he is entitled by law to five per cent. upon the amount collected. On the other hand a district cannot vote to pay more than five per cent. [See the forms for warrants and tax lists.]

Trustees. One or three trustees are to be appointed by a district at its annual meeting, but the decision, as to one or three, should be made before the election of any. If by any accident an election is not made then, or if a vacancy occurs, the district may elect afterwards. Trustees hold their offices until their successors are qualified, and can only be removed from their office, before the expiration of the term for which they were elected, for cause, and after notice and trial.

If there are three trustees, a majority can act, but the action of only one would be void. All business must be done at a meeting of the board, of which due notice was given to all the members. "Where a body or board of officers is constituted by law to perform a trust for the public, or to execute a power or perform a duty prescribed by law, it is not necessary that all should concur in the act done. The act of the majority is the act of the body. And where all have due notice of the time and place of meeting in the manner prescribed by law, if so prescribed—or by the rules and regulations of the body itself, if there be any,—otherwise if reasonable notice is given, and no practice or unfair means are used to prevent all from attending and participating in the proceeding, it is no objection that all the members do not attend, if there be a quorum."

The trustees must employ the teachers. In employing a teacher or assistant teacher, trustees should be cautious to employ no one who has not a legal certificate, and not to employ one after notice that his certificate is annulled, as in such a case the trustees would be held personally liable for the teacher's wages. The trustee has no power either to annul a certificate, or to dismiss a teacher before the expiration of the time for which he was hired. The trustees should see that the teacher keeps a proper record of attendance, as is required by the authorities, in order that the district returns may be properly made; and when the school is over, the register should be deposited with the committee. They should require the teacher to furnish them with such items of information as are necessary to make out their annual report to the town committee, which report should be made on the first of May, or sooner if the school is out, or at such time as the committee shall fix. Forms for these reports will be furnished to the districts, and can be obtained from the committee or from the superintendent.

If trustees appropriate any of the public money to pay a teacher not legally qualified, they are liable to a penalty. The uses for which the public money may be employed are teachers' wages, fuel, janitor's service, with some other current expenses.

If any scholars from without the town or State can more conveniently attend school in any district and desire to do so, the trustee of that district is authorized to make the necessary arrangements, subject to the approval of the school committee. The trustees should also take care that the school is kept in a house which will not be disapproved of by the committee of the town. To that end the trustees are authorized to make repairs that are immediately necessary for the preservation of the property and the maintenance of the school, without a vote of the district, and the district would be obliged to pay for such repairs. While the control and care of the school property is in the hands of the trustee he has no right to remove or dispose of any of it, except by vote of the district. As the custodian of the schoolhouse he may allow its use for purposes connected with education, even against the wish of the district, but he cannot be compelled to allow its use for such a purpose, provided he does not think it best. Nor *can* he allow its use for religious meetings, if a single taxpayer objects. If, however, the schoolhouse has been *given* to the district under certain conditions, the trustee will be bound thereby.

Trustees should regard the visiting of the schools as one of the most important of their duties, which should by no means be neglected.

When a district is organized and has trustees, they are the persons first authorized to notify all annual and special district meetings, and they cannot delegate this power; and if there is no district schoolhouse, or place appointed by the district, they are to fix the place of meeting. If the trustees and clerk on application neglect to call a meeting, the school committee may call it.

Trustees are liable to a penalty for refusal to discharge any duty,—call a meeting, assess a tax, etc., etc. And the Supreme Court would probably, upon application, compel any school officer, by writ of mandamus, to discharge any duty plainly imposed on him by the law. A trustee may, however, resign his office at any time.

Trustees should encourage meetings of teachers in their neighborhoods for mutual improvement, and also insist upon their attendance upon all institutes and other similar gatherings, and as far as possible aid them in going to and from such meetings. If any teacher neglects or refuses to attend a teachers' institute, when organized under proper auspices, and when he can conveniently, it should be regarded as a sign of unfitness for the place. No one is so well qualified as not to be able to learn from his fellows many useful hints as to methods of teaching, books, etc., and no one should be unwilling or too proud to learn.

If the committee authorize schools to be closed, the trustee has no power to prevent it and cannot compel a teacher to make up such days or legal holidays, except by special agreement.

Trustees have no authority to make any rules and regulations in regard to the school, such as times of sessions, recesses, studies, etc. They can however fix the limits of the school terms, subject to some general rules of the committee. And in this connection they should be very particular to notify the committee or superintendent of the beginning and ending of *every* term, in order that the schools may be properly visited.

Trustees should see that an inventory of all the maps, books, and other property belonging to the district, is made from time to time, and preserved among the papers of the district.

Every district should possess a dictionary, maps of the United States and other countries, and of the town (if there is one), a globe, and such other apparatus and works of reference as the means of the district, or the public spirit thereof, will allow. With the liberal aid now given by the State, no district or school need be without these essentials to a good school.

Trustees should recollect that in order to obtain from the school committee any order for money, they must have made a proper return from their district, for the year ending on the first of May previous, and must also furnish to the committee evidence that the "teachers' money," (that is, the money which the district received from the town treasurer as their part of the State appropriation,) for the year ending the first of May previous, has been applied to the wages of teachers, and to no other purpose whatever.

The return of the district should include the whole

time during which any portion of the public money has been used to support the school, and should include *all* expenditures for the benefit of the school, whether from district funds or any other source, and should state *all* the sources whence the moneys were obtained.

Trustees are cautioned in reference to these returns, that the committees have been instructed to refuse to draw their orders except upon the receipt of the proper return fully and accurately made out.

If a trustee removes from the district he ceases to be trustee from the date of his actual removal, and therefore cannot act at all as trustee after that date.

In assessment of taxes, which *must* be done by the trustees, and not by assessors, the trustee has no power to remit, or alter valuation. He has no discretionary power in the matter, but must follow exactly the town assessment.

Where a district maintains an evening school, the trustee would sustain exactly the same relation to it as to the day schools.

Qualifications for office. In order to be eligible to any district office, a person must possess the qualifications of a voter for said office; and any voter may be elected to any district office.

It is sufficient if the person elected have the qualifications of a voter at the time of his election; and it is not necessary that his name be upon the voting list of the town.

Engagement. Every district officer except the moderator must be engaged by some one duly authorrized to administer oaths before he enters upon the discharge of his duties. The following officers may administer the oath to school district officers: the moderator of the district, district clerk, town clerk, president of town council, trial justice, justices of the peace, and public notaries. When an officer is engaged at any other time than in the district meeting, he should always receive a written certificate of his engagement. [See form.]

The same person may hold more than one office at the same time, where the duties of the two do not conflict, or where the law does not make one officer responsible to the other: that is, one person may be both moderator and trustee or collector; but the two offices of moderator and clerk cannot be filled by the same person at the same time, neither the offices of trustee and collector, nor those of collector and treasurer.

Vacancies in office are always created by absolute removal from the district, and an officer has no authority to act after such removal. But great care should be taken before proceeding to fill any such vacancies, to see that the evidence of the removal and consequent vacancy is incontestible; for there is often a temporary removal or absence which could not be regarded as a legal removal, and any attempt to fill the so-called vacancy would lead to difficulty.

Resignations should always be given in writing, addressed either to the clerk of the district, or to the trustee. Oral resignations are so liable to be the source of misunderstanding that they should never be used. A resignation can be withdrawn any time before it has been accepted, either formally, or by filling the vacancy.

All district officers are to be elected annually, but

all school officers, whether town or district, will hold over till their successors are not only elected, but qualified. A pecuniary interest in the introduction of any school text-book disqualifies any school officer whatever from continuing in his office.

Voting. To enable a person to vote in a district meeting, he must reside in the district and possess the qualifications requisite to entitle him to have his name put upon the voting list of the town at that time; but his name need not actually be upon the list. To vote as a taxpayer, a man must pay, or be liable to pay, a portion of the tax in question.

Taxpaying residents alone have the right to vote on questions involving the expenditure of money, but a non-resident, though a taxpayer, has no vote at all, not even upon tax questions.

If a person residing in a joint district moves from one *town* to the other, he loses his vote in that district till he has gained it in the other town.

Certificate voters, so-called, cannot vote for school district officers.

Meetings. As to notifying meetings, see chapter 56, section 5. A meeting called by only one notice is never legal, nor where the notice is signed by any other person than the trustees, clerk, or school committee; and all business transacted at an illegal meeting is void. The notice for an *annual* meeting need not specify any of the items of business. Anything which it is lawful for a district to do, even the voting of a tax, can be done at an annual meeting without being mentioned in the notice. But every notice of a *special* meeting *must* state specifically what business is to be done, or it will be illegal. All notices must be posted at least five days before the meeting. (See form.) The annual meeting must organize by choosing a moderator and clerk. The moderator is an annual officer, the same as the clerk, and presides at all meetings during his year of service. He need not be engaged. The clerk, whether regular or *pro tem.* should be engaged before he enters upon the discharge of his duties. He may then engage all other district officers, and his record will be evidence of his own and their engagements. If there is a failure to appoint officers at the annual meeting they may be appointed afterwards, and vacancies may be filled at any time. If either moderator or clerk is absent from any meeting, a moderator or clerk *pro tem.* should be elected.

If the moderator refuses to put questions to vote, or if he or any other district officer violates the law, or refuses to perform his duties, he is liable to pay a fine, or to be brought before the Supreme Court and compelled to act.

The annual district meeting is to be in April, but special meetings may be called by the trustees at any time as their judgment may decide; *provided*, that no special meeting shall be called, without the consent of the school committee, to consider any subject that shall have been acted upon by the district within six months. Any legal meeting may adjourn to a special time and continue at that adjournment the business which was specified in the call, or which it was proper to consider at the first meeting.

Inhabitants of districts may be witnesses in all cases, and so may prove (if disputed) the legality of the notice and meeting, but the clerk's record that the meeting has been duly notified will be *prima facie* evidence of the fact.

Quorum. It has been repeatedly decided in the courts of England and this country, that at common law, where there is no statute provision, when a meeting of a corporation, consisting of an indefinite number of persons, (as towns, districts, etc.,) is properly notified, no particular number is necessary to form a quorum, but a majority of those present may act.

To require a majority of the voters of the district to be present would in many cases prevent the doing of any business at all. And to fix any particular number would be difficult, because, there are some districts where this number would be more than the whole number of voters. The law has therefore required the notice of the meeting to be given with great particularity, and then presumes that every voter who does not attend assents to what is done by those present.

At the same time it will not be advisable to proceed in any matter of importance, such as laying a tax, etc., unless a respectable proportion of the voters attend.

Order of business. A district has full power to make its own rules of order, and any district meeting is competent to overrule any decision or ruling of the moderator, and he is bound to conform to their votes in such matters.

In the election of officers where only one person is nominated, it is generally enough to call for all in favor of his election to say, "aye," and all opposed to say, "no." If there is the least doubt in the moderator's mind as to the vote, he should take it again, by show of hands. Where two or more persons are nominated for the same office, a ballot should *always* be taken by the moderator. If a ballot is called for on any question and the call is seconded, the moderator should put the question to the meeting, whether they will have a ballot. If the call is not seconded he can act his own pleasure. If a request is made for a record of the voters and how they voted on any question, it *must* be taken, but the request must be made before the voting begins. A district may therefore reconsider a vote at any time as well upon the motion of one who did not vote for it, as upon that of one who did; and the district may also rescind any vote at any time, before any contract has been made under it. But after a contract has been made, or an individual has incurred any expense or liabilities in consequence of a vote of the district, they cannot with justice rescind it. And if it is rescinded, they will be held liable to make good all damages and losses incurred.

A subsequent meeting cannot by vote legalize the illegal action of a preceding meeting.

TAXATION.

General provisions. The districts have power to build, purchase, hire, and repair schoolhouses, provide blackboards, maps, furniture, and all necessary and useful appendages. The law gives them a general power to tax for school purposes. They may tax to pay rent of a hired house. They may also tax to repair a hired house, provided they have a valid lease of it for a definite period. They may also tax to maintain a day or evening school, but they cannot impose any tuition tax or rate bill on the resident pupils. And to guard against any abuse of this power, the tax must be approved by the school committee, and the plans for building and repairs must also be approved by the committee, or, on appeal, by the commissioner; but this approval is simply an approval of the *amount* of tax, and not an endorsement of the accuracy or validity of the tax bill. And in all cases of levying taxes, it is necessary to vote either a sum certain, or a sum not less than a certain sum, and not more than a certain sum, or a certain percentage on the valuation of the ratable property of the district. The amount levied may be greater than the indebtedness of the district. Indeed it is desirable that there should be some funds in the treasury all of the time. Every vote to levy a tax should specify a time when it shall be due and payable, and it is usually wise to provide a penalty for non-payment at the required time.

All school district taxes must be voted, assessed, and collected according to the present school act, all former acts being repealed.

On laying a tax, or on any question relating to the expenditure of money, those only are entitled to vote who shall have paid, or are liable to pay, taxes; and no tax can be assessed or money hired on the credit of the district without the direct vote of the district to that effect.

Assessment of taxes. Unless the district vote to have their tax assessed according to the *next* town valuation, the trustee or trustees must proceed to make out the tax bill according to the *last* town valuation. If there are any complaints of wrong valuation, it would be well for the district to postpone the tax until the *next* town assessment is completed, to give the parties an opportunity to be heard before the town assessors.

There are no such officers recognized by the law as district assessors, and if a district should elect such, and they should assess a tax, it could not be collected; nor would a tax be collectible if assessed by trustees, one or all of whom were subsequently found to be disqualified, or illegally elected.

A vote to assess by the next town valuation is the only way for a district to avail itself of any increase in the taxable property of the district. The trustee, either by himself or by assessors, has no right to make a new valuation for individuals, or for the whole district indeed, apart from the rest of the town.

If any property within the district is assessed to any person together with property out of the district, so that there is no separate valuation of that portion which may lie within the district lines, and so in the other cases referred to in cap. 58, § 2, the trustees must *first* endeavor to agree with the parties interested as to the valuation of the property, and in case they cannot agree they must then apply in writing to one or more of the town assessors, living out of the district, stating the names of the parties so situated; and the assessors will immediately issue three notices, and at the expiration of the ten days proceed to decide and apportion the valuation; and in their return to the trustee they should certify over their official signatures to all of the material facts. As the assessors are called upon to act in these cases solely upon business of the district their fees should be paid by the district.

The following is an abstract of the general tax laws of the State; but a trustee or assessor, before proceeding to act, should always inquire if they have been altered or amended.

In assessing a tax, real and personal estate must be valued separately, and put in separate columns. Taxes on real estate must be assessed to the owner or tenant for life, and separate tracts or parcels should be separately described and valued, as far as practicable. They should not be assessed against a person deceased, but may be assessed to the estate or heirs of the deceased until the assessors have notice of a division, and each heir is liable for the whole tax. If a tax be assessed on real estate by mistake to a person not the owner thereof, the tax may be collected from such real estate, provided it can be identified, and that the real owner has notice of the assessment.

If any real estate has changed owners since the last town valuation, it, of course, must be assessed to the actual owners at the time the school-tax bill is made out. This is the reasonable construction of the law. If the new owner resides out of the district, the purchase does not carry the property out of the district too. It is still taxable where it is situated.

Persons must be taxed for personal property according to their residence for the greater portion of the twelve months next preceding the first day of April in each year, unless otherwise provided. But a person moving into the State will be taxable in the town and district where he resides when the tax is assessed. If a person moves out of the State before the assessment, he is not liable. The general rule as to taxation is, that personal property shall be taxed to the owner where he resides, and real estate where it lies. A few exceptions from this rule, made by statute, are hereafter referred to.

Buildings on leased land, where the lease is recorded, are to be deemed real estate, but in other cases they would be regarded as personal property. Standing wood to be cut and removed, if there is no deed of the land, is to be regarded as personal property. It has been decided in Massachusetts, that a person residing on land ceded to the United States, and where the State has only reserved a right of serving process, is not taxable. (8 Mass. 72; 1 Metcalf, 680.) Machinery in cotton and woolen factories, merchandise, stock in trade, lumber and coal, stock in livery stables, being permanently located in any town, are to be taxed in the towns where located, in the same manner as if the owner resided there.

Personal property in trust, the income of which is to be paid to some other person, must be assessed to the trustee in the town where such other person resides, if in the State; but if such person lives out of the State, then it is to be taxed where the trustee, executor, etc., resides.

Personal property in the hands of the executors, guardians, etc., is to be taxed to them in the town where the deceased dwelt, or the ward resides, if a resident of this State; but if not, then in the town where the guardian resides.

Collection of taxes. The taxes must be collected by the district collector, or by the town collector, if the district so votes. A tax paid to the treasurer or any other person does not release the party. If the town collector serves, he does not need to be engaged as district collector.

Before the collector proceeds to the collection of the taxes he should see that the provisions of the law regarding the assessment have been complied with.

The mode of distraining and selling personal property is pointed out in the General Laws. The mode of notifying and selling land for taxes is also prescribed by law. In either of the above cases the collector should be very particular to follow the exact letter of the law, keeping *within*, rather than overstepping, its bounds. If a person is taxed for more than one parcel of land, the whole tax may be collected out of any one parcel, and the real estate is liable for the tax on both real and personal property.

A tax warrant remains in force until the whole tax is collected, even though a second or third tax may have been levied in the meantime.

If the collector dies, resigns, or is removed, the new collector, in order to complete the collection, should receive a new warrant. The oath of the collector is admitted to prove a demand. Any district may offer a deduction to those who pay on or before a certain time, or impose a percentage on those who do not, not to exceed the rate of twelve per cent. per annum.

All property which is exempted from attachment by the laws of this State, or of the United States, such as the uniform, arms, ammunition and equipments of an officer or private in the militia, household furniture, family stores, tools, etc., cannot be distrained for taxes.

Owners of real estate sold for taxes may redeem within one year after sale, on paying to the purchaser the amount paid therefor, with twenty per cent. in addition.

Any person neglecting to appear before the assessor, after notice given, has no remedy. Any tax or assessment not appealed from cannot be questioned in court afterwards. Provision is made for correcting errors and re-assessing a tax by application to the commissioner.

All claims for abatement of taxes must be made to the district, who alone have authority to make the same; save in cases where the plea is based upon a change of boundaries, when an appeal is allowed to the committee, or the commissioner.

[See the forms and notes, and especially the notes to the form of a vote for levying a tax.]

TEACHERS.

Every teacher is required to keep a record of all the pupils attending the school, their sex, names, ages, names of parents or guardians, the time when they enter and leave school, their daily attendance, and the dates when the school is visited by any school officer. These registers should be furnished by the committee, to whom they are sent by the commissioner. From the register the teacher must furnish the trustees with such information as may be necessary to make the returns required by the school committee.

It would be well for the teacher to inform the committee of the time of commencing and closing his school, in order that they may know when to visit it, as the trustee sometimes neglects this duty.

It is important that the register be correctly kept

in all its details. Accuracy in all of the statistics is of the highest importance, and the teachers are especially cautioned to follow carefully the directions to be found in the registers.

The teacher should assist the trustees, by all the means in his power, in making the proper returns, as upon their accuracy and fullness may depend the success or failure of many provisions of the law, as well as the wisdom of future alterations of it. Full directions for making out these returns are to be found on all the blanks which are furnished, and these directions should be strictly followed.

The teacher should conform to all regulations of the school committee, in regard to hours, studies, discipline, text-books, etc., as for any violation of them his certificate may be annulled, or he may be dismissed. He may, (if the school committee by regulation authorize it), suspend a scholar temporarily, until a hearing can be had before the committee, in which case he should immediately notify the committee, and the parents or guardian of the child.

The law fixes no minimum standard of qualifications, but it is left for the school committee of each town to determine their own standard. Each teacher should, however, endeavor to add to his acquirements, and should realize that all knowledge is valuable and of use in a schoolroom.

There is no appeal to the commissioner from a refusal of a committee to grant a certificate.

No member of the committee, or superintendent, or trustee, can teach any school, supported wholly or in part by the public moneys, in the town where he resides.

If the teacher has a proper sense of the importance

of his position, and conducts himself accordingly, he will secure to himself the affection and respect of the people of his district, by exerting his utmost powers to promote the moral and intellectual advancement, not only of his scholars, but of the community around him. The moral influence he may exert by his example and instructions can hardly be estimated. And he may aid in diffusing much useful information by encouraging lectures and literary meetings.

Moral instruction should by all means be inculcated by the teacher, but yet so as to avoid all sectarian comments or bias.

The rule as laid down in the law of the State of Massachusetts, while it points out and inculcates the duty of the teacher to give moral instruction, is carefully drawn to avoid giving countenance to any attempt to impart sectarian instruction, and may well be followed in this commonwealth.

"It shall be the duty of the teachers to use their best endeavors to impress upon the minds of the youth committed to their care and instruction, the principles of piety, justice, and a sacred regard to truth, love to their country, humanity and universal benevolence, sobriety, industry, frugality, chastity, moderation, temperance, and those other virtues which are the ornament of human society and the basis upon which a republican constitution is founded; and they shall endeavor to lead their pupils, as their ages and capacities will allow, into a clear understanding of the tendencies of these virtues to preserve and perfect a republican constitution, and secure the blessings of liberty, as well as to promote their own happiness; and also to point out to them the evil tendency of the opposite vices."

Reading the Bible and praying in schools. The Constitution and laws of the State give no power to a school committee, nor is there any authority in the State, by which the reading of the Bible or praying in school, either at the opening or at the close, can be commanded and enforced. On the other hand, the spirit of the Constitution, and the neglect of the law to specify any penalty for so opening or closing a school, or to appoint or allow any officer to take notice of such an act, do as clearly show there can be no compulsory exclusion of such reading and praying from our public schools. The whole matter must be regulated by the consciences of the teachers and inhabitants of the district, and by the general consent of the community. Statute law and school committees' regulations can enforce neither the use nor disuse of such devotional exercises. School committees may recommend, but they can go no further.

It is believed to be the general sentiment of the people of Rhode Island that this matter shall be left to the conscience of the teacher; and it is expected that if he read the Bible as an opening exercise, he shall read such parts as are not controverted or disputed, but such as are purely or chiefly devotional; and if he pray at the opening of his school, he shall be very brief, and conform as nearly to the model of the Lord's Prayer as the nature of the case will admit. And in all this he is bound to respect the conscientious scruples of the parents of the children before him, as he would have his own conscientious scruples respected by them in turn; always, of course, taking care that in the means he uses to show his respect for the consciences of others he does not violate the law of his own conscience.

In regard to the use of the Bible in schools, two observations occur here. If the committee prescribe, or the teacher wishes, to have the Bible read in school, it should not be forced upon any children whose parents have any objections whatever to its use. In most cases the teacher will have no difficulty with the parents on this subject, if he conducts with proper kindness and courtesy. In the next place, no scholars should be required to read the Bible at school until they have learned to read with tolerable fluency. To use it as a text-book for the younger scholars often has the effect of leading them to look upon it with the same sort of careless disregard, and sometimes dislike, with which they regard their other schoolbooks, instead of that respect and veneration with which this book of books should always be treated and spoken of.

In the last part of this manual will be found certain forms of prayer, which are given simply as a guide to those who wish to use this service and as an indication of that form which would be generally acceptable to any community. These particular forms are those allowed by law to be used in the public schools of Canada, and are both comprehensive in their scope and appropriate in their diction.

Power to punish. The teacher should maintain a careful supervision over the conduct of his pupils at all times when they are upon the school premises. Recesses and the brief periods at the beginning and close of school, when the children are mingling together in the school yard, are times above all others when the watchful eye of the teacher should be on the alert. The conduct of pupils on their way to and from school should also not escape the notice of the teacher, though the extent of the teacher's authority to enforce obedience in such circumstances is much more restricted than in cases occurring on the school premises.

This question of the extent of the teacher's authority has been very widely discussed, and has been the subject of many controversies and judicial decisions in various states; and while it is impossible to lay down a rule which shall cover all cases, the general principles have been quite well defined, and were very clearly set forth in a recent case in the Supreme Court of this State where a teacher was sued for damages on account of unlawful and excessive punishment. The court, Mr. Justice Tillinghast presiding, instructed the jury substantially as follows:

An assault and battery is any unlawful physical force used against the person of another. It matters not how slight or how great the force, so that it be unlawful and wrongful, it is an assault and battery. This defendant is charged with the use of such force against the person of the plaintiff. She admits that she did use physical force against him—that she did punish him with the instrument which she has produced before you,—so that, the force being admitted, the first and principal question for you to determine is whether it was unlawful or wrongful. If so, she is guilty as charged. If not, she is not guilty.

The defendant justifies her conduct, or seeks to justify it, on the ground that she was a teacher in a public school; that this plaintiff was a pupil under her charge; that the only force she used was the infliction of such reasonable and judicious bodily punishment as she lawfully might inflict for the disobedience and misconduct of the pupil. That a teacher of a public school has the right to inflict corporal punishment upon a pupil, for sufficient cause, is not disputed. He stands, practically, for the time being, in place of the parent, and may lawfully and properly inflict such punishment as may be reasonable and necessary to compel obedience and a due regard for the well-ordering and good government of the school.

Judge Blackstone says, "The master is *in loco parentis*, and has such a *portion* of the powers of the parent committed to his charge as may be necessary to answer the purposes for which he is employed."

Punishment of this sort should, however, be administered with special care and prudence, and always with temperate zeal and moderation. If in any case the punishment is clearly excessive, it then becomes unjustifiable, and the teacher is liable.

It being admitted then, that the teacher has the right to punish his pupil for acts of misbehavior committed in school, we will enquire as to his right to punish for such acts committed before the school was commenced, or after it was dismissed. Upon this point there is some difference of opinion in the community, but the law seems to be well settled, and is this:—that for such misbehavior out of school as has a direct and immediate tendency to injure the school, to subvert the master's authority, and to beget disorder and insubordination, the teacher may inflict corporal punishment. "It is not misbehavior generally," says ALDIS J., "or towards other persons, or even towards the master in matters in no ways connected with or affecting the school. For as to such matters, committed by the child after his return home from school the parents, and they alone, have the power of punishment." But where the offence has a direct and immediate tendency to injure the school and bring the teacher's authority into contempt, as in this case, when done in the presence of other scholars and of the teacher, and with a design to insult her, she has the right to punish the scholar for such acts, if he comes again to school.

"The misbehavior," says the same judge, "must not have merely a remote and indirect tendency to injure the school. All improper conduct or language may perhaps have, by influence and example, a remote tendency of that kind. But the tendency of the acts so done out of the teacher's supervision, for which he may punish, must be direct and immediate in their bearing upon the welfare of the school, or the authority of the teacher or respect due him.

"Cases may readily be supposed which lie very near the line, and it will often be difficult to distinguish between the acts which have such an immediate, and those which have such a remote, tendency. Hence each case must be determined by its peculiar circumstances.

"Acts done to deface or injure the schoolroom, to destroy the books of scholars, or the books or apparatus for instruction, or the instruments of punishment of the master; language used to other scholars to stir up disorder and insubordination, or to heap odium and disgrace upon the master; writings and pictures placed so as to suggest evil and corrupt language, images and thoughts to the youth who must frequent the school; all such or similar acts tend directly to impair the usefulness of the school, the welfare of the scholars, and the authority of the master. By common consent and by the universal custom in our New England schools, the master has always been deemed to have the right to punish such offences.

"Such power is essential to the preservation of order, decency, decorum, and good government in schools."

Of course any direct personal insult or indignity to the teacher, as snowballing her, stoning her, and other like conduct out of school would come within the same rule. The reasonable exercise of the teacher's authority over her pupils both in and out of school, as to those things which pertain directly to the well-being of the school, must be upheld and sustained, or our public school system will prove worse than a failure.

If you find, therefore, that the punishment inflicted by the defendant in this case was either for misconduct committed in school, or out of school, under such circumstances as I have described to you and that it was not clearly excessive under the circumstances of the case, then the justification set up by defendant is made out, and you will find a verdict of not guilty. If you find that the punishment was wrongfully inflicted, or excessive, then you will find a verdict of guilty and assess such damages in favor of the plaintiff as you think him fairly entitled to.

The jury returned a verdict of NOT GUILTY.

The teacher should remember that while the law

holds him responsible for his acts in the schoolroom, it also protects him while therein employed from all external or unofficial interference. No private person has any right, in any circumstances, to enter a schoolroom in school hours to make any complaint or to disturb the school in any way. The statute law provides a specific penalty for such an offence.

APPEALS.

The law has wisely provided a cheap and efficient mode of settling all disputes arising under the school law. It was intended to save the expense of litigation to districts and individuals, and it is believed that it has already had the effect of saving a great expenditure of money in this way, as well as effecting a more speedy settlement of difficulties, which, if continued, would interrupt the harmony of the districts and injure the schools. An appeal may be taken to the commissioner [see the forms], and he will hear the parties without cost, and his decision is to be final as to the facts or merits of the case. When questions of law arise, provision is made for laying them before one of the judges of the Supreme Court, but the judges will not examine or hear the parties upon the facts of the case. When a case is submitted to one of the judges, it has been decided that the commissioner must make a statement of the facts as he finds them to be established by the evidence, and that this statement is to be submitted, and not the evidence itself.

Any party neglecting to appeal from a vote to tax, or an assessment of a tax, cannot question it afterwards, provided the meeting was legally notified, and the tax approved, etc.

It has been settled that an appeal brings the whole question up, and the commissioner in many cases is not confined to confirming or reversing the proceedings appealed from, but may make a new decision.

All appeals, however, should be taken within a reasonable time, and before any contract is made, or liability incurred, under the vote or act appealed from. If the appeal is not made within such a reasonable time, that circumstance alone will be sufficient reason for dismissing it. And no appeal will be entertained unless made by the party aggrieved.

Written notice of the appeal should always be sent to the party whose action is appealed from, or to the officer whose title is questioned, and this notice should include a copy of the appeal itself, or of the reasons therein contained.

EDUCATION OF THE DEPENDENT AND DEFECTIVE CLASSES.

This State makes special provision for these unfortunate children. For the dependent children, *i. e.*, those having no home and dependent on public charity, she has provided the State Home and School, which is located upon a large farm about three miles from the centre of the city. It is under the care of a board of seven persons, four of whom are to be men, and three, women.

The aim is indicated by the name,—to provide a home for the children, together with such training and education as shall fit them to become self-respecting, self-supporting men and women.

The general care of the education of the defective

classes is placed in the hands of the State Board of Education, upon whose recommendation children are appointed by the governor as State beneficiaries at any institution selected by the Board. The policy of the State with reference to these unfortunates is very liberal, and it is of great importance that the school officers and others should take pains to see that cases of blind and feeble-minded children are brought to the attention of the Board, in order that their education may be secured.

For the education of the deaf the State has established a boarding, or home, school, called the R. I. Institute for the Deaf, which is situated in the city of Providence. It is thoroughly equipped with new buildings and the best appliances for its work. The oral method of instruction is pursued exclusively, hence it is of great importance that the child should be placed there at an early age, or soon after the loss of hearing.

The school is under the care and direction of a board of six men and three women, together with the governor and lieutenant-governor, *ex-officiis*.

LIBRARIES.

Towns and districts are both authorized to maintain school libraries, and a slight annual expenditure added to the State aid for the supply of school apparatus would soon suffice to equip every school with a good working library, than which no better educational power exists. In towns where there is no public library and where the population is so scattered as to preclude the maintenance of one central library, such school libraries should be established without fail, and maintained at a high degree of efficiency.

In addition to these school libraries, towns are authorized to establish and maintain free public libraries, and several of the towns have such libraries already established. In a large number of other towns there are free libraries, but they are controlled by associations, either chartered directly by the General Assembly, or organized under the general law relating to "Voluntary Associations." The State Board of Education is authorized to grant aid from the State treasury to all such free public libraries. The main condition is that the use of the library shall be entirely free to all the citizens, subject only to such rules as are necessary for the proper care of the property. This aid cannot be given until the library has attained to the size of five hundred volumes. The amount of aid is limited to fifty dollars annually for the first five hundred volumes, and twenty-five dollars additional for each subsequent five hundred. This increase is, however, optional with the Board of Education. The Board are authorized to make rules and regulations for the government of these libraries. Copies of these rules can be had always on application to the commissioner.

If possible it is desirable to establish these libraries upon a permanent basis, and that is best secured by making them town institutions, and special attention is called to chapter 43 of the General Laws. Provision is thereby made for their constant care and protection and the general public is more thoroughly interested in them. It often happens, however, that the first inception of such an enterprise must be in the minds of a few public spirited persons, and in that case they should associate themselves together. An outline of the necessary articles for such an association will be found among the "Forms."

FORMS.

These forms have been prepared in order to assist those who may be disposed to undertake any office or duty under the school laws, to save them expense and trouble, and to bring about a uniformity of practice, as far as that can be done. These forms, with the exception of the oath of office, are not prescribed by law, but are believed to conform substantially to the law, and to be safe precedents.

1. *Warrant or Certificate of Election of School Officers.*

To   of   greeting:

This certifies that you, the said   were at a   meeting of the town of   [*or* of   of school district No.   of the town of   ], held on the   day of   A. D. 18   , chosen to the office of   of said town [*or* district], and are by virtue of said appointment fully authorized and empowered to discharge all the duties of said office, and to exercise all the powers thereto belonging, according to law.

[L. S.] Witness my hand, and the seal of said town [*or* district]   hereto affixed by me, this   day of   A. D. 18   .

FORMS RELATING TO PUBLIC INSTRUCTION.

2. Form of Oath to be taken by all School Officers.

I, [*naming the person*] do solemnly swear (*or* affirm) that I will faithfully and impartially discharge the duties of the office of [*naming the office*] according to the best of my abilities, and that I will support the constitution and laws of this State and the constitution of the United States, so help me God; (*or*, This affirmation I make and give upon the peril of the penalty of perjury).

---

3. Certificate of Engagement of School Officers.

       Town of   A. D. 18

I hereby certify that   personally appeared before me and took an oath to support the constitution of the United States, the constitution and laws of this State, and faithfully to discharge the duties of the office of school committee [*or* clerk, trustee, treasurer of school district No. , *as the case may be*] so long as he continues therein.

       A. B., Justice of the Peace,
        or Notary, *as the case may be.*

---

4. Form for Annulling a Certificate.

To the trustees of school districts in the town of   and all others whom it may concern:

Whereas, the school committee of this town did, on the   day of   A. D. 18   issue to   of a certificate of qualification as a teacher in the public schools: Now, know ye, that upon further examination, investigation and trial, the said   has been found deficient and unqualified [*or* the said   has refused to conform to the regulations made by the committee, *as the case may be*], and we do, therefore, by the authority given us by law, declare the said certificate to be annulled and void from this date, of which all persons whose duty it is to employ teachers of public schools are hereby requested to take notice.

By order and in behalf of the school committee of the town of

Date.   Chairman *or* Clerk.

NOTE. If a complaint is made against a teacher, it will be imperative that he shall be notified for at least five days before a decision on his case. And notice of the annulling should be immediately given to the trustees of the district, and generally, in order to prevent his being again employed.

---

5. *Memorandum of Contract with a Teacher.*

This agreement, made this   day of   A. D. 18   between A. B., etc. [trustee, *or* school committee, *as the case may be*], of   on the one part, and X. Y., of   on the other part, witnesses, that the said X. Y. hereby agrees to teach, for the compensation herein mentioned, the   school in and for said district [*or* town], at   [*specify the building, if desired*], for the term of   months [*or* weeks] commencing   and ending   and the said X. Y. further engages to exert the utmost of his ability in conducting said school, and improving the education and morals of the scholars; to keep such registers and make such returns to the trustees and to the school committee as may be required of him, and in all respects to conform to all such regulations for the government of said school as may be made by the school committee of said town, and to the provisions of the laws regulating public schools. And in case the certificate of qualification of said X. Y. should be annulled, or if he shall not keep the register and make return, as aforesaid, or should violate such regulations as aforesaid, this agreement from thenceforth shall be of no effect. And the said [committee, trustee *or* agent] agree to pay the said X. Y. therefor at the rate of   per month [*or* per week], to be paid at the end of each month [*or* term] out of the school money by law appropriated to said district, and the legal assessments which may be made, and in no event out of the private property of the contractor. And it is further agreed, that the possession of the schoolhouse and its appurtenances shall at all times be considered as being in the trustees [*or* school committee].

[L. S.] Witness our hands and seals hereto, the day first above mentioned.

Sealed and executed
in presence of

6. *Notice of a Meeeting of a District called by the School Committee.*

Notice is hereby given that there will be a meeting of the legal voters of school district No.   in the town of   at the schoolhouse in said district [*if no schoolhouse, then the school committee must appoint a place*], at   o'clock P. M., on the   day of   A. D. 18   for the purpose of organizing said district, of electing officers for said district for the ensuing year, of considering the expediency of building [*or* repairing] the schoolhouse in said district, and laying a tax on the ratable property of the district therefor, and of transacting any other business which may lawfully come before said meeting.

By order and in behalf of the school committee of said town.

Date.   Chairman, *or* Clerk.

---

7. *Notice of Annual District Meeting.*

To the legal voters of school district No.   of the town of   . The annual meeting of   for the choice of officers and the transaction of any other business which may lawfully come before it, will be held at   on the   day of   A. D. 18   at   o'clock P. M.

Date.

Trustee *or* Trustees.

---

8. *Notice of Special Meeting.*

A *Special meeting* of the legal voters of school district No.   in the town of   will be held at the district schoolhouse, on the   day of

FORMS RELATING TO PUBLIC INSTRUCTION.   367

A. D. 18   at   o'clock P. M., for the purpose of [*here insert every object that is to be brought before the meeting*].

   (Signed)   A. B., Trustee.

NOTE. All notices of district meetings must be posted in two or more public places, or published in some newspaper, for at least five days before the meeting. That is, a notice for a meeting on a Saturday must be posted the preceding Monday. If called by the trustees at the request of five qualified voters, the notice should be posted within two days from the time the request was made. Care should always be taken to preserve evidence of the proper notification of the meeting. Every notice should be dated, and signed only by the committee, trustee, or clerk.

---

9. *Form of Request to be made by five Legal Voters of a School District to the Trustees for the calling of a Special Meeeting.*

To the Trustees of School District No.

The undersigned, legal voters of school district No.   of the town of   request you, in pursuance of the school law, to call a special meeting of said district, for the purpose of

Dated this   day of   A. D. 18
   (Signed)

---

10. *Commencement of District Records.*

For first meeting. At a meeting of the legal voters of school district No.   of the town of   called by the school committee of said town, and duly notified as the law requires [*here in some cases it may be advisable to state particularly how the notice was given*], and held according to notice at the district schoolhouse [*or as the case may be*], on the   day of   A. D. 18   at   o'clock P. M.

For annual meeting. At the annual meeting of the legal voters of school district No.   of the town of   duly notified by the trustees of said district as the law requires [*in some cases specify as above*], and held according to notice at the district schoolhouse [*or as may be*], on the   day of   A. D. 18   at   o'clock P. M.

For special meeting. At a special meeting of the legal voters of school district No.   of the town of   held (*or* in pursuance of an application to the trustees) at   on   , which meeting was duly notified by the trustees of said district as the law requires:

For adjourned meeting. At a meeting of the legal voters of school district No.   of the town of   held according to adjournment (from the   day of   , 18   ,) at   on

---

11. *Records of the Choice of Officers, etc.*

The following-named persons were chosen to the offices set against their respective names, viz.:

    C. D., Clerk.   A. B., Moderator.

Or, *instead of the above, say—*

Voted, that A. B. be appointed moderator of this meeting.

Voted, that C. D. be appointed clerk [*or* trustee, treasurer, etc.], of this district [*or* in place of O. P., resigned, etc., *if such be the case*].

The clerk then, in presence of the meeting, took the oath of office in the form prescribed in chapter 25, section 5, of the General Laws, administered by E. F., Esq., moderator [*or* notary public, justice of the peace, or town clerk, *as the case may be*].

It was moved by A. B., and seconded by C. D., that   and after discussion the question was put and the motion was adopted, (*or* rejected).

---

12. *Vote of District to devolve care of School on School Committee.*

Voted, (if the school committee of this town consent thereto and accept thereof), that all the powers and duties of this district, and of the trustees thereof, relating to keeping public schools in this district be, and they are hereby, devolved on said school committee, until this district shall choose a new trustee or trustees, or shall otherwise legally direct.

NOTE. A copy of this vote, with a proper heading, "At a meeting of," etc., attested by the clerk, should be furnished to the committee.

---

13. *Vote of District to build Schoolhouse.*

Voted, that a schoolhouse be erected at or upon   for the use of the public schools in this district, and that   be a committee to cause the same to be erected, the said committee first procuring the plans and specifications for the building, to be approved by the committee of the town, according to law, and that the said   shall have full power, in the name and behalf of the district, to sign, seal and execute any contracts which may be necessary to carry out this vote, to superintend the execution of said contracts, and to do any other matter or thing which may be necessary to carry out this vote.

NOTE. The location (unless before made) must be made by the school committee.

---

14. *Form of Contract to build Schoolhouse.*

Articles of agreement made and executed on the   day of   A. D. 18   between A. B., of   on the one part, and school district No.   of the town of   county of   State of   on the other part.

The said A. B., for himself, his heirs, executors, and administrators, doth hereby covenant and agree with the said school district No.   and their assigns, that he, the said A. B., his heirs, executors, and administrators, for the considerations herein expressed, shall and will, within the space of   months from the date hereof, erect, build, and completely cover over and finish upon [*here describe the lot*], and upon such spot in said lot as said school district or their proper officers may direct, a house, outbuildings, and fences, for the purpose of a district schoolhouse and appendages, according to plans, elevation, and specifications more particularly expressed in a schedule hereto attached and signed by said parties, and which is hereby made part and parcel of this agreement; and also shall and will perform and execute all the works mentioned in the said plans and specifications, and in the manner therein mentioned, and within the time aforesaid; and also shall and will furnish and provide at his own charge, good and sufficient materials of the sorts and quality expressed in said schedule, and all such other materials as may be necessary for the erecting and fully completing the house, outhouses, and fences aforesaid, according to the plans and specifications aforesaid.

And it is further agreed between said parties, that if the said A. B., his heirs, executors, or administrators, shall not, within the space of time above mentioned, finish and complete all said works as aforesaid, then said school district, or their agent, may go on and complete said works, at the cost and charge of the said A. B., his heirs, executors, and administrators, and may deduct the same from the compensation herein agreed to be paid for said buildings and works; and the said A. B., his heirs, executors, and administrators, shall also be liable for any other damages incurred by said district by said failure, and shall also be liable to said district for any damages incurred by any other unreasonable delay in completing the works aforesaid.

And the said school district No.   doth hereby covenant and agree with the said A. B., his heirs, executors, administrators, and assigns, that the said school district shall and will pay to the said A. B., his executors, administrators, or assigns, the sum of   dollars, as full compensation for his services in building and completing said works ; said sum to be paid within   days after the completion of said works, as aforesaid, (*or, in case that the money is to be paid in installments, specify the times and amounts and conditions*).

And it is further agreed, that if said school district or their agents shall direct any more work to be done upon or around said buildings than is hereinbefore agreed, the said district shall pay the expense thereof, in addition to the compensation aforesaid. And if said district or their agents shall direct any part of the work hereinbefore agreed to be done and expressed in said schedule to be omitted or diminished, then there shall be deducted from said compensation a reasonable sum, according to the proportion said work omitted may bear to the work herein first agreed to be done. And said district or their proper agents shall have a right to direct any additions or omissions as aforesaid, and the party of the other part shall be bound to comply with and perform the said directions.

[*Clause to refer to arbitration.*]

And lastly, it is hereby agreed between the parties aforesaid, that if any dispute shall happen between the said district or its agents, and the said A. B., his heirs, executors, administrators, or assigns, in relation to the buildings herein agreed to be erected, work to be done, the payment of the money, or concerning the value and expense of any work directed to be added or omitted as hereinbefore mentioned, or concerning any other matter or thing whatever, relating to the construction of this agreement, or the amount of any damages claimed by either party under its provisions, or for any alleged violation thereof, then in such case such dispute shall, upon the demand of either party, be left to the award and determination of three indifferent persons, one to be appointed in writing by each of said parties, immediately thereafter, and a third to be appointed in writing by the two persons so first named. And the said parties hereby covenant and agree with each other, that they will severally abide by, perform, and keep the award and determination of the said three persons, or any two of them, touching said disputes, provided said award be made under the hands and seals of said arbitrators or any two of them, within   from the time of said reference.

 In testimony whereof, the said A. B. hath hereto set his hand and seal, and said school district No.   have hereto affixed their seal by the hand [*or* hands] of   duly authorized for that purpose, who hath [*or* have] hereto also set his [*or* their] own hand [*or* hands.]

A. B. [L. S.]

    Names of committee or agents. [L. S.]

Sealed and delivered
in presence of   [L. S.]

NOTE. If the district wishes a surety for the performance of a contract of A. B., it may be taken by a bond, conditioned for the performance by A. B. of the covenants and agreements in an instrument dated   [and then briefly describe it.]

---

15. *Record of a Vote of District to Tax.*

At the annual meeting of the legal voters of school district No   of the town of   held at   on   according to legal notice issued and signed by   and posted up at   for the five days previous required by law [*or*, at a special meeting of, etc., called by, etc.]

Whereas, this district has voted to build a schoolhouse in and for said district [*or*, to repair the district schoolhouse, *or whatever the cause may be*],

Voted, that for the purpose of defraying the expense thereof, a tax of the sum of   dollars [*or* of   cents on the hundred dollars] be assessed upon, levied, and collected from the ratable property in this district, in manner provided by law, [*or*, according to the estimate, apportionment, and value which shall be affixed to said ratable estates in the assessment and tax bill of this town which shall next be completed after the date of this vote].

NOTE. The above form is a proper one to submit to the committee for their approval. It should be signed by the clerk of the district.

In case nothing is said about valuation, the law directs the tax to be assessed on the last previous town valuation. If, however, the district wishes it assessed on the next valuation, it can be done by including the last clause.

Cautions for district meetings about to assess a tax.

If there is any doubt about the boundaries of the district, have them defined by the committee.

Have the meeting notified for the proper length of time, the notices put up as required, and, if the meeting is a special one, let the notice express clearly the object of the meeting, and evidence of the notice should be preserved.

See that only taxpayers vote on the proposition.

Have all the officers properly engaged. Specify the amount or rate of tax, and when to be collected.

The district may give the collection to the regular collector, if there be one, or, if there be none, may appoint a collector, or may vote to have it collected by the town collector.

The district need not, but may, require bonds of the collector or treasurer; if they do they should fix the sum and approve the sureties.

They should agree with the collector for his fees, otherwise he will be entitled to five per cent.

They may offer a deduction to those who pay on or before a specified time, and may impose a percentage on those who do not pay until after such time.

The location of the house, the plan of the house or repairs, and the amount of the tax, must all be approved by the school committee before a tax therefor is collectible.

---

16. *Form of a Tax Bill.*

Assessment of the taxes upon the ratable estates in school district No.   of the town of   made by the trustees thereof, according to law, this   day of   A. D. 18   according to a vote of said district, passed on the   day of   A. D. 18

Names.	Real.	Personal.	Total.	Tax.

NOTE. The trustees must sign the tax bill. The real and personal lists must be kept separate. If the town assessors are applied to, they should make a certificate of their doings to the trustees, and it would be well for them to attach this certificate, or a copy of it, to the tax bill or assessment.

---

17. *Warrant to Collect a Tax.*

To A. B., collector of taxes of school district No.
   of the town of   county of   and State of Rhode Island and Providence Plantations :—

GREETING.

You, having been appointed collector of taxes for said district, are hereby, in the name of said State, authorized and required to proceed and collect the tax specified in the annexed rate bill, according to law, and to pay the same to the treasurer of the district, or to his successor in office, and for so doing this shall be your sufficient warrant.

Given under my hand and seal, at   this   day of   A. D. 18

C. D.   [L. S.]

Trustee of school district No.
Town of

NOTE. The trustee must issue and sign this warrant in addition to the tax bill as above. The collector should also receive from the district clerk a warrant or formal certificate of election, which may be in substance according to the form No. 1, and then his engagement can be certified upon the back.

If a bond is required the district should approve the sum and sureties of the bond, and the clerk should certify the fact thereon.

If the town collector is appointed to collect the tax, the above will need to be changed in the first line by striking out the words "of school district No.   " and in the fourth line by striking out the words "for said district" and inserting the words "by school district No.   of said town."

---

18. *District Treasurer's Bond.*

Know all men, that we, A. B., of   county of   and State of Rhode Island and Providence Plantations, as principal, and C. D., of   county of   and State aforesaid, as surety [*or* sureties *to the satisfaction of the district*], are firmly held and bound unto the school district No.   of the town of   said State aforesaid, in the full sum of [*to be fixed by the district*] to be paid to the said school district or their assigns, to which we hereby jointly and severally bind ourselves, our several and respective heirs, executors, and administrators.

Sealed and dated the   day of   A. D. 18

The condition of the foregoing obligation is, that whereas the said A. B. was, at a meeting of said school district, holden   , appointed treasurer of said district. Now, if he shall faithfully discharge the duties of said office during his continuance therein, and, at the expiration of his office, he or his executors or administrators shall exhibit a true account, if required, and deliver over to his successor, or the order of the district, all books, papers, and moneys belonging to the district, in his hands, then the above obligation is to be void, otherwise to remain in force.

Executed in presence of
Witness.   A. B. [L. S.]
                                  C. D. [L. S.]

NOTE. It may be advisable for the treasurer to receive a formal certificate of appointment, or warrant, and then his engagement can be endorsed upon it. The above bond need not be given unless the district require it.

---

19. District Collector's Bond.

Know all men, that we, A. B., of   State of Rhode Island and Providence Plantations, as principal, and C. D., of   as surety (or sureties), are firmly held and bound unto E. F., of   , treasurer of school district No.   in the town and State aforesaid, in the full sum of [to be fixed by the district, not exceeding double the tax] to be paid to said   his successors in said office, or assigns, to which we jointly bind ourselves, our several and respective heirs, executors, and administrators.

Sealed and dated this   day of   A. D. 18

The condition of this obligation is, that whereas the said A. B. was, at a meeting of the legal voters of school district No.   of the town of   appointed collector of the rates and taxes assessed and to be assessed in, by, and upon said district, and the said A. B. has accepted said office ; and whereas said district on the   day of   A. D. 18   voted that a tax of   be assessed on all the ratable property in said district, for the purpose of   and said tax has been legally assessed, and the trustee of said district hath issued his warrant to said collector, with said rate bill annexed, for the collection of said tax, the receipt of which said rate bill and warrant is hereby acknowledged, and by which said warrant said tax is to be collected and paid over, on or before the   day of   A. D. 18   Now if the said A. B. shall faithfully perform and discharge said office and trust, and with diligence and fidelity levy and collect, as far as may be done, all the taxes that have been, or may be, so committed to him for collection, during his continuance in office, and he, his heirs, executors, or administrators shall, at all times on proper demand, render an account and pay over all the proceeds of such collections to the treasurer of said district, or his successors in office, according to the directions contained in the warrants for their collection, then this obligation is to be void, otherwise to remain in force.

Executed in presence of

Witness.   A. B. [L. S.]
                                                        C. D. [L. S.]

NOTE. The district collector need not give bond unless required, but the law requires the town collector to give a bond satisfactory to the school committee. The above form can be readily changed so as to render it suitable in case of the town collector.

20. *Form of Tax Collector's Deed.*

To all to whom these presents may come. I, A. B., of   county of   and State of Rhode Island and Providence Plantations, collector of taxes of school district No.   in said town, send greeting :—

Whereas said school district No.   at a meeting duly notified, and held on the   day of   A. D. 18   voted that a tax of   dollars be assessed on the ratable property in said district, for the purpose of   and said tax was afterwards, viz.: on the   day of   A. D. 18   assessed according to law, and the tax bill in due form delivered to me the said collector, with a warrant attached thereto, signed by the trustees of said district, requiring me to proceed according to law and collect the said tax, and pay over the same to the treasurer of the district, or to his successor in office, and whereas C. D., of   neglected to pay the tax assessed against him, and expressed in the said tax bill, amounting to the sum of   dollars, and in consequence thereof, I did on the   day of   levy said warrant upon a certain lot or tract of land belonging to said C. D., in said district, and did advertise the same for sale according to law, at two [*or more*] public places in said town, for twenty day previous to sale [and also in the   newspaper printed in   ], and on the   day of   A. D. 18   at   o'clock in the   noon, on the premises, being the time and place appointed, I proceeded to sell at auction so much of said land as was necessary to satisfy said tax and the incidental expenses, and E. F., of   was the highest bidder therefor.

Now, know ye, that in consideration of the sum of   dollars, being the amount of said tax and expenses paid me by the said E. F., I, the said collector, do hereby give, grant, bargain, sell and convey unto the said E. F., his heirs and assigns, all the right, title and interest which said C. D. had at the time of assessing said tax, in and to the following described tract of land, situated in the district and town aforesaid, containing   acres [more or less], and bounded [*describe*,] or however otherwise bounded, with all [buildings] and appurtenances, being so much of said land of the said C. D. levied on as was necessary to satisfy said tax and expenses; to have and to hold the same to said E. F., his heirs and assigns forever, subject to the right of redemption provided by law. And I, the said A. B., for myself, my heirs, executors, and administrators, do covenant with said E. F., his heirs and assigns, that I [have given bond and] have advertised said property as hereinbefore stated, and have complied with the terms of the law regulating the collecting of taxes, in respect to said sale, as hereinbefore stated.

Witness my hand and seal, this   day of   A. D. 18

         A. B.   [L. S.]

Signed, sealed, and delivered
  in presence of

Town of, etc.,   A. D. 18   Before me, the subscriber, appeared A. B., collector of taxes of school district No.   of the town of   and acknowl-

FORMS RELATING TO PUBLIC INSTRUCTION. 381

edged the foregoing to be his free act and deed, and his hand and seal to be thereunto affixed.

O. P.

Justice of the Peace, Notary Public, *or* Town Clerk.

NOTE. In case where town collector acts, the only change in the above will be in the third line, by dropping the words "of school district No." In case of unimproved lands owned by persons out of the State, and also of improved lands when neither the owner nor occupant lives in the State, notice of the sale must be given twenty days in a newspaper. The purchaser under a tax collector's deed should see that the law has been complied with, and that his evidence of advertising is preserved.

---

21. *Form of a Lease.*

These articles of agreement made this   day of   A. D. 18   witness that A. B., of   doth hereby demise and let unto the school district No.   of the town of   [*describe the room or building*] with the appurtenances, in consideration of the rents and covenants by said school district herein mentioned to be performed, to have and hold the same to the said school district and their assigns for the space of   year, commencing on the   day of A. D. 18   and ending on the   day of A. D. 18   for the purpose of keeping a district school therein, and holding such schools or lectures or other literary meetings, or meetings of business, as the school committee or the officers of said district may deem advisable for promoting the cause of education. And the said district agrees to pay therefor the sum of   per annum as rent, and at that rate for any less time than a year, the payment to be made to the said A. B., his heirs or assigns, at his residence, on the last day of the year [*or* on the last day of each year in the term], without any notice or demand therefor [*provisions about repairs, loss by fire, etc., may be here inserted*].

Witness the hand and seal of said A. B., and the seal of the said district hereto affixed by , by said district duly authorized, the day and year first above mentioned.

Sealed and executed
in presence of

.... [L. S.]
.... [L. S.]

---

22. *Vote to take a Lease.*

The district may authorize a person to execute a lease for them by a vote as follows:

Voted, that the trustees of the district [*or* treasurer] be and they are hereby fully empowered to hire for the purposes of a schoolhouse for the district [*here specify the building, and fix the time and conditions or leave them at discretion*], and to make and execute the necessary contracts therefor, and to seal, deliver, and acknowledge the same in the name and behalf of the district.

NOTE. If the above lease is to be acknowledged. see the form of acknowledgment to No. 26.

A certified copy of the above vote should be given by the district clerk to the person authorized to take the lease.

23. Deed to a School District.

Know all men, that I, A. B., of   in the State of Rhode Island and Providence Plantations, in consideration of the sum of   paid me by C. D., treasurer of school district No.   in the town of   and State aforesaid, the receipt of which I acknowledge, and am therewith fully satisfied and paid [*if a gift, say*, in consideration of my desire to aid and assist in diffusing the benefits of a good common school education among the inhabitants of school district No.   etc., *as the grantor pleases*] do hereby give, grant, enfeoff, convey, and confirm unto said school district and their assigns, a certain lot of land situated in said town of   [*describe*] or however otherwise bounded, with all the appurtenances and privileges thereto belonging, to have and to hold the same forever to said school district and their assigns, [*but if there is a desire to prevent the lot ever being used for any other purpose, omit* assigns *and say*, for the purpose of maintaining thereon a district schoolhouse and its appurtenances, for the benefit of the district school of said district, and for no other use or purpose whatever]. And I, the said A. B., do hereby for myself, my heirs, executors, and administrators, covenant and engage to and with said school district [and their assigns] that the premises are free of all incumbrances, and I have good right to sell and convey as aforesaid, and that I, my heirs, executors, and administrators shall and will forever warrant, secure, and defend the premises to said school district [and their assigns *or* to and for the purpose aforesaid], against the lawful claims of all persons whatsoever. And I, E. F. wife of the said A. B., for the consideration paid my said husband, hereby release unto said school district [and their assigns] all my right of dower in the premises. [*If the premises are under mortgage, a release may be here inserted.*] And I, G. H., of   in consideration of the sum of   paid to me by   to my full satisfaction, do hereby give, grant, bargain, sell, assign, and convey unto said school district [and their assigns], all the right, title, and interest which I have in the premises by virtue of any mortgage deed thereof [or of any other claim or title whatsoever.] In witness whereof we have hereunto set our hands and seals this   day of   A. D. 18

[L. S.]
[L. S.]
.... [L. S.]

Signed, sealed, and delivered
  in presence of

State of   county of   town of   A. D. 18   This day personally appeared before me   and acknowledged the foregoing instrument to be   voluntary act and deed and   hand and seal to be thereunto affixed.

Before me, O. P., Justice of the Peace, Notary Public, *or* Town Clerk (*if executed in Rhode Island*).

NOTE. If the land belongs to a married woman, her name should be inserted as one of the grantors, and the deed altered accordingly. She must acknowledge separately from her husband. Use the words of the law in the certificate of acknowledgment. See General Laws.

24. *Vote appointing an Agent to sell land belonging to the District.*

At a meeting of the legal voters of school district No.   of the town of   etc., notified as the law requires, and held at   on the   day of   A. D. 18

Voted, that A. B., treasurer of said school district, be and he is hereby appointed the agent and attorney of the district, to sell at his discretion, [*or insert the terms or condition*] a certain lot of land, situated in and belonging to the district, containing   bounded   with the buildings and appurtenances, and with full power to affix the seal of the district to a deed or deeds conveying the same [*with covenants of warranty or not, as the district may vote*], and in the name of the district to acknowledge and deliver the same, and receive the purchase-money, and give a full discharge therefor.

A true copy of record : Witness,
E. F., Clerk of said District.

25. *Deed from a District.*

Know all men, that the school district No.   of the town of   county of   State of Rhode Island and Providence Plantations, in consideration of the sum of   paid to A. B., treasurer of said district, to and for the use of said district, by M. N., of   the receipt of which is hereby acknowledged, does hereby give, grant, bargain, sell, and convey unto the said M. N., his heirs and assigns, all the right, title, and interest of said school district, in and to a lot of land situated in said district, containing   bounded   or however otherwise bounded, with all buildings and appurtenances, being the same lot conveyed to said district by deed of H. I. To have and to hold the same to said M. N., his heirs and assigns, forever. In testimony whereof, the said school district have hereunto fixed their seal, by the hands of said A. B., their treasurer, duly appointed for that purpose, at a legal meeting of said district, and the said treasurer hath hereunto affixed his own hand, this   day of   A. D. 18

A. B., Treasurer [*as aforesaid.*]   [L. S.]

Signed and sealed in presence of

Acknowledgment.

State of Rhode Island and Providence Plantations, county of   town of   A. D. 18   The school district No.   of said town, by A. B., their treasurer, agent, and attorney for that purpose, by vote of said district appointed, acknowledged the foregoing to be their voluntary act and deed, and their seal to be thereto affixed; and the said A. B., treasurer and attorney as aforesaid, also acknowledged his own hand affixed thereto, and that the same was the voluntary act and deed of himself and of the said district.

Before me,

P. Q.,

Justice of the Peace, *or* Notary Public, *or* Town Clerk.

NOTE. It will seldom, if ever, be advisable for a district to give anything more than a quit claim deed. If they wish to insert any warranty, it would be best to consult a well informed attorney.

26. *Vote to hire Money.*

Voted, that the treasurer of this school district be and he hereby is authorized to hire   dollars for the purpose of [*here specify the uses to be made of the money*] and to give the note of the district for the same.

NOTE. If any instructions as to rate of interest or time are to be given they should be inserted immediately after the word "dollars."

27. *District Note.*

$............

.... R. I., ...18

For value received school district No.   of the town of   of the county of   and State of Rhode Island, promises to pay A. B., or order,   dollars on demand [*or if a time note, state the time*], with interest, at .   per cent. per annum, in accordance with the vote of said district, passed at a meeting held on the   day of   A. D. 18

C. D., Treasurer.

28. *Vote Prescribing Form of District Seal.*

Voted, That the clerk of the district cause to be made a seal for the use of the district, with the figure of   engraven thereon, and the letters or inscription   around its margin, and that the same is hereby adopted, and declared to be the common seal

of this corporation, and shall be kept by the clerk of
the district.

NOTE. Every town, district, or other corporation, shall have a common
seal, with a suitable device; but if they have no regular seal, any seal may
be affixed to any instrument by their authority; for instance, a piece of
paper attached by a wafer will be considered to be their seal.

29. *Order on School Fund.*

To   treasurer of the town of
  Pay to   on account of school district No.
   of this town, or order, the sum of   for
By order of the school committee of the town.
                                Chairman *or* Clerk.
Date.

NOTE. No order can legally be given on the town treasurer except in
payment for services rendered or expenses actually incurred.

30. *Vote of School Committee to form Joint District.*

Voted, [the school committee of the town of
concurring herewith] that a joint district be formed
according to the provisions of the acts relating to
public schools, to consist of school district No.
of this town, and school district No.   of said town
of   and that said districts shall constitute a joint
district from the time that the school committee of
said town of   shall concur herewith [*or if they
have already passed a similar vote say*, from and
after the passage of this vote].

Voted further, that the chairman be authorized, in

conjunction with the school committee of said town of   to cause notices to be posted up [in two or more places in each of the two districts—*specify them*] for the first meeting of said joint district, to be held at   on   at   o'clock in the   noon [*or* to be held at such time and place as he may agree upon with the school committee of said town of   ] and that the clerk of the committee furnish a certified copy of this vote to the school committee of the said town of

NOTE. A notice signed by the chairman or clerk of each committee should be posted up in two or more places in each district. After trustees are elected, they will notify the subsequent meetings.

31. *Notice of Change in Text-Books.*

Notice is hereby given that a change in text-books in the study of   will be proposed for consideration at the next regular meeting, [*or* at a meeting to be held on (*here state the time*)].

   Signed,

NOTE. The above notice must be given at a *regular* meeting of the committee. .

32. *An Appeal.*

To A. B., commissioner of public schools of the State of Rhode Island and Providence Plantations:

Whereas, the school committee, [trustees of school district No.   of the town of   No.   ], did at a meeting on the   day of   A. D. 18

pass a vote—[*here copy or insert the substance, as nearly as can be procured*]. I, the subscriber, according to law, do hereby appeal to you from said vote or decision, and claim that the same may be reversed. [*Here state plainly and briefly the reasons*].

Signed,

33. *Notice of Appeal.*

To the School Committee of the town of
 [trustees of school district No.   in the town of   ]

I hereby notify you, that in conformity with the provisions of the laws regulating public schools, I appeal to A. B., commissioner of public schools, from [*here specify the vote or decision of the committee, trustees, or district, which is complained of*] for the following reasons: [*here give the reasons specified in the appeal*].

Signed,

Date.   C. D.

A copy of this notice should be immediately served upon the clerk of the committee, clerk of the district, or upon the trustee, or trustees who have done the act complained of, or upon the parties interested, whoever they may be. In general it is full as well to send a copy of the appeal to the parties.

34. Form of Incorporation for a Public Library.

The following is submitted as a suitable form for the constitution of an association for establishing and maintaining a free public library:

We, the subscribers, agree to associate and incorporate ourselves for the purpose of maintaining a public library, by the name of the   , under the provisions contained for that purpose in chapter 176 of the General Laws, and to be governed by the following constitution:

ARTICLE 1. This association shall be called the

The library shall be established and maintained at   in the town of

2. The officers of the association shall be a president, vice-president, secretary, treasurer, and one or more trustees, who shall constitute a board of directors for the management of the business of the association, according to such rules as the association may from time to time adopt.

3. The annual meeting shall be held at   on   when the above-named officers shall be elected. Any officer shall be elected by ballot if demanded by any   members. Special meetings may be held at any time upon the call of the president or secretary, public notice having been given at least five days before holding the meeting.

4. Any member, for disorderly or immoral conduct, may be expelled, and any officer, for miscon-

duct, may be removed at any regularly notified meeting of the society.

5. The directors shall appoint a librarian, and fix his compensation, and make all such regulations as they may deem proper for the government of the library, and prescribe fines for non-compliance, and may, in any case of misuse of books, prohibit any person from using the library until satisfaction is made.

6. The library shall be held by the association, not in shares for the benefit of shareholders, but in trust for the public benefit; to be open to all who shall comply with such reasonable rules as shall from time to time be made by the association or directors; and for the purpose of continuing the existence of the corporation, the association will from time to time elect as members such persons as they shall think most likely to coöperate zealously in promoting its objects. No member shall be admitted unless proposed at a previous meeting.

7. This constitution may be amended at any annual meeting, provided notice of the intended amendment has been given at some previous meeting.

The above are all the provisions necessary to be inserted in the constitution. All other provisions are better made in the shape of rules or regulations, which may be altered from time to time with less trouble.

This agreement, or constitution, must be filed with the secretary of state, and a fee of five dollars paid for his certificate thereof, before the corporation is legally organized.

Whenever it is intended to establish a permanent

library, it will always be most prudent to be incorporated as above. If a library is owned by several persons unincorporated it will be liable to division, and each one's interest liable to attachment. In a corporation, the share only could be attached, and where the corporation hold the library merely as trustees (as provided in Art. 6, above), no individual would have any attachable interest whatever.

35. *Forms of Prayer.*

BEFORE ENTERING UPON THE WORK OF THE DAY.

O Lord our Heavenly Father, Almighty and Everlasting God, who hath safely brought us to the beginning of this day, defend us in the same by Thy mighty power; and grant that this day we fall into no sin, neither run into any kind of danger, but that all our doings may be ordered of Thee to do always that which is righteous in Thy sight, through Jesus Christ our Lord. Amen.

O Almighty God, the giver of every good and perfect gift, the fountain of all wisdom, enlighten, we beseech Thee, our understandings by Thy Holy Spirit, and grant that whilst with all diligence and sincerity we apply ourselves to the attainment of human knowledge, we fail not constantly to strive after that wisdom which makes wise unto salvation; that so, through Thy mercy, we may daily be advanced both in learning and godliness, to the honor and praise of Thy name, through Jesus Christ our Lord. Amen.

Our Father which art in heaven, hallowed be Thy name. Thy kingdom come. Thy will be done in earth, as it is in heaven. Give us this day our daily bread. And forgive us our trespasses, as we forgive them that trespass against us. And lead us not into temptation ; but deliver us from evil: for Thine is the kingdom, and the power, and the glory, for ever and ever. Amen.

AT THE CLOSE OF THE WORK OF THE DAY.

Most merciful God, we yield Thee our humble and hearty thanks for Thy fatherly care and preservation of us this day, and for the progess which Thou hast enabled us to make in useful learning: We pray Thee to impress upon our minds whatever good instructions we have received, and to bless them to the advancement of our temporal and eternal welfare ; and pardon, we implore Thee, all that Thou hast seen amiss in our thoughts, words, and actions. May Thy good providence still guide and keep us during the approaching interval of rest and relaxation, so that we may be thereby prepared to enter on the duties of the morrow with renewed vigor, both of body and mind ; and preserve us, we beseech Thee, now and ever, both outwardly in our bodies, and inwardly in our souls, for the sake of Jesus Christ, Thy Son, our Lord. Amen.

Lighten our darkness we beseech Thee, O Lord; and by Thy great mercy defend us from all perils and dangers of this night, for the love of Thine only Son, our Saviour, Jesus Christ. Amen.

INDEX TO GENERAL LAWS.

Abatement of taxes, how and when made, 55
Absentees, provisions and arrangements for, 77
Account of school commissioner to state auditor, 72
 of school moneys, penalty for neglect to deliver to successor, 80
Adjournment of tax sale of real or personal property, 29
Admission of children of soldiers to any school, 82
 to normal school, requirements of, 71
 to public schools, what does not exclude from, 80
Advertisement in sale of property for taxes, manner of, 25, 26
Agreement to submit dispute to commissioner, when, 63
Agriculture and Mechanic Arts, Rhode Island College of, 84–88
Aid, collector of taxes may require, 30
Alcohol, instruction as to effect of, upon human system, 60
Aldermen, Board of, words "town councils" construed to include, 13
 to appoint special constables under truant law, 74, 75
 penalty for neglect to appoint truant officers, 78
Apparatus, and reference books, appropriation for, 39, 40
 sale or exchange of, penalty for offering fee to school officers for, 82
Appeals, in school matters, to school commissioner, 67, 68
 from proceedings condemning land for school site, 60
Apportionment of school money among the towns, 38
 of State money for apparatus, 39, 40
  for libraries, 34
 of property where district is divided, 53
Appraisal of land for schoolhouse, 60

Appropriation by districts for school purposes, 47
    of money for schools, power of town to make, 17
    for free public libraries, power of town to make, 17, 18
    annual State, for free public libraries, 34
        for support of public schools, 38, 40
        for reference books and school apparatus, 39
        for support of evening schools, 40
        for traveling expenses of pupils of Normal school, 71
        for teachers' institutes, 72
        for educational publications, lectures, etc., 72
        for education of blind, deaf, and imbecile, 91, 92
        for free public libraries, how to be made, 20
        to Rhode Island school of design, how paid, 88

Arbor Day, programme for, 37
    to be a legal holiday, 104

Assessment of poll tax, by whom, when and how made, 23
    of school district taxes, 47, 53, 54

Assessors of Taxes, may administer oaths, when, 11
    to give notice of assessment of taxes on school district, 54
    to assess property in school district in what cases, 53, 69.

Associate School Districts, how formed and powers, 50, 51

Attendance of children in public schools, how regulated, 73–79
    rules for, to be made by school committee, 61
    average, money to be apportioned by, 62
    of non-residents, how to treat, 57, 58

Auctioneers, duties paid by, added to school fund, 15

Beneficiaries, blind, deaf, and imbecile, how appointed, 91, 92
    at Rhode Island school of design, provision for, 88, 89

Bequest to free public library, full discharge for, 21

Blackboards, school district may supply, 46

Blanks for schools, to be distributed by town clerk, 45
    for school census, how furnished, 45
    for report of school committee, how furnished, 64

Blind Persons, provisions for education of, 91

Board of Education, 33–36. See *Education, State Board of*.

Bond of clerk of school district, 47
 of collector of school district, 47
 of treasurer of school district, 47
Books, of public libraries, penalty for injuring, 103
  penalty for conversion of, 109
 penalty for unlawful refusal to deliver official, 16
 of office to be delivered to whom by retiring officer, 16
 of free public library, rules for character of, 34
 selection of, for school libraries, 37
Boundaries of school districts, power of school committee over, 59
 to be recorded by town clerk, 45
Bribery of school officers prohibited, and penalty for, 82

Census of children of school age, how to be taken, 45
 blank forms for, furnished by commissioner, 45
 returns of, to be received before school money paid, 46
Certificates of school teacher, when may be annulled, 60
  good for how long, 66
  required and by whom signed, 65
 of attendance at school under the truant law, 76
 relating to school money, penalty for false, 80
 of vaccination required from pupils in school, 83
Chairman of school committee, election, removal, powers, 58
Children. See *State Home and School for Children.*
 annual census of school, to be taken, 45
 new district not to be formed with less than forty, 59
 employment of, in certain cases prohibited, when, 75–77, 89
 factory inspectors may visit establishments employing, 90
 provision for education of deaf, blind, and imbecile, 91
 what, may be received into State home and school, 96, 97
Christmas Day, to be a legal holiday, 104
City, word included in meaning of word "town," 13
 mayor of, may administer oaths, 11
 management and control of free public library by, 20
City Clerk, included in words "town clerk," 13

City Council, may accept free public library or funds for, 19
    trustees of free public library to be elected by, 20
    penalty for neglect of, to make truant ordinances, 78
Clerk. See *Town Clerk*.
    commissioner may employ, 37
    of school committees, election, removal, and duties, 58
    of school districts, election, powers, duties, 47-49, 70, 80
Collectors of school districts, election of ; to have powers of collectors of taxes, 47
    to give bond, when, 47, 69, 70
    to receive tax bill from trustees, 56
    compensation of, 32
    collection of poll taxes by, 24
    may collect school-district taxes, when, 47
College of Agriculture and Mechanic Arts, 84-88
Commissioner. See *School Commissioner*.
    of public schools, election and duties, 37, 38
Committee, school. See *School Committee*.
Compensation of assessors, town clerks, collectors, 32
    of secretary of State home and school, 96
    of superintendents of schools, 44
    board of education to receive no, 36
    trustees of Rhode Island institute for deaf to receive no, 93
    of trustees, 57
Complainant in cases of truancy, etc., 75
Consolidated school districts, how formed, powers, 51
Constitution of the State, extracts, 1-4:—
    declaration of rights, 2
    qualification for office, 3
        officer must be qualified elector except for school committee, 3
    education, 3
        duty of general assembly to provide, 3
        permanent school fund, 3
        donations for schools, 3, 4
        alienations of school money forbidden, 4
Construction of statutes, rules of, how applied, 12-14
    of certain words, "town," 13

Construction of statutes, of certain words, "town council," 13
Contract of district, remedy, if not fulfilled, 54
Corporations, school districts are, 46
    literary and scientific, how formed, 105, 106
        powers of, 107
Costs, not to be taxed against school officers when, 68
    security for, in suit against school district, 69
Council. See *City Council; Town Council.*
Cranston, probate court, jurisdiction of, over what vagrant children, 99

Deaf, blind, and imbecile children, public provision for, 91
    what persons admitted to R. I. Institute for the, 93
Declaration of rights and principles, 2, 3
Deduction from taxes may be provided for, 31
Design, R. I. school of, State beneficiaries at, 88
Dictionaries, etc., for schools, appropriation for, 39, 40
Diploma, graduates from normal school to receive, 71
Directors of R. I. school of design to make report to board of education, 88
Dismissal of teacher, when and how, 60, 66
Dispute relative to school matters may be submitted to commissioner, 68
Distraint from taxes, mode of conducting, 26-30
    fees of collector, 32
District Clerk included in words "ward clerk," 13
District Council included in "town council," 13
District Court, to have jurisdiction of truancy cases, 79
    clerks of, may administer oaths, where, 11
    justices of, may administer oaths, where, 11
    assistant justices of, may administer oaths, where, 11
District Meetings, school, 48-50. See *School District.*
District of Narragansett included in word "town," 13
    district council of, included in words "town council," 13
Districts. See *School Districts.*
District Schools. See *Schools.*
District Taxes, levy and assessment of, 53-55. See also *School District.*

District Taxes, how to be collected, 47
Disturbing public meetings and schools, how punished, 108
Documents, penalty for unlawful refusal to deliver official, 16
    school, distribution of, by town clerk, 45
Dogs, licenses of, when applied to support of public schools, 102, 104
Donations for public schools, how to be applied, 3, 4

Education, provisions of constitution for, 3. See *Schools*.
Educational purposes of property, effect of, on taxes, 21, 22
Education, State board of, 33-36
    division, and term of office of members, 33
    vacancies in, how filled, 34
    to elect commissioner of public schools, 33
    meetings of, when and where to be holden, 34
    to prescribe rules for carrying into effect school laws, 34
    to appropriate money and make rules for free libraries, 34
    to report annually ; expenses how allowed, 36
    when consent of, required for change of text-books, 65
    may consent to remission of fines in school matters, 70
    to have management of the normal school, 71
    to provide for educational publications and lectures, 72
    school committee to report annually to, 78
    may visit any school aided by State, 81
    control of beneficiaries at school of design, 88, 89
    to recommend a blind, deaf, or imbecile child as State beneficiary, 91
    to have supervision of education of same, 91
    to make annual report on to general assembly, 92
    may purchase clothing for beneficiaries, 92
    bills for same to be approved by, and how paid, 92
    to include, in report to general assembly, what, 100
    to receive report of State home and school, 100
    secretary of, to furnish form of certificate of school attendance, 76
        to file applications for school of design, how, 89

Election Day, State, to be a legal holiday, 104
   national, to be a legal holiday, 104
Elections, rights and qualifications of voters in, 5-9
   registering, listing, and returning lists of voters, etc., 7-9
Electors, rights and qualifications of, 5-9. See *Voters*.
   registering, listing, and returning lists of, 7-9
Employment of children in certain places prohibited, when, 75, 76, 89
Engaged, word to include either "sworn" or "affirmed," 13
Engagement. See *Oath of Office*.
Evening Schools, appropriation for support of, 40
Evidence that district meeting has been duly notified, 70
   that school district officer has been duly engaged, 80
Examination of pupils for normal school, 71
   of teachers, 60, 66, 71
Exclusion of pupils from school, by school committee, 62
   on account of age, race, or color forbidden, 80
Exemption from taxation, 21, 22
   for schooling, 82, 83
   of schools, when to cease, 81
Expenses of State board of education, how paid, 36

Factory, word how construed for special purposes, 90
Factory Inspectors, appointment, duties, powers of, 90
Factory laborers, regulations as to employment of, 89, 90
Fees of collector of taxes, 32
   for books in free public library not to be exacted, 20
   not to be offered to school officers, 82
   not to be received by school officers, 82
Fines in school matters, commissioner may remit, 70
   under truant law, to be applied to use of schools, 79
   for disturbing meetings or schools, 108
   for employment of children in factories, 76-77
   for injury to property of libraries, 108
   for neglect of duty, 80, 81
Flags, foreign, not displayed on public schoolhouse, 109
Forfeiture of school money by town or district, 39, 63, 78
Fourth of July, to be a legal holiday, 104
Free Public Libraries. See *Library*; *Schools*.

34*

Fund, permanent. See *School Fund.*
  for free public libraries may be accepted by town or city council, 19
General Assembly, relations of, to school fund, 4
  report to, of Rhode Island institute for deaf, 94
    of State board of education, 36, 92
General Treasurer, to have custody of school fund, 15
  how to pay appropriations for free public libraries, 35
  when to pay traveling expenses of board of education, 36
  to add to school fund school money when forfeited, 39
Gift to free public library, how receipted for, 21
Governor may administer oaths anywhere in the State, 10
  to advise as to investment of permanent school fund, 15
  member and president of State board of education, 33, 34
  to appoint State beneficiaries, blind, deaf, etc., 91
  to approve bills for blind, deaf, etc., 92
  to appoint board of control for State home and school, 95
    commissioner of public schools, pro tempore, 37
    factory inspectors and may remove them, 90
    trustees of Rhode Island institute for the deaf, 93
Guardian, board of control of State home and school to be legal, of inmates, 97

Holidays, legal, what are, 104, 105
Home. See *State Home and School for Children.*
Human System, instruction as to effects of stimulants on, 60
Hygiene, instruction in, to be provided, when, 60

Idiot, included in meaning of words "insane person," 12
  provisions for education of, 91
Imbeciles, provisions for education of, 91
Income of permanent school fund, for support of schools, 15, 38
Incorporation, act of, how far deemed a public act, 14
  need not be specially pleaded, 14
Insane person, words to be construed to include whom, 12

Institutes, teachers', 72
Instruction in physiology and hygiene, 60
Insurance of schoolhouse, 47
Investments of permanent school fund, 15

Joint school district, how formed and powers of, 50-53
    how regulated and supervised, 52
    See *School District.*
Judgment, to issue how against school district, 69
Justice of supreme court, statement in appeal made to, 68

Labor Day is a legal holiday, 104
Land or lands, words, how construed, 13
    aliened, not to be sold by collector of taxes, when, 25
    how condemned for school purposes, 59
Lectures on subjects of education, how provided, 72
Legacy to free public library, how discharged, 21
Letters, retiring officer to deliver official, to whom, 16
    penalty for unlawful refusal to deliver official, 16
Levy of school district taxes, 53-55
Library, incorporated, how far exempt from taxation, 22
    how may be incorporated under general law, 105-107
    public, penalty for injuring property of, 108
        of unlawfully converting books, etc., of, 109
    free public libraries, powers of town to appropriate money for, 18, 20
        may be accepted by town or city council as a, 19
        establishment and control of, by towns, 18
        trustees of, election and duties, 20
        exempt from taxation, 22
        board of education may appropriate for and establish rules for, 34
        payments to, by State, how to be made, 35
    school, powers of town to vote money for, 17
        commissioner to assist in establishment of, 37
        appropriation for works of reference and apparatus, 39
        school districts may maintain, 46
Lieutenant-Governor may administer oaths, 10
    ex-officio member of State board of education, 33

Lieutenant-Governor member of board of trustees, Rhode Island institute for deaf, 93
Literary Associations, how organized as corporations, 105
   how created ; powers and liabilities of, 105–107
Malicious mischief to books of free library, how punished, 108
Manufacturing establishments, employment of minors in, when, 75–77
Maps and other school apparatus, provision for, 39, 40
   school district may supply, 47
   receiving or offering fees for exchange of, forbidden, 82
Masculine gender, words importing, may include feminine, 12
Mechanic Arts, college of agriculture and, 84–88
Meetings, district. See *School Districts*.
Meetings of school committee, 59
   of board of education, where to be held, when, 34
   penalty for disturbing, 108
Memorial Day is a legal holiday, 104
Mercantile establishments, employment of minors in, 75–77
Mileage for pupils in normal school, paid how, 72
Minors to attend school, 73
   convicted under truant law, commitment of, 78
   employment of, prohibited, when, 75–77
Moderator of school district, election of, 47
   may engage in office district officers, 47
   need not be engaged, 80
Money for schools, distributed how and when, 62
   statements of, to be made by town treasurer, 44
   to be received and paid out by town treasurer, 44
   tuition, used how, 57
Month to be construed to mean a calendar month, 13
Morality, instructions in principles of, in schools, 67
Newspapers, notice of sale by collector of taxes to be given in, 26, 28
Normal School, management and support of, 71
   qualifications for free tuition in, 71
   trustees of, how constituted, 71
   to prescribe examination of applicants for admission, 71
   to pay traveling expenses of pupils in, 72

Normal School—*Continued.*
    may give teachers' certificates, 71
    graduates from, entitled to diploma, 71
    to be open to children of deceased soldiers and sailors, 82

Notaries Public, to administer oaths, 10

Notice of appeal to be given, 67
    of proposed change of district boundaries, 59
    of sales of property for taxes, how given, 26–29
    of removal of personal property by collector of taxes, 28
    of school district meetings, 48, 49
    of assessment of school district taxes, 54
    in case of land condemned for site of schoolhouse, 60

Nuisances, near schoolhouses prohibited, 81

Oath, construed to mean affirmation, 13
    may be administered by notaries and commissioners, 10
    who may administer anywhere in the state, 10
        in certain counties and towns, 11
        in connection with certain offices, 11
    of school district officers may be before whom, 47, 80

Oath of Office, and how administered, 10
    of school district officers, evidence of, 80
    of school district officers, except moderator, 80

Office, oath of. See *Oath; Oath of Office.*
    tenure of. See *Tenure of Office.*

Officers. See *School District.*
    oath and engagement of, 80. See *Oath of Office.*
    joint authority to three or more, how construed, 12
    to surrender official records, when and to whom, 16
    of schools receiving State aid to report annually, 35
    violating laws relative to public schools, penalties on, 83
    of public schools, forbidden to receive fees, etc., 82
    offering of fees to, forbidden, 82

Orders for school money, given by whom, 44
    payable to whom, 63

Ordinances to be made for attendance of children in schools, 77

Ordinances concerning truants, district courts to have
    jurisdiction of, 79
Organization of districts, 48
    associate, consolidated, and joint, 51, 52

Parents to cause child to attend school, 73
    penalty on, for illegal employment of children, 76
Penalty for breach of ordinances respecting truants, etc., 78
    disturbing meetings or schools, 103
    employing children, what, 76
    making false returns or other neglect of duty, 80, 81
    malicious mischief to property of libraries, 108
    misappropriating moneys, 80, 81
    neglect of duty relative to taxes, 31
    non-payment of taxes, 31
    non-remittance of returns, 44–46, 64
    refusal to permit schools to be visited by school com-
        mittee and others, 81
    general, 83
Penalties, etc., school commissioner may remit what, 70
Permanent School Fund. See *School Fund.*
Person, construction of the word, 12
Physiology, instruction in, to be provided in what schools,
    60
Pictures, in public libraries, malicious injury to, how pun-
    ished, 103
Plural Number, construction of words in, 12
Poll Tax, assessment and collection of, 23, 24
    town treasurer to credit public school account with,
        24, 44
Powers of towns, 17
Private Schools to be registered, and report, 35, 36
    what, may be approved under truant laws, 74
Probate Court, jurisdiction of, to send children to State
        home and school, 98
    may appoint next friend to act for child, 98
    order of, and execution thereof, 99
    expense of such case to be paid by town, 99
Process against school district, how served, 70
    under truant law, by whom served, 75

Property, liable to and exempt from taxation, 21, 22
    surplus, returned to owner by collector of taxes, 28
    of free public library, penalty for malicious injury of, 108
        penalty for conversion of, 109
Providence, Title IX how far applicable to, 81
    schools, how regulated, 82
Public Libraries. See *Library.*
Public Schools. See *Schools.*
Pupils. See *Scholars.*

Qualifications of voters, 5-7. See *Voters.*
    of voters in school district meetings, 50
    for office, 3

Real Estate, taxes against either personal or real estate, a lien on, 25
    taxes against owner of, how long a lien on, 25
    or personal estate, tax may be collected from either, 25
    if aliened, not to be sold for tax, in what case, 25
    return of collector of taxes on sale of, to town clerk, 27
    how advertised and sold for taxes, 26
    deed of, for taxes, what title vested in purchaser by, 27
    right of owner to redeem, if sold for taxes, 27
    fees of collectors of taxes for levy on, 32
    how condemned for school purposes, 59, 60
Reasons of Appeal. See also *Appeals.*
Record of vaccination of pupils kept by teacher, 83
Records, public, when surrendered by officers, etc., 16
    of school district clerk prima facie evidence, 70, 80
Redemption by owner of land sold for taxes, 27
Register of scholars, to be kept by teachers, 66
    to be deposited where, 63
Religious Purposes, buildings and land held for, how far exempt from taxation, 21
Religious Societies, what property of, exempt from taxation, 21
Remittance of fines, penalties, etc., when and how, 70
Reports of board of control of State home and school, annual, 100

Reports—*Continued.*
   of board of education, annual, 36
   of commissioner of public schools, 37
   of school committee, 64
   of trustees of Rhode Island institute for the deaf, annual, 94
   by officers of private schools to board of education, 35, 36

Resignation of officers. See *Vacancies.*

Returns of school census, where deposited, and effect of failure, 46
   of teachers to school committee, 66
   of trustees, to whom and how made, 57

Rhode Island College of Agriculture and Mechanic Arts, 84–88
   to have use of United States money, 85
   location of, 85
   to be a corporation with what powers, 84
   board of managers of, appointment and powers, 86
   clerk of, appointment, 86
   faculty of, duties and appointment, 87
   treasurer of, appointment ; to give bond, 86

Rhode Island Institute for the Deaf, 92–95
   governor and lieutenant-governor, ex-officio trustees, 93
   board of trustees of, appointment and term of office, 93
   powers and dutes of, 94
   to make annual report to general assembly, 94

Rhode Island School of Design, State beneficiaries at, 88, 89
   to make annual report to State board of education, 88

Rights, declaration of, 1–3
   and qualifications of voters, 5–7

Rules and regulations, for appeals, made how, 68
   for libraries, 20, 34, 35
   for schools, made how, 61
   board of control for State home and school to make, 96

Sailors, children of dead or invalided, schools free to, 82

Scholars, without town, admitted by trustee, when, 57
   school committee to make rules for classification, 61

Scholars—*Continued.*
authorized to attend in adjoining town or district when, 61
may be suspended, when, 62
if less than five, school may be suspended, 63
text-books and supplies to be loaned to, 64
register of, to be kept by teachers, 66
to be taught principles of morality and virtue, 67
in normal school, privileges of, 71, 72
not to attend school unless vaccinated, 83

Schoolbooks, uniformity in, how secured, 37
works of reference and apparatus, appropriation for, 39
school committee to place in school rules for use of, 61
to be furnished at expense of town or city, 64
how may be changed, 65
    how, in Providence, 65
receiving or offering fees for exchange of, forbidden, 82

School Commissioner, power to administer oaths, 11
to be elected by board of education, 33
to be secretary of board of education, 34
payments to free public libraries to be made on order of, 35
order for books for free libraries to be made by, 35
pro tempore, may be appointed by governor, 37
may employ a clerk, 37
to visit school districts, when and for what purpose, 37
duties of, in relation to text-books and school libraries, 37
to prepare programme of exercises for Arbor Day, 37
to report annually to board of education, 37
how to apportion appropriation for public schools, 38
how to draw appropriation for public schools, 39
how to apportion appropriation for reference works, etc., 39
when may withhold school money from a town, 45, 64, 78
to furnish blanks for census of children of school age, 45
not to draw money due town, when, 46
town treasurer to transmit to, certificate of amount of money voted by town, 44

School Commissioner—*Continued.*
    erection and repairs of district schools to be approved by, on appeal, 47
    when order assessment and collection of district tax, 54
    power of, to correct errors in assessing, or to re-assess, tax, 55
    power of, to order abatement of tax, 55
    when to approve tax, repairs, etc., of joint district, 55
    powers of, in case of tax by joint or associate district, 55
    powers of, in formation of new district, 59
    school committees to prescribe rules and studies under direction of, 61
    report of school committee to, and of blank therefor, 64
    duty of, in appeals and disputes on school matters, 67, 68
    may submit statement to justice of supreme court, 68
    power of, to remit fines, penalties, and forfeitures, 70
    with board of education, trustee of normal school, 71
    to hold teachers' institutes, account for same, 72
    to notify authorities of neglect under truant law, 78
    may visit schools receiving aid from State, 81

School Committee, schools to be under care of, 41
    how and when chosen; vacancies, how filled, 43
    number may be increased, when, 43
    to have care of schools in discontinued districts, 48
    to have entire control of districts abolished, 43
    officers of, and powers, 58
    meetings of, 59
    to elect superintendent of schools, 44
    town treasurer to report to, 44
    school census returns to be deposited with, when, 46
    to approve plans for erection and repairs of school-house, 47
    to approve amount of tax ordered by school district, 47
    when may exercise powers and duties of district, 48
    to approve bond of collector of district tax, 47
    when establish district school and employ teacher, 48
    when and how call meeting to organize district, 48
    when call special meeting of school district, 49
    no special district meeting without consent of, when, 49

School Committee—*Continued.*
    may fix time and place to organize associate district, 51
    to draw order for public money for associate districts, 51
    to approve organization of consolidated districts, 51
    power of, to form and regulate joint school districts, 52
    to apportion property, etc., when district divided, 53
        public money, in some cases of joint districts, 52
    power of, to abate tax in certain cases, 55
        to approve tax for erection and repairs of schoolhouses in joint districts, 55
    to be notified by trustees of opening and closing schools, 56
    trustees to provide for care of books furnished by, 56
    when may admit pupils from without district, 64
    powers of, over boundaries of districts, 59
    to locate schoolhouses, 59
    when land taken by, without owner's consent, 59
    to examine and dismiss teachers, and to annul certificates, 60, 66
    when not to sign certificates for teachers, 66
    duties and powers of, in regard to visiting schools, 61, 81
    duties and powers of, as to pupils, text-books, schools, 61
    powers of, when town not divided into districts, 62
    how to apportion among the districts the public money, 62
    how to apportion receipts from poll tax, etc., 62
    to draw orders only for districts making returns, 63
    restrictions on powers of, to draw orders, 63
    how to divide forfeited money, 64
    to report annually, to whom, 64
    expense of printing report of, how paid, 64
    power of, to change schoolbooks, 65
    fees to, prohibited, 82
    members of, ineligible to teach public schools, 66
    appeal from, how taken, proceedings thereon, 67, 68
    may excuse child from attending school, when, 74
    powers and duties of, concerning attendance in schools, 73–78

School Committee—*Continued.*
    chairman of, election, and removal by, 58
    clerk of, election, and removal by, 58
School District, how established, 41
    powers of, and how designated, 46
    providing schoolhouses, not to be taxed for others, 42
    may be abolished, 42
    what powers remain to discontinued, 42
    boundaries of, to be recorded by town clerk, 45
        power of school committee over, 59
    may build and repair schoolhouses and furnish same, 46
    power of, to raise money by tax, 47
    to make return to receive proportion of school fund, 63
    money appropriated to, if forfeited, how expended, 64
    officers of, who and when elected, 47
        tenure of office of, 80
        except moderator, in what form to be engaged, 80
    evidence of engagement, 80
    moderator of, may administer oath to other officers, 47
    clerk, collector, treasurer of, duties, powers of, 47
    clerk of, may administer oaths, 11
        may call meetings, when, 48, 49
        when to record votes in meetings of, 50
        provide record book, 70
        records of, to be prima facie evidence of what, 70
        record of, evidence of engagement of officers, 80
    in case of neglect by, school committee may establish
        school, and employ teacher, 48
    may delegate powers and duties to school committee, 48
    meetings of, for organization, how notified, 48
        annual, when held, how notified, 49, 50
        special, how called, how notified, 49, 50
        where held, 49
        appeals from doings of, how taken, 67, 68
        who entitled to vote in, 50
        votes in, when, how recorded, 50
    associate, for having advanced schools, how formed, 50
        to constitute school district for what purposes, 51
        meeting for organization, how called, 51

School District—*Continued.*
    associate, public money how drawn for, 51
        assessments in, how determined in certain cases, 55
    consolidated, how formed from districts in same town, 51
        how organized and entitled to receive public money, 52
        title of, to incorporate property of the several districts, 52
    joint, how formed by districts in adjoining towns, 52
        how organized and powers of, 52
        how entitled to share in public money, 52
        tax of, and schoolhouse plans, how approved, 55
        assessments, how, if town assessments vary, 55
    when divided, property of, how apportioned, 53
    contribution, how made, 53
    school commissioner to visit, 37
    trustees of, when, and how many, elected, how engaged, 47, 80
        how may call meetings, 48, 50
        when to call upon assessers of taxes, 54
        to have custody of property; to employ teachers, 56
        duties of, relative to schools, fuel, schoolbooks, 56
        to provide bookcases in each schoolroom, 56
        to make tax bills, to issue warrants to collectors, 56
        to make returns to school committee, 57
        entitled to no pay, except from district tax, 57
        may admit scholars from without the town, 57
        when school committee may exercise powers of, 57
        ineligible to teach in the public schools, 66
        appeals from decision of, how taken, 67, 68
    power of school committee over, 59
    when not to be formed, 59
    suits against, who may answer, 69
    judgment against, how satisfied, 69
    legal process against, how may be served, 70
    taxes, Title VIII how far applicable to, 32

35*

School District—*Continued.*
    taxes, amount of, to be approved by school committee, 47
        how levied and assessed, 53, 54
        person overtaxed, when to have no remedy, 54
        when school commissioner may order assessment and collection of, 54
        how errors in tax may be corrected, 55
        how and when abated, 55
        for schoolhouse, etc., in joint district, when to be approved by commissioner, 55
        assessment of, by joint or associate districts, 55
        how assessed, to satisfy judgment against district, 69
        proof of payment of, 8
    vote of, ordering tax, and assessment, when final, 68

School Fund of State, provisions of constitution relative to, 3
    general treasurer to have custody of, 15
    income of, how to be invested, 15
    what moneys to be added to, 15
    income of, to be paid for support of public schools, 15, 38
    town share of school money, when to be added to, 39
    penalty of a false certificate relating to, 80

School Fund of Town, when surplus moneys from dog licenses to be applied to, 102, 104

Schoolhouses, power of towns to vote money for, 17
    provided by towns or districts, 41, 46
    to be in custody of trustees, 56
    how supplied with furniture, fixtures, etc., 41, 46
    how provided by associate districts, 51
    district, when school committee may establish schools in, 48
        district meetings to be held in, 49
    contribution to, to be paid by annexed district, 53
    when built by joint district by tax, amount and plans how approved, 55
    to be located by school committee, 59

Schoolhouses—*Continued.*
    land for, how condemned, 59
    rules and regulations to be put in, 61
    what legal process served by posting copy on, 70
    nuisances near, prohibited, 81
    foreign flags not to be raised over, 109

School Libraries, power of town to vote money for, 17
    commissioner to assist in establishment of, 37
    State appropriation for works of reference, etc., for, 39
    school districts may maintain, 46

School of Design, Rhode Island, State beneficiaries at, 88, 89

Schools, income from school fund for support of, 15
    general supervision of, vested in board of education, 33
    support of, power of towns to vote money for, 17
        poll tax to be applied to, 24, 44
            State appropriation for, how to be apportioned, 38
                duty of town treasurer relative to, 44
                how apportioned among districts, 62
                when may be withheld, 45, 46, 64, 78
    works of reference for, how provided for, 39, 40
    free public, building for, exempt from taxation, 21
    private, to register and report to board of education, 35
    when to be visited by school commissioner, 37
    duty of towns to maintain sufficient number of, 41
    census of school children, when and how taken, 45
    school committee may establish, when, 48
    time of opening and closing, trustees to give notice of, 56
    moneys for tuition in, how received and used, 57
    scholars may attend, in another district, when, 64
        in another town, 57, 61
    average attendance in, how determined in such case, 57
    teachers in, qualifications of, duties, 65, 66, 67
        when dismissed, 66
        what school officers ineligible to be, 66
            trustees of normal school may give certificates to, 71
            to keep record of pupils vaccinated, 83

Schools—*Continued.*
    rules as to instruction and government to be posted in, 61
    of towns without districts managed by school committee, 62
    may be suspended in case attendance falls below five, 63
    legal proceedings relating to, 67-70
    appeals relating to, to school commissioner, 67
    provisions concerning attendance and truancy, 73-79
    fines under truant law to be applied to support of, 79
    no person to be excluded from, except by general rule, 80
    aided by State, may be visited and examined by whom, 81
    in Providence how governed, 81
    no person connected with, to take fee for sale of books, 82
    fee to children of dead and invalided soldiers and sailors, 82
    no pupil to attend, without certificate of vaccination, 83
    Title IX is subject to special statutes respecting, 83
    penalty for violation of law regulating, by officer, 80
    penalties under dog law to be applied to support of, 102, 104
    public or private, willful disturbance of, how punished, 108

School Supplies furnished at expense of town or city, 64

Seal, word how construed, 14

Secretary of Board of Control of State Home and School for Children, appointment of, 96

Smallpox, no one to attend school without certificate of vaccination for, 83

Soldiers, children of dead and invalided, schools free to, 82

Special school district meetings, how to be called and for what business, 48, 49
    notice required, 49, 50

State Auditor, school commissioner to render annual account to, 72
    to draw order for payment of education of deaf, blind, and imbecile children, 92

State Home and School for Children, 95–100
    control and maintenance of, vested in whom, 95
    probate courts have jurisdiction of commitment to, 98
    order of court to, on hearing case, 99
        expenses of, to be paid by town, 99
    what children may be sent from State almshouse to, 99
        expense to be paid by State, 99
    board of control of, to consist of whom, 95
        appointed by governor ; tenure of office, 95, 96
        to provide books for registry of children, 99
        to make annual report to board of education, 100
        to appoint secretary, 96
        members of, not to receive compensation, 96
        to establish rules and regulations, 96
        may admit what children, 96
Studies in schools, how prescribed, 61
Successors in office, what officers continue in office until successors qualify, 80
    retiring officer to deliver official possessions to, 16
    penalty for neglect to deliver school accounts to, 80
Superintendent of Schools, election and duties, 44
    compensation of, 44
    to be notified of opening and closing of schools, 56
    ineligible to teach in public schools, 66
    receiving or offering to, fee for exchange of school-books, forbidden, 82
Supreme Court, justices of, to hear and decide on school appeals, when, 68
Suspension of pupils by school committee, 62

Tax, to qualify persons to vote, 6–8
    proposition to impose, who not permitted to vote on, 6
    proof of payment of, what, 8
    penalty on officers refusing certificate of payment of, 9
    officers when to furnish certified list of persons paying, 8, 9
        when to grant certificate in particular cases, 9
    for free public libraries, what and when, 17, 18
    assessment and collection of poll, 23, 24

Tax—*Continued.*
    real estate, holden for tax, how long a lien, 25
        how advertised and sold for, 26, 27
        what title to, vested by deed, under sale, 27
        aliened, not to be sold, if other property, 25
        notice given owner and others interested, 26
        proceeding of sale, when and where returned, 27
        how and when owner may redeem, 27
    personal property, whole tax collected out of, 25
        if advertised for sale, what notice is given, 28, 29
        what not liable to distraint, 28
        distraint and sale of, for, 28
    school district, collection of, 32, 47. See *School District.*
    compensation of assessors, town clerks, collectors, 32
    town to raise by, for schools, amount equal to State appropriation, 39

Taxation, property liable to, exempt from, 21, 22

Teachers, State appropriation for schools to be applied to wages of, 39
    school district neglecting to employ, school committee may employ, 48
    duty of trustees to employ, 56
    duty of school committees to examine, 60, 61, 66
    what certificate of qualification necessary, 65, 66
    when may be dismissed, 66
    what school officers ineligible as, 66, 67
    to keep register of scholars and make return, 66
    to impart what moral instruction, 67
    certificates to, by trustees of normal school, 71
    to keep record of pupils vaccinated, 83

Teachers' Institutes, appropriation for, how expended, 72

Teachers' Money, State appropriation to be so denominated, 39

Telephone Companies, certain minors not to be employed by, when, 75, 76

Tenure of Office, of State board of education, 33, 34
    of commissioner of public schools, 37

Tenure of Office—*Continued.*
    of school committee, 43
    of school district officers, 80
    of board of managers of Rhode Island College of Agriculture and Mechanic Arts, 86
    of trustees of Rhode Island Institute for the Deaf, 93
    of board of control of State Home and School, 95, 96

Text-books. See *Schoolbooks.*

Thanksgiving Day appointed by general assembly, governor, president, legal holiday, 105

Time, reckoned by calendar months and years, excludes day from which reckoned, 13

Town, word construed to include city, or district of Narragansett, 13
    oath of office of persons elected to office by, 10
    powers and duties of, relative to schools, 17-19, 41-43
    power of, to establish free public libraries, 17
    may appropriate money for maintenance of such libraries, 18
    may appropriate money for free public library not its own, 18
    power of, to incur debt, limited; exceptions, 18, 19
        to assess ratable property, limited; exceptions, 19
    management and control of free public library by, 19-21
    entitled to what part of State appropriation for schools, 38
    school money due from State, forfeited when, 39
        when withheld from, 45, 46, 64, 78
    to establish and maintain public schools, 41
    may be divided into school districts, 41

Town Clerk, words may include city clerk, district clerk, 13
    may administer oaths, 11
    to record boundaries of school districts, alterations, 45
    to take census of children of school age, 45
    to distribute school documents, 45

Town Council, words may include board of aldermen, or district council, 13
    may prescribe rules for public libraries, when, 17, 18

Town Council—*Continued.*
    may accept free public library or funds for, 19, 20
    board of trustees of free public library to be elected by, 20
    power of, to fill vacancy in school committee, 43
    to appoint special constables under truant law, 74, 75
    to make ordinances, etc., concerning truants, 77, 78
    penalty for neglect of, to appoint officers or make ordinances concerning truants, 78

Town Meetings, report of school committee to be submitted at annual, 64

Town Treasurer, words may include city or district treasurer, 13
    duties of, in receiving and paying school money, 44

Treasurer, General. See *General Treasurer.*

Treasurer of school district, election, powers, etc., 47

Truant Officers, appointment, duties, 73–79

Truants, town councils to make ordinances for, 78
    may be committed to suitable places of instruction, 78
    may be discharged, when, 78
    district courts have jurisdiction of, 79

Trustees, of free public libraries, how elected, duties, 20
    of schools receiving State aid, to report annually, 35
    of Rhode Island Institute for the Deaf, tenure of office, 93
    of school districts, election of, 47
    how engaged, 80
    how call meetings of districts, 49, 81
    when determine place of meeting, 49
    of associate districts, how appointed, 51
    how to ascertain valuation of property in certain cases, 54
    duties and powers of, relative to schools, taxes, etc., 53–57
    to make returns to school committee, 57
    to receive no compensation unless from district tax, 57
    may admit scholars from without the town, 57
    when school committee may exercise powers of, 57
    to be notified of revocation of teacher's certificate, 60, 61

INDEX TO GENERAL LAWS. 421

Trustees—*Continued.*
    ineligible to teach in public schools, 66, 67
    appeals from decisions of, how taken, and proceedings, 67, 68
Tuition money received by districts and towns, how used, 57
    fees not required of attendants at normal school, 71
    fees of beneficiaries at school of design, 89

Vacancy in office of trustee of free public library, how filled, 20
    in State board of education, how filled, 34
    in school committee, how filled, 43
    in school district offices, how filled, 47
    in board of managers for college of agriculture, how filled, 86

Vacation in public schools, children employed during, 75, 76
Vaccination, to attend school to have certificate of, 83
Vagrants, when received in State Home and School, 96
Virtue, instruction in principles of, in schools, 67
Visits of committee required, 61
    of trustees required, 56
Voluntary Associations, how formed, 105-107
Voters, rights and qualifications of, 5-7
Voters in school districts, qualifications of, 50. See *School District.*

Warrant for collection of tax to satisfy judgment against school district, how issued, 69
Washington's Birthday, to be a legal holiday, 104
Words, construction of, in statutes, 12-14. See *Construction.*

Year, word construed to mean calendar year, 13

INDEX TO DECISIONS.

Abolition of school districts, 115, 288
Annual district meetings, notice of, 166
Annulment of certificate, causes for, 252
Appeal to commissioner, on tax, when, 201
    must be taken in reasonable time, 208
    rehearing allowed, when, 261
    when not allowable, 245
Appraisal, new one not needed when land is sold, 264
    void, when, 270
Approval of a judge shuts off rehearing, 265
Apportionment, school, not district, basis of, 247
Arnold, S. C., *vs.* school committee, Scituate, 244, 281
Assessment, by per cent. legal, 192
    greater than sum voted, illegal, 203
    legal if clear to whom, 192
Assessors appointed by commissioner, how proceed, 199
    of town called by trustee, when, 194, 202
Award of appraisers void, when, 270

Barrington, District No. 1, 133
Boundaries of district how determined, 203
    change of, effect on district, 206
Building committee, powers of, 132
Bull, I. M., et al. *vs.* school committee, Woonsocket, 229
Burrillville, District No. 7, 126, 152, 259
    District No. 12, 125

Carpenter, G. B., *vs.* Joint District 2 and 4, Hopkinton, and 8, Westerly, 277
Certificate of teacher, can be annulled by school committee, 224

Certificate—*Continued*.
    may be annulled when, 225, 252
    may be limited by school committee, 223, 224
    not necessary when no districts, 255
Change in text-books, action on, when may be taken, 244
Clarke, Joseph O., case of, 131
Clerk, of district, error in records of, effect of, 192
              how to record proceedings, 184
    not clothed with discretionary power of committee, 227
Collector of taxes, not liable for damages when, 199
    has percentage on payments to treasurer, 197
Commissioner. See *School Commissioner*.
Committee. See *School Committee*.
Condemnation, proceedings in, how conducted, 139, 144
Constitution, plurality amendment to, effect of, 181
Coventry, Emma A. Frink *vs.* school committee of, 156
    L. E. Seamans *vs.* school committee of, 249
Crandall, Jos., *vs.* School District No. 2, Exeter, 194
Cranston, abolition of districts in, 115
    L. A. Freeman et al. *vs.* school committee of, 254
    J. Nevins *vs.* school committee of, 241
    District No. 1, 220
    District No. 2, 153, 214
Cumberland, District No. 5, 222
    and Lincoln, Joint District Nos. 15 and 13, 175, 182

Decision of commissioner how to be enforced, 260
Debt of district not limit of tax, 197
De facto officers, acts of, are valid, 135, 164, 208
Discretionary powers of school committee not transferable, 227
Dismission of teacher to be by school committee, 223
District, cannot hire teachers by vote, 213
    can tax for more than debt, 197
    entitled to official notice when, 198
    joint. See *Joint District*.
    liable for costs in suit, 127
    limitations of, as to building, 129
    may be changed after vote to tax, 208
    may be divided, how, 129

District—*Continued.*
    may give note, 126, 131
    may open more than one school, 122
    no longer basis of division of money, 245
    no right to overdraw, 136
    not town, liable for teachers' wages, 276

Districts, abolition of, constitutional, 115
        provisions for, interpreted, 119
    discontinued by school committee, 233
    originally formed by school committee, 230
    powers of, 122–146

District boundaries, how determined, 203
    change of, effect of, 206

District meetings, 147–188
    notice of annual, 166
        special, 151, 166, 170
    when consent of school committee required, 174
    records of, 166

District officers, powers of, 122

District taxes, 189–207

District tax, confided to town collector when, 193
    cannot be approved by commissioner, 201
    may be approved when, 167
    to whom to be paid, 191
    when to be questioned, 169

Douglass, Josephine E., *vs.* G. E. Barber, 234

East Providence, F. E. Hovey *vs.* town of, 282
Enforcement of decision lies in Supreme Court, 260
Examination must precede election, 257
    other means than, to determine qualifications, 256
Exempt from taxation, what buildings, 113
Exeter, Jos. Crandall *vs.* School District No. 2 of, 194
    District No. 11, 196
Expulsion of a pupil in hands of school committee, 229

Failure to govern or instruct, cause for annulling, 252
Fires, teacher cannot be required to make, 253
    scholar cannot be required to make, 226
Forfeiture of office not caused by loss of qualification, 208

Freeman, L. A., et al. *vs.* school committee, Cranston, 254
Frink, Emma A., *vs.* school committee, Coventry, 156

General laws modify special only when so stated, 235
Gift to a district not contrary to law, 240
Gradation of schools cannot be forced on a district, 224
Grievance, what may be, 272

Hopkinton and Westerly, Joint District, G. B. Carpenter *vs.*, 277
Hovey, F. E., *vs.* town of East Providence, 282
Howland, E. W., *vs.* District No. 3, Little Compton, 137, 140, 144
Husband, right of, to vote on wife's estate, 155

Incidentals, paid for out of town money 228, 237
Illegal votes, effect of, 152
Insurance of schoolhouse illegal unless voted, 196
Irregularities in district meeting, effect of, 176
Interruption of school is breach of peace, 284

Johnston, District No. 1, 173
    vote of, to abolish districts, 288
Joint district, limitations on establishment of, 228
    when abolished, 182
Jurisdiction, of school commissioner, 260, 261, 262, 267, 269 272, 281
    where school committee have none, 245

Kenyon, A. W., *vs.* school committee, Richmond, 245

Land in two districts valued by town assessors, 194
Legal proceedings, 259-291
Length of residence fixes tax on personal property, 197
Little Compton, District No. 3, 137, 140, 144, 165
    District No. 5, 209
Locate schoolhouse, who has power to, 138
    vote to, not a vote to erect, 138
    when to, 141
Location of schoolhouse may be appealed, 271

Majority vote, when unsafe, 125
Mechanic's lien not good against schoolhouse, 283
Meetings, of district, 147-188
        special, notice of, 151, 166, 170
    of school committee, no fixed mode of notice of, 222
Middletown, District No. 4, 198
Moderator, duty of, 147
    may vote when, 184
Moral character, lack of, reason for not examining, 249
Motive for gift no reason for appeal, 239

Narragansett, district of, considered as a town, 115
Negative acts of school committee no basis for appeal, 245
Nevins, J., vs. school committee, Cranston, 241
North Kingstown, Districts Nos. 3 and 4, 159
    District No. 5, 170
    District No. 10, 122
    school committee of, 226
North Providence, District No. 2, 210
    District No. 3, 128, 148, 149, 151, 223, 224, 260, 261
    District No. 7, 270
    District No. 8, 135, 262
    District No. 10, 269
    P. B. Stiness, Jr., vs. school committee of, 227
    E. S. Wilkinson vs. District No. 1 of, 192
North Smithfield, District No. 6, 183
Notice, for school committee meetings, no fixed mode of, 222
    of change, of boundaries, when waived, 205
        in text-books, how to be given, 243
    of district meeting, how many required, 156
        annual, 166
        special, 151, 166, 170
    official, to be sent to district when, 198

Office, eligibility to, 130
Offices, incompatibility of, 134
Officers, acts of de facto, valid, 135, 164, 208
    district, powers of, 122
    rights of, 136

Order of trustees fixed by district records, 219

Per cent. on taxes paid treasurer goes to collector, 197
Plurality amendment to constitution, effect of, 181
Preventing school from assembling is unlawful disturbance, 285
Property, liable to assessment when, 206
    when not to be relieved from tax, 206
Power, to enforce decisions only in a mandamus, 260
    to annul certificates cannot be delegated, 224
Powers and duties, of towns, 115–121
    of districts and district officers, 122–146
    discretionary, cannot be delegated, 225, 227
Providence, St. Mary's Church *vs.* city of, 113
Public money, cannot be used for repairs, etc., 238
    not drawn by teacher without certificate, 222
    uses of, 237
Public place, what constitutes, 161

Qualification, loss of, not work forfeiture of office, 208

Real and personal estate, how treated on tax list, 190
Re-approval of tax, necessary, when, 196
Recognition of school, lack of, by committee, 157
Records, of districts, how amended, 148
    of district meetings, 166
    of school committee, show district boundaries. 203
        subject to their own control, 282
Record vote, how to be taken, 177
    on what questions, may be called for, 178
    refusal to allow, effect of, 175
    when to be called for, 158
Registry voters, can vote to abolish districts, 288
    may vote when, 129, 147
Rehearing of appeal, may be allowed for cause, 261
    not possible after approval by judge, 265
Removal of trustee, only for cause, 209
Resignation may be withdrawn before acceptance, 220
Residence, change of, 186
    length of, required, 155
    what constitutes, 150, 184

Richmond, District No. 1, 202
    and Hopkinton, Joint District, Nos. 7 and 13, 177
    A. W. Kenyon *vs.* school committee of, 245

Scholars cannot be compelled to make fires, 226
School, not district, basis of apportionment, 245
Schools, district may open more than one, 122
School commissioner, jurisdiction of, 260, 261, 262, 267, 269, 272, 281
    has no jurisdiction when, 269
        over records of school committee, 282
    cannot approve district tax, 201
    cannot compel trustees to perform duties, 262
    cannot interfere with other officers, 263
    has no power to enforce decisions, 260
    may allow rehearing for cause, 261
    not to order tax save as law provides, 201
    power over district boundaries, 259, 260
    to submit statement, not evidence, 266
School committee, powers and duties of, 222-248
    act of one member of, not act of all, 251
    can annul certificate or dismiss for cause, 223, 225
    can discontinue districts, 233
    can examine or not, 256
    can expel pupils, 229
    can refuse to examine on moral grounds, 249
    cannot compel gradation of schools, 224
        scholars to make fires, 226
    cannot delegate general powers, 225, 227
        power to annul certificates, 224
    cannot make conditions after appointment, 257
    have no criminal jurisdiction, 245
    have power to lay off districts, 230
    may limit their certificates, 223, 224
    need not issue certificates, when, 255
Schoolhouse, location of, may be appealed, 271
    not a grievance, 240
    not subject to mechanic's lien, 283
    not to be insured without vote, 196
    uses of, 122, 138

School year, legal, begins May 1, 210
Scituate, District No. 7, 191
    S. C. Arnold *vs.* school committee of, 244, 281
Seabury, B. C., collector, *vs.* E. W. Howland, 165
Seamans, L. E., *vs.* school committee, Coventry, 249
Smith, E., *vs.* school committee, Smithfield, 251, 264
Smithfield, District No. 14, 190
    E. Smith, *vs.* school committee of, 251, 264
Soldiers and Sailors, children of, provision for, 278
    estates of, not exempt from tax for schools, 280
South Kingstown, District No. 3, 239
    District No. 19, 200, 271
    and Richmond, Joint Districts Nos. 17 and 4, 158
Special laws modified by general when so stated, 235
Special district meetings, notice of, 151, 166, 170
        when consent of school committee required for, 174
Spencer, D. P., *vs.* District No. 17, Warwick, 275
Statement of facts, what constitutes, 266
    is not evidence, 266
Stiness, P. B., Jr., *vs.* J. H. Willard, clerk school committee, North Providence, 227
St. Mary's Church *vs.* City of Providence, 113

Tax of district, may be approved when, 167
    committee's approval of, not appealed from, 189
        may be rescinded from, 189
        when to be secured, 190
    for more than amount of debt legal, 197
    may be ordered by one legal voter, 197
    ordered by commissioner, when, 200
    re-approval of, necessary when, 196
    when can be rescinded, 125, 126
    who may vote on, 152, 153
Taxation, what buildings exempt from, when, 113
Tax collector not liable for damages, when, 199
Teachers, 249-258
    cannot be compelled to make fires, 253
    cannot be dismissed by trustee during term, 212
    cannot be hired by district, 213

Teachers—*Continued.*
    cannot draw public money without certificate, 222
    claims of, against district, not town, 276
    dismissed by school committee, 223
    if dismissed draw public money no longer, 250
    may be dismissed for cause, 225
    wages of, fixed by trustee, 210

Text-books, change in, may be made when, 244
    change of edition of, not change of books, 242
    notice of change in, what kind needed, 243

Tiffany, W., *vs.* District No. 4, Warwick, 215

Time, how reckoned, 173

Town, powers and duties of, 115–121
    not liable for teacher's wages, when, 276

Town appropriation can be used for incidentals, 228, 237

Town assessors, called on by trustee, when, 202
    land in two districts valued by, 194

Town collector, bond of, not held for district, 189
    can collect district tax when, 193

Transfer of title does not call for new appraisal, 264

Trustees, 208–221
    can hire at any price, 210
    cannot be made to act by commissioner, 262
    cannot compel scholars to make fires, 226
    cannot dismiss teacher during term, 212
    cannot reduce wages during term, 212
    if one elected, later meeting cannot add, 214
    meetings of, not determined by law, 214
    must act as a board, 213
    number of, how decided, 162
    only removable for cause, 209
    order of, fixed by district records, 219
    to call on town assessor, when, 194, 202
    to respect orders of school committee, when, 209
    two do not make legal board, 216

Uses of public money, 228, 237

Verry, N. T., *vs.* school committee, Woonsocket, 235

Vote to abolish districts not direct vote to tax, 289

Votes, fixing time for taxes, how interpreted, 190
    illegal, effect of, 152
Voter, one legal, can order tax, 197
    qualifications of, 128, 149
    residence of, 150

Wages of teachers, at discretion of trustee, 210
    cannot be reduced during term, 212
Warwick, District No. 7, 193
    D. P. Spencer *vs.* District No. 17 of, 275
West Greenwich, District No. 4, 204
    District No. 8, 213
Wilkinson, E. S., *vs.* District No. 1, North Providence, 192
Woonsocket, I. M. Bull *vs.* school committee of, 229
    N. T. Verry *vs.* school committee of, 235

Year, school, begins when, 210

INDEX TO REMARKS AND FORMS.

Accounts of school committee, how to be kept, 321
Admission to school, at what ages, 318
Adjourned meeting, what business legal at, 340
Annulling certificates, reasons for, 312
Appeals to commissioner, form of, 389
    notice of, to be served, 358
        form of, 390
    restrictions thereon, 357, 358
    suggestions relating thereto, 357, 358
Apportioning money, under what restrictions, 319, 320
Assessment of taxes, 343–346

Bible reading in the schools, 351, 352
Blind and feeble-minded, education of, 359
Board of education. See *State Board of Education.*
Bond of district treasurer and collector, form of, 376, 377

Casting vote, moderator has none, 329
Certificates, of election, form of, 362
    of engagement, form of, 363
    of teachers, annulling, reasons for, 312
        form for annulling, 363
        given on what diploma, 312
        how granted, etc., 306–312
Choice of officers, form of record of, 368
Clerk, town. See *Town Clerk.*
Collection of taxes, 346–348
Commissioner of public schools. See *School Commissioner.*
Contract, to build schoolhouse, form of, 370
    with teacher, form of, 364

Course of study, need for, 318
    to be fixed by school committee, 318, 319

Deaf, education of, 359
    blind, and imbecile, education of, 292, 359
Deed, tax collector's, form of, 379
    to and from school district, form of, 383, 385
Discipline, need of precise rules thereon, 316
Dismissing teacher, causes for, 312
Distraint and collection, method of, 347
    what not subject to, 347
Districts, attendance in other, how regulated, 302, 303
    boundaries of, how determined, 301, 302
    how dissolved, 329
    how laid off by school committee, 301
    may tax for what purposes, 342
    should possess what equipment, 336
    three ways of uniting, 328
District assessors, no such officers as, 344
    boundaries, provisions for keeping record of, 303
    clerk, duties of, 330, 331
        records of, should be kept how, 330, 331
            when prima facie evidence, 331
    collector, engagement and duties of, 332
        form of bond of, 377
        legal fee of, 332
    meetings, how to be notified, 339
        mode of conducting, 340
    note, should be signed by treasurer, 332
    taxes, abatement of, how made, 343
    treasurer, engagement and duties of, 331, 332
        form of bond of, 376
        must give bonds, when, 331
Dog taxes, when to be credited to school account, 296

Education, board of. See *State Board of Education.*
Education of dependent and defective classes, 358, 359
Engagement, of officers should be recorded, 340
    who may administer, 338
    who must take an, 337

Equipment needed for each school, 336
Evening schools, appropriation for, and care of, 292
    place for, 324
Examination, points of, 307-311

Fines and forfeitures, remission of, 292
Form, of appeal to school commissioner, 389
    of annulling certificates, 363
    of bond of district collector, 377
        treasurer, 376
    of certificate of election of school officers, 362
        engagement of school officers, 363
    of commencement of district records, 367
    of contract to build schoolhouse, 370
        with a teacher, 364
    of deed from a school district, 385
        to a school district, 383
    of incorporation of public library, 391
    of lease of building by district, 381
    of note given by a school district, 387
    of notice of appeal, 390
        of annual district meeting, 366
        of special district meeting, 366
        of district meeting by school committee, 365
        of change in text-books, 389
    of oath to be taken by school officers, 363
    of order on school fund, 388
    of prayer for opening and closing school, 393, 394
    of record of choice of officers, 368
        of vote to levy tax, 373
    of request for special district meeting, 367
    of tax bill, or assessment list, 375
    of tax collector's bond, 377
        deed, 379
    of treasurer's bond, 376
    of vote to build a schoolhouse, 369
        to devolve care on school committee, 369
        to fix form of seal, 387
        to hire money, 387
        to sell land of district, 385

INDEX TO REMARKS AND FORMS. 435

Form—*Continued.*
    of vote to take a lease, 382
        by school committee to form joint district, 388
    of warrant to collect a tax, 375
Free public libraries, as town institutions, 295, 360
    care of, 292
    form for incorporation of, 391
    how organized, 360

Govern, power to, how discerned, 310, 311
Gradation of schools, to be urged, 323

Holidays, to be fixed by school committee, 319

Instruct, ability to, importance of, 310

Joint districts, when desirable, 303, 304

Kindergarten, age of admission to, 318

Lease of building by district, form of, 381
Libraries, free public, may be maintained by towns, 295, 360
    suggestions concerning, 359–361
Literary attainments of teachers, 307–309
Moral instruction, nature of, to be taught, 350
Meetings, district, adjourned, legal business at, 340
    conduct of, 340–342
    form of notice of, 365, 366
        of request for special, 367
Moderator, election and duties of, 329
    has no casting vote, 329
    no judge of voter's qualifications, 329
    should maintain order, 330
Moral character, how to be considered, 307
Normal school. See *State Normal School.*
Note given by school district, form of, 387
Notice, of district meeting, by school committee, 323
    form of, of appeal, 390

Oath, form of, to be taken by school officers, 363
Offices, qualifications for, 337
    when same person may not hold two, 338

Order, of business, in hands of district, 341
    on school fund, form of, 388

Parliamentary law, force of, in district meetings, 329
Plans for building or repairs, to be approved, 304, 305
Poll taxes, when to be credited to school account, 296
Prayer, forms of, for use in schools, 393, 394
    in schools, 351
Punishment by teachers, extent of, allowable, 352-357
    for acts done out of school, 354-356
Pupils, admitted to school at what age, 318

Qualifications, for office, 337
    for voting, 339
    of teachers, what constitute, 307-311
Quorum of district meeting, none fixed, 341

Reading of Bible in schools, 351, 352
Records, of district, forms of commencement of, 367
    of meeting may be proved by testimony, 340
Record vote, when moderator should call for, 329
Redemption of tax sale, how done, 347
Refusal, of certificate, no appeal from, 349
    of officers to act, remedy for, 335, 340
Register, teacher's duty with reference to, 348
Resignations, how to be made, 338
Restrictions upon paying out school moneys, 320, 321
Returns, importance of, 322
    how and by whom made, 322
    teacher's duty with reference to, 349
R. I. Institute for the Deaf, 359
Rules and regulations, nature and extent of, 317-319
    to be made by whom, 317
School commissioner, duties of, 293
    election of, 292
    judicial functions of, 293, 294
School committee, annual report of, 298
    condition of membership, 297
    duties of, 298-324
        as to schoolhouses, 304, 305

School committee– *Continued.*
        have final power over certificates, 311
        meetings of, 300
            records of, how to be kept, 300, 301
        not to be relieved by superintendent, 325
        number of, how fixed, 299
        organization of, 298, 299
        synopsis of duties of, 327, 328
        vacancies in, how filled, 299
        what disqualifies one for, 297, 339
        women eligible to, 297
School libraries, how to secure, 359
School moneys, how to be kept and disbursed, 296
School officers, tenure of, 338
School superintendents, 324–326
        not civil officers, 324
        not to relieve committee, 325
        suggestions concerning, 326
Schoolhouses, location of, 304, 305
Schools, how may be carried on, 294
    small, how to be treated, 320
State board of education, composition of, 292
    duties of, 292
    meetings of, 293
State Home and School for Children, 358
State normal school, trustees of, 292

Taxation, general provisions concerning, 342, 343
Taxes, district, assessment of, 343–346
    collection of, 346–348
    how should be voted, 343
    must be assessed by trustee, 337
    must be paid to collector, 346, 347
    who can vote for, 343
    why to be approved by school committee, 305
Tax bill, or assessment list, form of, 375
Tax laws of the State, abstract of, 345, 346
Tax warrant remains in force, how long, 347
Teachers, cause for dismission of, 312
    certificates of, 306–312

Teachers—*Continued.*
    duties of, and suggestions to, 348-357
        as to registers, 348
        as to returns, 349
    form of contract with, 364
    meetings of, should be encouraged, 335
    power of, to punish, 352-357
    qualifications of, 307-311, 349
    to impart moral instruction, 350

Text-books, notice of change in, form of, 389
    selection of, 316
    uniformity in, when desirable, 317
    what, should be excluded, 317

Town, each, fixes its own limit of education, 294
    may abolish districts, 295
    may establish and maintain free libraries, 295, 360
    required to maintain schools, 294

Town clerk, duties of, relating to schools, 295

Town system, advantage of, 295

Town treasurer, duties of, as to returns, 296, 297
    relating to schools, 296
    to school committee, 296

Trustees, are legal custodians of schoolhouse, 334
    duties and powers of, 332-337
    election of, 332
    have no power over rules and regulations, 336
    number of, when to be decided, 332
    returns of, nature and importance of, 336, 337
    subject to penalty for neglect of duty, 335
    to call on town assessors when; how proceed, 344
    when three, to do all business at a meeting, 333

Vacancies and resignations, how to be treated, 338

Visiting schools, benefits of, 313
    duty of school committee as to, 312
    how to be conducted, 313-316
    two phases of, 316

Vote, to levy tax, form of record of, 373
    form of, to build schoolhouse, 369

Vote—*Continued.*
　　form of, to devolve care on school committee, 369
　　　　to fix form of seal, 387
　　　　to hire money, 387
　　　　to sell land of district, 385
　　　　to take a lease, 382
　　　　by committee to form joint district, 388

Voting, qualifications for, 339

Warrant to collect a tax, form of, 375